The Lakeside Classics

Army Life in Dakota

PHILIPPE REGIS DENIS DE KEREDERN DE TROBRIAND

The Lakeside Classics

—

Army Life in Dakota

Selections from the
Journal of Philippe Régis Denis
de Keredern de Trobriand

TRANSLATED FROM THE FRENCH BY
GEORGE FRANCIS WILL
VICE-PRESIDENT
NORTH DAKOTA STATE HISTORICAL SOCIETY

EDITED BY
MILO MILTON QUAIFE
SECRETARY OF
THE BURTON HISTORICAL COLLECTION

CHICAGO
The Lakeside Press
R. R. DONNELLEY & SONS CO.
Christmas, 1941

Publishers' Preface

W E have turned again to a Frenchman's journal for the subject matter of this year's volume of the Lakeside Classics. Like the journal of Thomas Vercheres de Boucherville, the journal of de Trobriand also had been printed in its original language, but as only five hundred copies were printed by the family for gratuitous circulation, its appearance in English will come to most of its recipients with all the interest of a new book.

De Trobriand's Journal was called to the attention of the Publishers by Mr. George F. Will, a business man of Bismarck, North Dakota, who in his spare moments had translated it as an expression of his deep interest in the historical literature of the upper Missouri area. Mr. Will most generously offered his manuscript for publication as one of the Lakeside Classics, but, unfortunately, the manuscript contained some 140,000 words, which automatically ruled it out of consideration as 80,000 words have proved to be the maximum limit of the established format unless the proportion of thickness to over-all size was to be distorted.

vii

Publishers' Preface

Upon perusing the manuscript, it became apparent that here was recorded an unusual understanding of the character and ideology of the Indians, both friendly and hostile. General de Trobriand, as commanding officer for two years of three forts spread along the Upper Missouri, had both opportunity and time to study the many tribes that occupied his district. The General was a man of broad cultural background and an experienced writer and journalist. Having no preconceived convictions that the Indian question could only be settled by the rifle, he approached the subject objectively and was able to give credit and sympathy where they were deserved and criticism where it was due.

The Publishers decided that at least those entries in the journal that pertained to the Indians should be made available to the readers of the Lakeside Classics. Mr. Will was asked if, under these circumstances, he would permit an elimination of sufficient material that covered other phases of life at Fort Stevenson in order to bring the size of the book within the necessary limits. To this request Mr. Will graciously acceded. As printed, all important entries covering Indian relations have been included; also sufficient other entries to give the reader a fair

Publishers' Preface

picture of the many trials and few pleasures that were the lot of military men in the frontier forts of Dakota during the late 60s.

The Publishers wish to express their appreciation of Mr. Will's cooperation with Mr. Quaife and themselves in the editing and putting this volume to press. We believe it will be an important addition to the Lakeside Classics, and hope the recipients will enjoy its reading.

Even though the daily press continuously emphasizes the dismal prospects for all concerns which are not engaged in some form of defense work, we still have the temerity to wish all our patrons and friends a Merry Christmas and a New Year that will turn out not so bad as prophesied.

THE PUBLISHERS

Christmas 1941

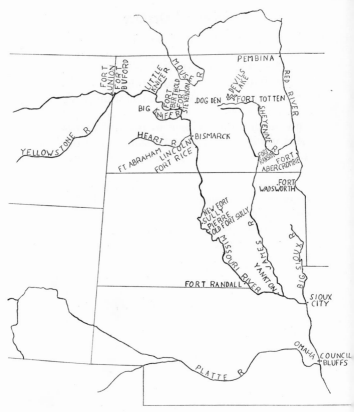

MAP OF THE De TROBRIAND COUNTRY

Historical Introduction

FOR the twenty-sixth successive year the Editor is privileged to address the readers of the *Lakeside Classics*. In the quarter-century that has passed since our editorial task was first assumed the narratives printed have ranged widely in both time and space; from the mid-eighteenth-century adventures of John Long and Alexander Henry to the late-nineteenth-century careers of Martha Summerhayes and John R. Cook; and from the arid deserts of Mexico and the Far Southwest to the snow-girt valleys of the Peace and the St. Lawrence. Always, however, the narratives have illustrated one common theme, the tremendous story of the exploration and occupation of the American continent.

In *War on the Detroit*, published a year ago, the experiences of an American and a Canadian soldier in the War of 1812 on the western front were detailed to the reader. With our present offering, the Journal of General De Trobriand, the scene shifts to the Upper Missouri area in the troubled years of the later 1860's. A better reporter of the life he observed and shared than General De Trobriand could scarcely be imagined or desired. He came of ancient military stock, of a family that had been ennobled in Brittany in 1426, and whose members for many generations had been found "anywhere in Christendom or out of it where fighting was going on." Although he was the eldest son of one of Napoleon's generals, he did not turn to the profession of arms until comparatively late in life. He was born in 1816 and after attending the university studied law and for several years held a governmental appointment in Paris, meanwhile dabbling in literature. In 1841 he made an impulsive visit to the New World, toured both the United States and Canada, wrote a book, and fell in love, all in a single year. Thereafter for many years he alternated between Europe and America, devoting himself to literary and artistic pursuits and enjoying the wealth and social station to which he had been born. Eventually he fixed upon New York as his permanent home, where during the later fifties he became a familiar figure in the leading literary and social circles of the time.

The Civil War opened in 1861 and a French Regiment was organized in New York. Although De Trobriand was the descendant of a long line of soldiers he seems to have had no military experience of his own. Notwithstanding this, he was appointed colonel of the regiment and served until the end of the war, attaining the rank of brigadier-general and major general by brevet. Upon the reorganization of the army following the close of the war he was selected as one of the officers to be retained and was commissioned a colonel in the regular army. He had already gone to France to prepare a history of the Army of the Potomac,[1] to be published there, and by permission of General Grant he remained to complete this task before assuming the duties of his new military station.

At this point, in the summer of 1867, his journal begins, continuing until his removal from Fort Stevenson in North Dakota to Montana in the spring of 1869. His subsequent service in Montana, Utah, and Louisiana, until his retirement from active service in 1879, lies beyond the scope of our present narrative. Following his retirement he made New Orleans his home, until his death in 1897. During these years "he read much,

---

[1] *Quatre Ans de Campagnes à l'Armée du Potomac* (Paris, 2 vols., 1867–68). Republished in English translation as *Four Years with the Army of the Potomac* (Boston, 1889).

cultivated his roses, visited in France, and spent the summers with his daughter on Long Island."

A thorough cosmopolite, familiar with the best society of Europe and America, De Trobriand's removal to the Upper Missouri marked his entry upon a new world. Instead of bemoaning his fate as an exile from civilization, he looked upon the scenes of his new environment with lively curiosity, and beguiled the weary hours of his isolation from all that he knew and loved by recording the lengthy entries which constitute his Journal. Quite possibly this was intended to supply the basis for a book, which he never got around to write. The bulky manuscript is still preserved in the Long Island home of his grandson, Mr. Waldron Kintzing Post of New York City.

Mr. Post's mother was Mrs. Marie Caroline Post, eldest daughter of General De Trobriand. Toward the close of her life she determined to publish her father's manuscript, and with the coöperation of her sister who was living in France it was privately printed in Paris in 1926 under the title of *Vie Militaire Dans Le Dakota*, *Notes Et Souvenirs* (1867–1869), constituting an octavo volume of more than 400 pages. The edition numbered 500 copies and each sister received one-half of it for distribution to friends and otherwise as circumstances might determine.[2]

Mrs. Post published the Journal both as a memorial to her father and as a contribution to the history of the region in which it was written.[3] Until the present moment however, these objectives have remained largely unrealized, for owing partly to the circumstances of its publication and distribution, the Journal's wealth of scientific and historical data still remains practically unknown to the world of American scholarship. But one review of the book seems ever to have been published, and this one appeared seven years late, in 1933.[4] Inquiry instituted at ten outstanding libraries which might be expected to possess copies disclosed that five of them have the book, but more significant is the fact that such institutions as the

[2]Mrs. Post had died before the Journal was actually printed, but her share of the edition came to her family. Letter of Regis H. Post, Istanbul, to Lawrence K. Fox, Secretary, South Dakota State Historical Society, Jan. 16, 1938.

[3]Statement of Regis H. Post to Lawrence K. Fox.

[4]See *Miss. Valley Hist. Rev.*, XX, 127–28. Florence S. Hellman, Chief Bibliographer of Congress, reports the finding of no other review notices, and further that an examination of recent books on the Dakotas disclosed but one which mentions De Trobriand's Journal as a source. Report to the Editor, Sept. 16, 1941.

University of Chicago, the Wisconsin State Historical Library, the Detroit Public Library, and the Nebraska State Library do not; while the extensive catalogs of the Manuscript Division of the Library of Congress do not contain "any entry whatever" concerning it.[5]

That these things should be true is a great pity, and our present reprint, in English translation, of a considerable portion of the Journal should be correspondingly welcomed by its readers. Because the size of the original Journal far transcends the modest limits of *The Lakeside Classics* volumes,[6] only a portion of it is presented here. In determining what to include, the plan has been adopted of retaining as much of the data dealing with the life and activities of the Indians as possible. Records of the weather, of steamboat and other visitations, botanical and

---

[5]Report of Dr. St. George L. Sioussat, Chief of the Division, to the Editor, Sept. 26, 1941. However, Lawrence K. Fox reports that several Dakotans who knew the volume have at different times conceived the project of translating all, or portions, of it. Letter to the Editor, Oct. 3, 1941.

[6]Mr. Waldron Kintzing Post doubts that the published volume is a complete printing of the original Notes; "presumably my mother edited it," he writes, "and left out a good deal." Letter to the Editor, Sept. 15, 1941.

other scientific observations, details of army
life and personages, routine military move-
ments, hunting and other expeditions, have
been regretfully but ruthlessly excised. For
this wealth of material the reader must
turn to the original French edition of 1926,
until such time as some Editor with more
space at his disposal than the present one
commands shall publish the Journal in English in its entirety.

The task of the Editor has been made
easier by the patient work of Mr. George F.
Will, who in addition to translating the
Journal into English has supplied an ex-
planatory introduction and numerous foot-
notes. Mr. Will is a business man of Bismarck who specialized in the field of American anthropology while in college and who
during the ensuing years has continued a
diligent student of the archeological and
other backgrounds of the Upper Missouri
area. He is the author of numerous mono-
graphs and articles in his chosen field of
work, and author or co-author of several
books. To him in particular, and to the busy
librarians and other scholars who have interrupted their own tasks to respond to the
Editor's appeals for information, our in-
debtedness is gratefully acknowledged.

We conclude with this pertinent story,

relayed by Lawrence K. Fox, Secretary of
the South Dakota State Historical Society.

"Soon after we received the copy of the
Journal (about eight years ago) a G.A.R.
encampment was held in Pierre. An aged
veteran from Iowa came into the office, and
chancing to mention the General to him I
was much surprised to find that he had
served under him in North Dakota. To make
certain, I showed him the General's picture,
as reproduced in the frontispiece; 'That's
the blankety blank blank blank!' he ex-
claimed, and from other statements I gathered that the General was not overly popular
with his men. In fact, he was quite a mar-
tinet—something like my topkick in 1917–
19." Thus accidentally, after the lapse of
two-thirds of a century, came incidental
confirmation of certain facts concerning the
state of the army in the sixties disclosed by
Mr. Will in his Translator's Introduction; as
well as by certain observations recorded by
the General himself in his Notes.

M. M. QUAIFE

Detroit,
October, 1941.

Translator's Introduction

IN the story of the final preparation of the
Northern Great Plains for the coming of
permanent settlers, the Journal of General de Trobriand is outstanding on many
counts. It covers the period in a portion of
the Northwest which has to a considerable
extent been neglected. We have a whole
library on the final dramatic conclusion of
the Sioux wars, comprising numerous works
on the Battle of the Little Big Horn and the
final subjugation of the Sioux, on the many
battles in Wyoming and Montana, on the
Sibley and Sully expeditions of the Sixties,
and on the Indian campaigns of the central
Great Plains. Of the years from 1865 to
1870 in the Northwest we have, however,
only very meager published chronicles, and
of the territory of the Upper Missouri and
the country now comprising North Dakota
there are practically no authentic and full
published accounts.

General de Trobriand's journal deals with
the region and the period mentioned. The
General was a writer of long and varied experience, the author of several books, and a

music and art critic for some years on the leading French paper of New York. As a result the journals are written in a charming literary style and the statements they contain are unusually accurate.

The period was one of great turbulence among the tribes of the Great Plains. Despite the punishment visited upon the Sioux following the Minnesota uprising of 1862, the rather equivocal results of the Sibley and Sully expeditions and the tendency during the Civil War of the Federal authorities to temporize with the recalcitrant tribes had bred in them a feeling of contempt for the United States Army, which was shared by the frontiersmen and white residents of the Indian country generally. It was a common saying among them that ten cowboys were worth a company of soldiers, while the Indians went so often unpunished for their frequent outrages against the whites that they conceived the idea that the latter were afraid of them.

The Indian community with its loose government seldom recognized the right of any chief to deal for it or to bind it. While the elders of the tribe might follow a wise chief, the young men were seldom, if ever, under control. The social organization forced the youths to make their names and reputation on the war path. Consequently, in spite of wise counsel or definite orders, the young men were beyond restraint and at any time might embroil a whole band in undesired hostility with other bands or tribes. As a result, the treaties made by the chiefs were even less valid and binding than were those made by the whites.

The period dealt with was a particularly crucial one in the history of the Great Plains region. Thousands of discharged soldiers from both the Union and Confederate armies returned to their homes with the thrill of danger and adventure still in their blood, to find no satisfactory places for themselves, or to discover a permanent distaste for hard and humdrum labor. The West was developing, and talk of it was everywhere rife; railroads building across the Plains, gold and silver to be dug in the hills of Montana, free land for the settlers, profitable hunting for fur and for buffalo robes, big money from the sale of firewood to the steamboats. Naturally the most turbulent and adventurous were drawn to the West; and the United States Government was almost as powerless to control them as the Indian chiefs were to manage their young men. As a result, there were continuous clashes between the two races, and the deeds of the plainsmen were scarcely less cruel and terrible than those of the wild Indians of the Plains. The Indians saw their lands invaded, their game destroyed or driven away, and the buffalo on the road to extinction. Without the buffalo their old life was dead. Food, clothing, and shelter all derived from him. It is no wonder, therefore, that the bravest and strongest leaders felt that their only hope was definitely and finally to expel all whites from their lands, killing them wherever and whenever they found them. The struggle they initiated lasted for a full decade, and the horsemen of the Plains tribes are fully entitled to rank with the great fighters of the world.

Within the United States Army at this trying period, conditions were most unsatisfactory. The officers were unfamiliar with Indian fighting, which had almost nothing in common with the campaigns of the Civil War, in which they had received their military training. The enlisted personnel consisted largely of the dregs from the Union and Confederate armies, and of recent emigrants from Europe, Germans and Irish with a sprinkling of others. They knew almost nothing of life on the frontier and were unable to take care of themselves under the conditions of the country. The life at the isolated army posts was tedious and monotonous, and desertions were frequent and very often successful. Little help in capturing deserters was to be got from the natives, and in many of the posts the officers were so inefficient or dissatisfied that discipline was relaxed almost beyond belief. Furthermore, the garrisons were at first nearly all composed of infantry, and it was almost impossible for such troops to make a successful expedition against mounted Indians. Even the cavalry, as the General observes, with their heavy equipment and soft, grain-fed horses, were no match for the light-horse Indian warriors, who could outspeed and outdistance them. Thus the only possibility of success lay in taking the Indians by surprise, and even then most of them usually escaped.

The Indians' methods of conflict were also undergoing a tremendous change during these years of their final stand. As has been noted, Indian warfare was primarily a sort of game for the most part, through which, by excelling, high honors might be acquired. The Journal gives us a picture of the Indian idea of warfare. No advantage or booty was considered great enough to compensate for heavy losses, and a successful foray was one with very light losses even if only a single scalp or one lone horse were the spoils. Com-

plete conquest was never thought of, and
even much-heralded invasions by one tribe
against another usually degenerated into a
swift surprise attack and immediate withdrawal or a series of skirmishes between
scattered detachments on both sides. It was,
therefore, an achievement of rather a high
order when Red Cloud, Crazy Horse, Gall,
Sitting Bull, and others finally adopted the
idea of attacks in large numbers and the
overwhelming of the whites by dogged and
persistent attack, regardless of losses. This
development came only in the latter years
of the Sioux Wars and accounts for the several successes in Wyoming and the last one
of the Little Big Horn. Fortunately for the
small isolated garrisons of the frontier forts,
it was not developed in the earlier years.

A brief historical summary of the territory
where General de Trobriand was stationed
may aid in a fuller understanding of the
Journal. The places mentioned are nearly
all in the present state of North Dakota.
This region was first explored along two
quite different lines and in two quite different portions. The northwestern portion was
explored by French and British fur traders
during the eighteenth century. A French
population along the Red River grew up,
mostly developed by intermarriage between

the French and Scotch employees of the fur
companies and Indian women of the Chippewa and Cree tribes, and many expeditions
were made by traders across the Plains to
the Missouri, but without any great effect
on the Indians there.

The real penetration of the western and
Missouri River section of the State came
only after the Lewis and Clark Expedition,
which wintered near one of the Mandan
villages in 1804. Several American fur companies took part in it, establishing numerous
so-called forts along the Missouri, which was
the one great artery of transportation for
the whole Great Plains region. In North
Dakota the best known of these fur posts
were Fort Clark, at the Mandan and Hidatsa villages near the mouth of Knife River,
and Fort Union, near the confluence of the
Missouri and the Yellowstone. Fort Berthold was established much later, after the removal of the Mandans and Hidatsa to its
vicinity, and a number of other small and
temporary posts were erected at various
points advantageous for trade along the
river. With the fur trade there came into the
country both from Canada and St. Louis a
considerable number of employees, many of
them French, but with nearly every national-
ity represented. Many of them made the

scattered trading posts their permanent residences, married Indian women, and reared families of half-breed children.

During these early years there was little trouble between the whites and Indians in the region. White trappers roamed the country, alone or in small parties, with no danger except occasionally from chance small war parties of young men out for scalps and glory. As mid-century came, however, conditions began to change; the various Sioux bands were being gradually pushed westward by the whites in Iowa and Minnesota, and naturally they carried with them their animosity against those who had seized their old hunting grounds. As a result, travel on the plains became increasingly dangerous. Following the Sioux Outbreak of 1862 in Minnesota, and the two campaigns against them in Dakota by Generals Sully and Sibley, travel on the Plains and along the Missouri became unsafe, except by large parties. To the Sioux, almost every white man had become an enemy, and fair prey for every war party of any of the tribes. Since the United States Government had few troops to spare from the Union forces, it preferred to placate the red men until the arrival of a more favorable time for final dealing with them. At the same time, the War Department had to make some show of authority against the Indians, and a number of military posts were established in the region.

Up to this point the region was for the most part in its natural state. With the building of the military forts, however, and the opening of migration over the prairies to the Montana gold fields, the white population was very greatly increased. Artisans and laborers came in to work on the military establishments and remained to engage in civilian activities around the posts or along the Missouri. These pioneers, with the addition of discharged soldiers and trappers, formed the nucleus from which gradually the white population of the region was built up by the addition of emigrants from the East and from Europe, after the railroads began to move westward into the territory.

There was a military post at Pembina, close to the international boundary, at an early date, but it was not continuously occupied. Aside from this, the first military post in the State was Fort Abercrombie, built in 1856 on the west bank of the Red River in the southeastern part of the State. Fort Ridgely in Minnesota was established on the Minnesota River even earlier, and Fort Wadsworth, later called Fort Sisseton, in the northeastern part of what is now South Dakota, was built in 1864. Fort Rice on the Missouri River was built by General Sully in 1863 about thirty miles south of present-day Bismarck. Fort Totten on the southern shore of Devils Lake was built in 1867, about the same time as Fort Stevenson. Fort Ransom on the Cheyenne River, on the route between Fort Abercrombie and Fort Totten, was also built in 1867. Prior to the building of Fort Stevenson, about six miles southwest of the present town of Garrison, a small garrison was kept at Fort Berthold. Fort Buford, established in 1866, was on the Missouri near the present Montana-Dakota line, and not far from the famous fur post, Fort Union. In 1872 the largest military post on the Upper Missouri was built about five miles southwest of Bismarck. This was Fort Abraham Lincoln, whence Custer set out on his ill-fated Little Big Horn campaign. In 1880 a smaller post, Fort Yates, was built on the Standing Rock Indian Reservation at the present town of Fort Yates, some of the buildings being still in use by the Indian Department.

All of these forts were finally abandoned during the twenty years following the Battle of the Little Big Horn in 1876, and for the most part hardly any traces of them remain. The site of Fort Abraham Lincoln has become a state park and some of the military works there have been restored. The site of Fort Stevenson is now a farm, the only remaining souvenir of the old military post being a part of one of the adobe buildings which is incorporated into one of the barns or sheds.

In view of the prominence of the Indians in the Journal it seems proper to devote a little space to clarifying the relationships of the different tribes and bands who are mentioned. In the earlier historical period there were seven different tribes of Indians in North Dakota. They were the Mandans, Hidatsa, Arikara, Assiniboine, Chippewa, Cheyenne, and Sioux. The Mandans had been dwellers along the Missouri in North Dakota for several hundred years. They lived in lodges built of logs and covered with willows, dry grass, and earth, ranging from 25 to 90 feet in diameter, and accommodating an average of twenty persons. At the center of the village was an open plaza, where public performances and tribal ceremonials took place. Facing this was a large lodge with a flattened front, known as the medicine lodge. The village was surrounded by a stout wall of logs, set in a wide embankment of earth and sometimes covered in places with hides. There were salients or bastions at intervals along these walls. Outside was a ditch some nine feet deep and fifteen feet wide, and entrance to the village was over a rude drawbridge. In early days the Mandans lived mainly on the fruits of their agriculture. The crops grown were corn, beans, squash, pumpkins, sunflowers, and tobacco. Large quantities of these various crops were dried and stored in caches or cellars, such as are described in the Journal, and the tribes regularly enjoyed a lucrative trade in them with their more nomadic neighbors. In their full power the Mandans were in complete control of a large region on either side of the Missouri. Successive attacks of the smallpox, however, beginning in 1780, reduced them to a handful, who took up their residence with the Hidatsa and Arikara in the vicinity of Fort Clark, and when the Hidatsa removed to Fort Berthold about 1850 the Mandans went with them. A village was built there in which each tribe had its own section. There we meet them in the Journal.

The Hidatsa, like the Mandans, were of the Siouan stock. They were taller and larger than the Mandans, more aggressive and rougher, and with considerably less stability. According to their own account, they gave up a rather nomadic life on the eastern prairies some time in the seventeenth century to settle near the Mandans. From the latter they learned how to grow corn and the other crops and they built in the Heart River region one or more earth lodge villages much like those of the Mandans.

Some time after their arrival here there was a quarrel between two divisions of the tribe and one large group separated and moved westward into the Yellowstone Valley and the foothills of the Rockies. This division has come to be known as the Crow tribe. Their language is practically a dialect of the Hidatsa, and the Crows have always visited back and forth with the Hidatsa, down to this day.

Before the smallpox visitation of 1780 the Hidatsa moved up the Missouri to the mouth of Knife River and there built three or four villages. Here they continued to live until their final removal to Fort Berthold.

The Arikara, the third of the Three Allied Tribes, formed the most northerly extension of the Caddoan stock, which was scattered through the plains region from Texas northward. They were originally closely allied with the Skidi Pawnee in Nebraska, but after a quarrel they left and traveled northeastward to the Missouri, where they first fought but eventually became allied with the Mandans and the Hidatsa. They had many disputes with the early fur traders, which culminated in the famous Ashley-Leavenworth expedition of the United States Army against them in 1825. At that time they were forced to abandon their villages near the mouth of Grand River, and after various removals, about the year 1860 they joined the Mandan-Hidatsa village at Fort Berthold, adding to it a quarter for themselves. There we shall find them in the Journal.

Physically the Arikara are somewhat shorter and usually more stocky than their Siouan neighbors, with strong features and a proud and haughty appearance and manner. They have always been excellent warriors and for many generations, though fewer in numbers, have maintained an excellent defense against their Sioux enemies.

The Sioux or Dakota Nation was and still is perhaps the largest group in the Plains. They are generally divided into three great divisions, each of which is composed of several tribes. These divisions are the Santee or most easterly group, the Yankton or middle group, and the Teton or western group. In the Santee group are the Mdewakanton, the Wahpeton, the Wahpekute, the Sisseton; the Yankton include the Yank-

ton proper and the upper and lower Yanktonais; the Teton include the Brule, Oglalla, Sans Arcs, Blackfoot, Minneconjou,
Two Kettle, and Uncpapa. There were many
small bands under individual chiefs and bearing special names, but belonging to one or
other of the seven tribes last mentioned.

Prior to the Minnesota troubles the Santee group lived along the Minnesota River
from its mouth to Big Stone Lake in the
northeast corner of South Dakota. They
were driven from that region, and thoroughly
scattered over the plains and among the
other tribes, by both the Sibley and the
Sully expeditions. Later the Sissetons had a
reserve west of Lake Traverse in northern
South Dakota; the Devils Lake reservation
was set up for other remnants, predomi-
nantly the Mdewakanton, and some fled to
Canada or took up residence on some of the
other Sioux reservations; still others were
given land in southern and southeastern
South Dakota.

The Yanktons for many years held the
region in southern and central South Dakota between the Missouri River and the
Big Sioux River. North of them the Yanktonais ranged east of the Missouri, especially in the James and Cheyenne valleys up
to the country of the Chippewa and Assini-

boine. This group was for the most part generally friendly to the whites. Most of the Teton division ranged within historical times west of the Missouri to the Black Hills and the Powder River, touching the Yellowstone and disputing western Nebraska with the Pawnees. At the time of our Journal most of the eastern division was scattered among the hostile bands, which were largely of the Teton group, who were particularly incensed at the invasion of their hunting grounds. The Yanktonais were wandering through North Dakota on both sides of the Missouri and far east into the James River valley. The Teton group was largely west of the Missouri, but small bands were wandering much farther east looking for opportunities to attack the whites, solitary or in small groups.

The Dakota were an extremely warlike race, the conquerors of nearly all their neighbors except the Chippewa. Physically they are unusually tall, straight, spare but strongframed, active and with great endurance. Mentally they are intelligent but headstrong, impatient of control and authority. Their religious and ceremonial life is but little developed, although they are famous dancers. Ever since they obtained the horse they have been outstanding horsemen, perhaps the equal of any in the world. The horse made possible their nomadic and hunting life and their last great struggle against the United States Army.

With the coming of peaceful times they have been unwilling to learn to support themselves, and have apparently felt that it was their right to be supported by the government. With the younger people this feeling is apparently on the wane, and many of them are gainfully employed, giving satisfactory service.

GEORGE F. WILL
Bismarck, N. Dak.

Army Life in Dakota

Army Life in Dakota

NOTES

I LEFT Paris on Tuesday, June 11, 1867. Paris *en fête*, at the height of the Universal Exposition, gathering her birds of passage from every corner of the world, and rejoicing in visits from foreign sovereigns. For the official world was nothing but grand dinners, grand receptions, grand balls, grand celebrations of all sorts. For the common herd, theaters and places of amusement of every kind at the maximum of attractiveness; horse races two or three times a week, grand review succeeding grand review to do honor, today to the Emperor of Russia, tomorrow to the King of Prussia, then for the Sultan, and again for the Emperor of Austria. Foreign crowned heads literally overran the streets. The Emperor Alexander laid aside his majesty, and incognito from a box at the *Varietiés*, listened to "La Duchesse de Gerolstein." The King of Prussia, attired as a plain citizen, took his schooner of beer at the cafe. The heir to the crown of England—but we will pass that by. Every afternoon, in the Bois de Boulogne, appeared around the lake so many Royal and Imperial Highnesses, so many foreign dukes and princes, that one could no longer keep track of them. From nine o'clock in the morning until six in the evening, the entire Universe crowded the concentric ellipses of the Champ de Mars throughout the length of the marvelous galleries of the exposition.

The great whirlwind caught me an hour after my arrival. It bore me along for several weeks, and never let me go until an hour before my departure. And now I am leaving Paris to pass directly to the Upper Missouri. From the radiant summits of civilized life, I am about to plunge abruptly into the shadowy depths of existence in the wilderness. Never was contrast more violent. But contrasts are the salt of life; they banish monotony and boredom, and give a savor that one searches for in vain in sedentary occupations. To know life, one must attack it from different angles, study it from different points of view. The text-book *par excellence* is the book of personal experience. In its chapters, I fear, an orderly progression serves only to dull the sensations and weaken the judgment. The greater the contrasts the stronger the impressions, the truer, or I should say the more natural, become the

4

appreciations. In such case the mind takes a Russian bath, and my mental Russian bath is to pass from Paris to Dakota, as one would pass from the steam room to the icy shower.

The last ten days of my sojourn in France was devoted to my family, and on June 22, 1867, I embarked at Brest on the *Ville de Paris*.

* * *

I landed in New York on the morning of July 3. My first duty was to report my arrival to the Adjutant General of the Army, and to devote to my relatives the few days that remained to me before the orders of the War Department should reach me. They arrived on the 12th, and on the 16th, having completed my preparations and passed the examination prescribed for all officers transferred from the Volunteer to the Regular Service, I set out to join my command on the Upper Missouri. Fort Rice, in Dakota, is designated as my headquarters. I am to proceed there by the shortest possible route.

JOURNAL

I left New York the morning of July 16, and arrived in Chicago, Illinois, the evening of the 17th, after thirty-six consecutive hours on the train. I put up at the Sherman

House, and gave up the morning of the 18th to going about this city, marvelous for the rapidity and extent of its development. It must be remembered that thirty years ago— thirty years only—Chicago did not exist. It was then a village grouped around a military post, of two companies, barracked in log houses surrounded by palisades; a very dirty village, squatted down in the mud of the prairie, on the bank of a natural creek at the end of Lake Michigan. Only two years before, it had been acquired from the Indians, who had sold immense quantities of land in the region, and whom the government had transferred to the other side of the Missouri. Bears and wolves still frequented the neighborhood, and commerce did not exist.

And now behold the prodigy. The population of Chicago that in 1836 was less than two thousand souls, has passed in 1866 the figure of two hundred thousand . . . . Thirty years ago, Chicago could only be reached on horseback, or by primitive carts. The first locomotive appeared there in 1849,[1] and today an average of two hundred trains ar-

[1] The statements about early Chicago are not wholly accurate. The growth of the modern city began in 1833. The Indian title to the 6-mile-square tract on which Chicago was built was acquired by the United States at the Treaty of Greenville in 1795. The first stage line

rive and depart each day, over a network of
about 5,000 miles of railway radiating from
the city as a center. And so it is with everything else.

* * *

I left for Omaha at three in the afternoon.
The sleeping cars on the railroad from Chicago to Omaha are not so luxurious as those
that are pompously called "silver palaces"
on the route from New York to Chicago.
There are no private staterooms; mirrors are
not as plentiful and the ornamentation is
more sober; but nevertheless they are sufficiently comfortable—really much more
comfortable than one would have the right
to expect on a route that does not touch any
center of population, any city, or any town,
but which runs straight across the almost
desert prairies of Iowa, for a distance of 490
miles, to end at a miserable village on the
bank of the Missouri,—for the railroad stops
at Council Bluffs, four or five miles from
Omaha, which is on the other side of the
river.

My trip across Illinois and Iowa initiated
me to the spectacle of the great plains of the

entered Chicago in 1835, and the city was incorporated
in 1837. The first railroad locomotive, on the Galena
and Chicago Union Road, made its initial run—a distance of 5 miles—October 25, 1848. M. M. Q.

West as seen from a car window. These flat immensities, where not a mountain nor a hill rises, where only some tiny stream barely traces a bed in its lazy flow, are known as prairies. Nothing interrupts the view except here and there, where some scattered groves mark the line where the sky meets the earth at the horizon. . . . The population of the prairies is still so scattered that one sees only here and there, far apart, log houses, surrounded by cultivated fields, and shaded by a grove of young trees. Everywhere no real roads; only a few paths for travellers on foot or beasts of burden. The only wagon roads that I saw were the muddy ditches, that, long and narrow, marked the stations of the railroad, where several "rough sketches" of houses grouped around a waiting room and freight shed, served as a pretense at a village.

* * *

The passengers are in keeping with their surroundings. They are for the most part rough men of the West, not touched with refinement from any point of view, uncultured morally and physically, but endowed with vigor, and utilizing energetically the faculties that God has given them. Inside the coaches as on the outside, it is evident that the centers of civilization are receding; although here, as everywhere else, one meets the Yankee, precocious fruit of the civilization of the East.

Among the horde of men seeking their fortune, there are some who have already found it. These are easily recognizable by their jewelry, their speech and their carriage; much more so than by their manners. Almost without exception those that you meet of this class are lucky or able fellows who have won their dollars by the sweat of their brows, and at the risk of their lives. Emerged from the lemon, they have not had time to shed the peel. Living among savages, or semi-savages, plunged over their heads in the current of affairs, they are little anxious to raise themselves above the level of such material comfort and vulgar pleasures as they can get in exchange for their dollars. They may be able, intelligent, active, energetic, and even honest men; but, much as they invoke the name, they are certainly not "gentlemen." The fact is that they are ignorant of the true significance of the word, which has been strangely corrupted in the course of its transition from England to the banks of the Missouri.

* * *

Omaha City was—I speak in the imperfect tense, not on account of the complete state of imperfection that existed there at that time; but because in this devil of a country, everything goes so fast that from one year to another all things become unrecognizable. Certain towns have grown faster than the generation that was born at the same time with them, villages becoming cities before the children there have become men. And in 1867 Omaha was started on such a future, so that the sketch I draw of it today probably will not apply at all to the Omaha of 1870.

In the month of July, 1867, Omaha was no longer a village, and properly speaking, was not yet a town, although it rejoiced in the name of Omaha City.[2] The designation, after all, is of little consequence, for a group of a dozen shacks, will often, *motu proprio*, judge itself by the light of anticipation. I am assured that the population of Omaha now amounts to ten thousand inhabitants.

[2] Omaha as seen by De Trobriand was a typical frontier town. It was new and rough, a product purely of the railroad, its importance increased by the fact that it was the farthest north point of railroad contact with steamboat navigation at the time. This contact was important for a brief time only, for with the building of new lines the trans-shipping front changed, first to Sioux City, then to Bismarck, when the Northern Pacific Railroad was built. The whole great steamboat transportation system hardly lasted twenty years after the day that De Trobriand first took passage at Omaha. G. F. W.

It scarcely looks it. I should have said five
or six thousand; but I am probably wrong.
Two or three blocks of warehouses, shops,
and offices, among them a theater, part of
them of brick and part of wood, formed a
crowded center where all movement con-
verged, and where the greatest activity was
displayed. The principal street, Farnham
Street, connected this center with the river
bank by a straight line. It boasted of two
or three half-blocks in brick, a number of
frame shops, as well as bar-rooms and cheap
eating houses, all ending at the Herndon
Hotel, at the edge of the steep bluff which
stands well above the highest floods of the
Missouri. There, by a long ramp cut into
the perpendicular face of the bluff, the street
now becomes a road, plunges down to the
low, half-submerged ground, and is carried
by a raised grade of earth over the tracks of
the Pacific Railroad right to the bank of the
river.

* * *

In spite of the roughness of their aspect
and their manners, the men of the West are
generally kind and obliging. They readily
enter into conversation with a stranger, and
though they are apt to ask a lot of questions,
they willingly answer any that may be addressed to them. They even take the lead,

and show little reserve in this respect, and will of their own accord tell where they live, what they are doing, what brings them to town, etc. Their adventures in the deserts, among the Indians, are often really interesting, and it seems to me that they are not insensible to the attention they receive.

It can be imagined that I did not fail to gather as much information as I could about this country, absolutely new to me, where I am about to live. In the evening, taking the air on the hotel porch, I had many chats with these pioneers of the West. Especially the Indians, their customs, habits and ideas, were the subjects to which I constantly returned, the more so as my informants were never of the same opinion in the matter. The majority were convinced that the simplest and only means of settling the "Indian question" was to exterminate "all the vermin." This opinion prevails throughout all the frontier, especially in the towns and settlements of any importance. Others, more just and more moderate, believe that the whites have been far from blameless, and attribute to them, at bottom, the causes of the hostilities that broke out during the war, and that are still being carried on. These latter informants are few in number, and while they declare that the poor Indians have been treated like dogs, that they have been lied to, robbed, pillaged, and massacred, they would be just as prompt as the others in shooting on sight any red-skin suspect that crossed their path. The destiny of the white race in America is to eat up the red men, and in this rising tide of population that rolls towards the setting sun there is not one who is backward in taking his bite— no one except the government that temporizes and buys peace, to avoid doing the duty that the individual is performing from choice or from necessity. For example, in Montana, in the very heart of the Indian country, wherever the presence of gold attracts and holds the miners, the Indian must flee or disappear. If he attempts to defend his land, he is exterminated! The miner, interrupted in his work and his dreams of fortune, is in a terrible temper. He must have complete security, sheltered from hostile raids. Therefore he spares no one, and where he meets the red-skin, their women and children as well as warriors are left to fatten the land or the wolves. In many of the frontier settlements they do not consider any other course, and when the settlers take to horse they are never bothered by prisoners on the return from the expedition.

* * *

I waited sixteen days in Omaha: sixteen days of heat, of dust, and of boredom mixed with regret, for, from the lack of any means of communication with my destination, could I not have spent a dozen more days in New York and Newport with my relatives, without being an hour later in arriving at my post? Happily it is not my nature to worry over "Ifs." What is done is done. Goodbye to what is over with.

My first care, on arriving, was to find out when the first steamer going up the river would pass. But as to this, no one could give me any information, as the departures are not on fixed dates, but depend entirely upon the amount of freight that the steamers can pick up. I therefore turned to the notices in the two principal newspapers of St. Louis to find out what boat left first, and on what date. In this way I learned that the *Deer Lodge*, Captain Clark, would leave St. Louis on June 19. Some days later, I learned from the same source that her departure was postponed until the 25th of June. In the end, she did not start until the morning of the 29th.

* * *

Sunday, August 4: At last, here I am on board the *Deer Lodge!* She arrived at Omaha about six o'clock this evening, and is moored to the bank for the night. As I had been expecting her for several days, I was in readiness to embark at once. My preparations did not take long: time to close a trunk or two, to pay my bill at the hotel, to load my baggage on the wagon I had ordered for it, and I was at the landing—much preferring to settle myself on board this evening, and sleep without bothering about the hour of departure, than to stay on at the hotel, to be roused before daylight, and plunged into all the *tohu-bohu* of the last moment. The more so as my baggage had increased greatly in Omaha. Forewarned by the advice of officers accustomed to military life on the frontier, I had supplied myself with what was indispensable in the way of furniture. The rest will follow as circumstances permit. But even the indispensable could not be packed in a handbag. There was a wooden bedstead, mattress, blankets, sheets, table linen and towels, porcelain, glass, and a couple of rocking chairs. These, and four trunks, make a big enough load, and my servant was only just able to get it all on one spring-wagon.

Captain Clark appears to be a fine man. His clerk, Mr. Corbin, who acts as supercargo, is a very polite young man. Both have shown me the greatest courtesy, and have given me the best cabin available. My baggage was soon on board. Two of my trunks were put in my cabin, which I occupy alone; my servant sleeps on a mattress in the saloon near my door, and everything presages as comfortable a voyage as one could hope for.

An hour after me, Brevet Lieutenant-Colonel Chambers, Major of the Twenty-second Regiment, came on board. Longer even than I, he has been waiting at the Hotel Herndon for the steamer to take him to his post, with his young wife and her maid, an orphan whom Mrs. Chambers has cared for and educated, and whom she takes with her wherever she accompanies her husband. The Major is assigned to the command of Fort Randall[3], the first post above Sioux City; therefore he will be with us for only a few days. Included in his baggage is a light carriage, a horse, and two superb greyhounds of the large breed.

On board also, was Mrs. Elliott with her two little daughters. She is on her way to rejoin her husband, a Captain of the Twenty-second Regiment, who is in garrison at Fort Sully, where General Stanley, commanding

[3] Fort Randall, established by General Wm. S. Harney in 1856, was located on the Missouri River about 55 miles airline distance above Yankton, S. Dak. M. M. Q.

the district of southeastern Dakota, has his headquarters.

And last, the most agreeable meeting that I had on embarking was with my adjutant, Mr. Marshall, who is returning from leave, and bringing with him his young wife, whom he has only a few weeks ago married. The impression that Mr. Marshall made on me was in every way favorable. . . . From him, I learn that my command is composed of three posts; Fort Buford, at the confluence of the Yellowstone and the Missouri (5 companies): Fort Totten, on Devils Lake, to the northeast of the great bend that the Missouri makes below Fort Berthold (3 companies): and Fort Stevenson, fifteen miles below Fort Berthold[4] (2 companies). At Fort Stevenson is my headquarters, and therefore it is my destination. Fort Berthold is also under my command; but the garrison has been withdrawn, and it is no longer occupied, except by the agents of the American Fur Company

[4] For interesting comment upon most of these Upper Missouri posts, see Charles Larpenteur, *Forty Years a Fur Trader on the Upper Missouri*, the annual *Lakeside Classics* volume for 1933. Fort Buford was established in 1867, not far from the older American Fur Company Post, Fort Union. Fort Sully was established in 1863 by General Alfred Sully a few miles below Pierre, S. Dak. In 1866 the new Fort Sully, about 25 miles above Pierre, was established. M. M. Q.

and several other white traders. Around them is located an Indian village, containing the remnants of three tribes, formerly powerful and warlike, but today peaceful, few in numbers, and cultivators of corn.

* * *

Monday, August 5: Here we are en route on the great Missouri. At breakfast, I found that there were several more passengers on board than I mentioned last night; the wife and children of a carpenter employed at Fort Rice, very ordinary people with whom I had nothing in common, and a big fellow of unprepossessing aspect, who presented himself to me as the Indian Agent at Fort Berthold; still another source of information.

The country is monotonous. The banks of the river are flat and bordered here and there by bare hills. The river is most capricious in its course, and frequently changes its bed. For years it will build up magnificent alluvial flats; the vegetation there is flourishing and abundant; trees grow rapidly and to a great height; and then one fine day, the Missouri starts to destroy its own work, and from year to year it devours foot by foot these same flats that it had built up.

In the great woods that border the river, the wood-cutters chop down the trees that

are free to all, cut them into sticks of the
desired length, and cord them into long
piles on the bank. The steamboats short of
fuel moor alongside. The price is discussed,
the bargain made, and the crew leaps ashore
and loads on the run the wood purchased;
and then we proceed without loss of time.
The work of the woodcutters is very profitable to them, and pays them well for their
season's labor. A cord of wood brings from
£3 to £6, and even £7, according to the
abundance of the supply, and its proximity
to or remoteness from the point where it is
sold. A skillful and strong man can cut as
much as two cords a day; but supposing an
average of only forty cords a month at $5
each, it makes $200 per month, with no ex-
pense except food. The river being navigable
for six months of the year, there should be a
profit of a thousand to twelve hundred dollars for the season, if the woodcutter works
from April to October.[5] Is that not worth the
risk of a little danger from the Indians, and

[5] The men who cut and sold wood to the steamboats
were generally known as woodhawks. The occupation
was highly profitable, but was also highly dangerous.
The men who engaged in it usually organized into part-
nerships, cut wood all winter, and made their profit
during the season of navigation. Sometimes they were
employed on a share basis by some trader or contractor
who furnished the necessary tools and supplies for the

a life of absolute solitude from the melting of the snows until the first frosts?

* * *

Tuesday, August 6: ... The steamboat *Deer Lodge* is built after the plan that is uniform with all the vessels that navigate the Mississippi and Missouri. Nothing is more simple in design. The hull is very flat, almost without keel, so as to draw as little water as possible. Fully loaded, it draws no more than 4 feet; the average is $3\frac{1}{2}$ to 3 feet. The entire hull, below the deck, forms a hold where merchandise can be stowed. The deck is open for half, or two-thirds of its length forward. The after part is closed in the form of a room to house the engine and to act as repair shop. The fire pits and boilers are in front of the engine on the deck. To the right, left, and in front of the boilers the fire-wood, leaving on either side an outside passage for the crew. In front of the boilers is an uncovered stairway leading to the upper deck. This deck, supported for the entire length of the vessel on light cast-iron columns, contains the saloon or dining room in the middle, from which all the cabins open to the right and left.

winter season. Although the author states the prices received as from 3 to 7 pounds, he undoubtedly intended to write dollars, instead. G. F. W.

The rear part of the saloon is exactly above the boiler-room, which heats the floor, summer as well as winter. Outside the cabins, along either side, runs a gallery upon which each cabin has a glass door, and in summer, by opening the two doors that face each other, an agreeable current of air is created through the entire boat. In the *Deer Lodge*, the saloon, with its side cabins, is flanked by an open deck at either end, one forward and one aft. A stairway leads to the roof of the saloon, but it is seldom used, even though from this height the view is much more extended; if the sun is shining, one is roasted, while if the rain is falling, one is soaked; and if there is neither sun nor rain, the flaming cinders which escape in a shower of sparks from the two high funnels fall on the deck and burn the garments of those exposed to them full of holes.

The only difference in construction that divides the steamboats of the Missouri into two classes is that one type has the paddle-wheels on both sides, and the other has but one in the rear. The *Deer Lodge* is among these latter, the great paddle wheel which drives her taking up the entire width of the stern.

A screw can not be used on account of the shallowness of the water, the rapidity of the current, and above all the numerous obstructions in the river bed, such as stumps, sand banks, etc.

To complete the description, I should mention that the pilot house, where the steering wheel is located, is placed on the roof of the saloon, between the two high funnels, and a little behind them.

To the spectator, who from the bank watches this type of steamboat go by, the appearance is quite different from what we are accustomed to in the East, land of deep waters. The Missouri steamer resembles a long cabin built on piles, which a flood has left high and dry, and which is being moved on a big scow. Nothing could be less graceful; but nothing could be more appropriate to the navigation of the Western rivers, as they are the only system of transportation employed in these regions. The engines are of great power, and low compression. They snort noisily, like giants panting under the weight of mountains. At times they blow up, or the vessel may be sunk by a snag, but as a rule it arrives in safety at its destination.

* * *

Friday, August 9: . . . Towards noon we arrived at Fort Randall. Through the great trees that border the bank, we saw the buildings, only a part of which are surrounded by palisades. That is to say, it is

22

more a post than a fort, as the fortification is absolutely insignificant. There we left Major Chambers and his wife, with the orphan maid servant, the horse and the two greyhounds, in the midst of some twenty Indians who were helping to unload. Then, after the customary hand-shaking and good-byes, the steamboat swung away and resumed her route.

* * *

Saturday, August 10: . . . We lost a lot of time this afternoon. At a place where the river forks at a very wide place into two arms, separated by a long island covered with willows, and by wide banks of sand, we took the wrong channel which was found to have no practicable outlet. We were forced to return on our tracks, for a distance of over a mile; and then we bumped on a sandbank twenty or thirty metres thick. It ended in our having to force a passage, or a ditch, through this obstacle, by the force of steam, and the aid of two gigantic crutches, by means of which the bow of the boat could be raised. These crutches consist of two strong spars suspended from a powerful crane placed on each side of the bow.

They let the foot of the spar sink to the bottom of the water, which is only two and a half, or three feet, below the surface. Then

23

they attach to an enormous ring on the bow of the boat, a system of blocks and pullies of which one end is fastened to the end of the spar, and the other to a capstan worked by the steam engine. The boat, thus lifted by the bow, forces its slow passage over the surface of the shifting sand that the current partly sweeps away; and so, after an hour or more of repeated effort, we found ourselves once more afloat in the channel, and continuing on our way. It goes without saying that before beginning the operation, they launched a small boat and sounded in every direction to find the best passage—or to be more exact, the least bad.

* * *

Tuesday, August 13: Arrived at the landing for new Fort Sully toward ten o'clock in the morning. Needless to say, the landing consists only of half-a-dozen posts planted in the prairie, alongside which the steamboats moor. The post is a mile or two away on a point of bluff where not a shrub grows. It is a group of buildings for a garrison of four companies of the Twenty-second Regiment, and for the accommodation of General Stanley and his staff, as Fort Sully is the headquarters of the military district.

There is absolutely no justification for calling it a fort, for the location is not even protected by a moat or a palisade. General Stanley is of the opinion that with a despicable enemy like the Indian, the men should be trained to trust to their own vigilance and to their breech-loaders for their protection, rather than to the shelter of palisades which serve only to weaken their morale. I think the General is perfectly right.

* * *

We are now entering the region frequented by hostile Indians. At times they hide themselves in the bushes, to fire on the steamboats as they pass close to the bank. Several persons have been killed or wounded in this way: therefore, for the protection of the passengers, the Captain of the *Deer Lodge* has surrounded the upper gallery with bundles of shingles piled in a double row, which formed for us a bullet-proof rampart 4 feet high. The sides of the pilot house are also protected by a thick sheet-iron sheathing. Moreover, the steamboats on the Upper Missouri go armed. We carry on the forward deck two mortars, and in the saloon is a rack of guns and rifles,—not counting the revolvers that each male passenger is armed with as a matter of course.

* * *

Friday, August 16: . . . We arrived at Fort Rice towards dawn. This had been my first

destination, but after having visited it, I
give thanks to Heaven that I have been sent
elsewhere. On a raised point on the right
bank of the river stands a square enclosure
of palisades with block-houses projecting
from two of its corners. This is Fort Rice.
Outside are built several traders' cabins; inside, four companies of the Twenty-second,
commanded by Lieutenant Colonel Otis,
have their quarters, cramped by reason of the
lack of space necessary for the different
buildings. The officers' quarters are cabins
of squared logs, chinked with clay; one-
storied, whitewashed inside, and of very poor
appearance.[6] . . .

The Indians are numerous around the
Fort. They are principally Yanktonais and
Uncpapa, both belonging to the Sioux nation. The Government distributes goods to
them once a year, and the garrison gives
them supplies from time to time. These
tribes are divided. Part remain close to the
fort, without taking part in any hostilities
against the whites, with whom in conse-

[6] Fort Rice, about 25 miles south of Mandan, was
established by General Sully in the summer of 1864. For
a number of years it was an important post where
numerous councils were held. It is now distinguishable
only by the old foundations of the buildings. The
site is a state park and has been properly marked.
G. F. W.

quence they are on terms of friendship. The other part stick to the Plains and live a wandering life, having no contact with the military posts unless to commit an armed depredation when the opportunity presents itself. These latter are the ones who sometimes fire on the steamboats. Not infrequently their vagabond course leads them into the region that separates Fort Rice from Fort Stevenson, especially on the west bank of the river.

* * *

Sunday, August 18: ... The Indians do not bury their dead. They expose them on scaffolds supported by four long posts eight or ten feet high, probably to keep them from the teeth of the wolves. The body, wrapped in skins and blankets and corded from head to foot, is laid on its back. There it remains to dry in the sun, or to decompose through the action of the other elements. We saw from a distance a number of these aerial tombs which are generally perched on the top of a hill. ...

We continue to make good progress ... They tell me that this is the fastest trip that has been made between St. Louis and the spot where we have just tied up for the night. This feat is recorded in big letters on a long plank which they are now nailing to the trunk of a tall tree in plain sight. The inscription reads

"The Deer Lodge—20 days out"
August 18, 1867.

This will be the admiration and envy of all the steamboats that will pass here after us.

* * *

FORT STEVENSON

August 19, 1867: Here I am, landed and safe at my post. To reach here I have crossed half of France by rail, 17 hours—the Atlantic Ocean by steamer, 10½ days—7 States of the Union, in a trip of 1,400 miles, 60 hours; —and at last I have ascended the Upper Missouri for a distance of 1,235 miles in 20 days and some hours. I have the right to rest. But first let us examine my future residence.

At the 101st degree of west longitude and between the 47th and 48th degrees of north latitude, the Missouri, after having run for a long time towards the East, describes an abrupt curve and takes a new direction towards the South. At a few hundred meters above this curve, and on an elevated bench, at this spot, some forty or fifty feet above the water, the white tents of a little camp of two companies are baking in the sun. This is the temporary post awaiting the construction of Fort Stevenson. The steamboats

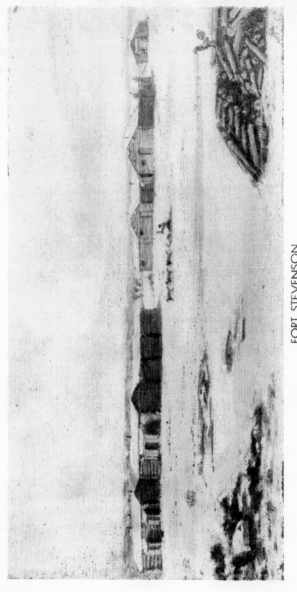

FORT STEVENSON

stop at a spot a little less elevated on the
upper side of this sharp curve, where the
current has eaten out a semicircle from the
edge of the bottoms. There, under make-
shift sheds, are piled the sacks of corn and
oats, miscellaneous supplies and the quantities of material requisite to establishing a
new post: cannon, caissons, shingles, am-
bulances, pine planks, lumber, bricks, etc.
At this landing they unload first all the
freight, which later will be transferred to the
tent warehouses back of the camp.

The tents of the officers, most of them furnished with plank floors, face toward the
river on a sort of natural terrace. The tents
of the companies are ranged at right angles
to these and in the direction of the slope of
the ground that falls away in the rear, giving a natural drainage for the water when it
rains, which seems to be very seldom. Below the companies are situated the quarters
of the civilian workmen, backed on one side
by a double corral, where they keep in one
section the cattle, and in the other the work
horses and mules. On a line with the corral
and more to the eastward is the steam saw-
mill where the logs are transformed into
planks, beams, or joists. The machine is in
full activity.

The warehouses of the commissary and

the quarter-master project forward on the
right flank of the camp, parallel to the hospital tents.

* * *

The sweep of the country is vast and the
eye traverses it easily. It consists of a wide
and long flat bounded on the north by a
chain of irregular hills, and on the south by
the river that runs parallel with them from
west to east. In its windings it leaves bare,
sometimes on one side, sometimes on the
other, great sand bars, or alluvial land covered with willows, with brush or tall timber.
These woods contain the only trees, except
one, that are visible within the horizon. The
one and only tree that makes the exception
grows, I do not know why, in the bottom of
a ravine that opens on the flat, and therefore
is visible from it. But neither on the chain
of hills to the north nor on the high and
steep bluffs that border the right bank of the
river to the south does anything appear but
a few bushes in depressions of the ground.
Everywhere else is nothing but a uniform
carpet of grass. The flat extends in the same
way a very great distance to the east and
west, where it ends by blending with the sky.
In the direction of Berthold, the hills approach the river, where little hills of alkaline
soil, bare of vegetation, dominate the view

and form the boundary of sight at eight or
ten miles from camp. In the opposite direction, the roll of the ground is less noticeable,
and the view extends without interruption
for even a greater distance. Finally, a mile
to the east, the plain is cut across by the
windings of a little stream called Douglas
Creek. There is a bridge here, built since our
coming; but as the water flows enclosed between banks below which only rushes and a
few bushes grow, its course is not apparent,
and to discover it, it is necessary to be literally on its edge. In all of that there is
nothing especially picturesque. The character of the country is absolutely of the desert;
space and solitude.

And now where are the buildings? Hardly
begun. The garrison only arrived here in
June last, when Fort Berthold was abandoned. It had been necessary all at one
time to choose at once the best location for
the construction of the fort, to measure the
ground, examine the slopes, and to seek the
most desirable conditions; afterwards, or at
the same time to draw a complete plan of the
buildings to be built, their location in respect to each other, and their size. That
done, the first work had been to lay the
foundations and to install the steam engine.
But to lay the foundations, stones were

needed, and these stones were detached rocks which were only to be found in the bluffs a mile and a half or two miles from camp. The transporting of them could only be done slowly, and when brought in, they had to be broken into the desired sizes. While the masons, for the most part civilian laborers, were busy with this work, fatigue parties crossed the river in a skiff, and cut down on the opposite bank the tall trees that would furnish the lumber. Over there is a permanent post of ten men, a sergeant and two corporals, who sleep there in log cabins, and look after a team of oxen, and one of six mules. When the trees are cut and stripped of their branches, one end of the trunks is raised and fastened by chains on the running gear of a wagon without a box and they are thus hauled to the river. When ten or a dozen of these logs are put into the water, they are lashed firmly together into a raft which the skiff takes in tow, and pulls to the opposite bank near the landing place. There the logs are hoisted up to the bench on an inclined chute made of boards, and from there dragged to the saw-mill in the same way that they were dragged to the river. I find that between four and five hundred great trees have already been felled, and a good part of them have been brought

to the left bank. The frame of the principal
warehouse for the new fort is already up,
and the frames for the windows and doors
are being put in place. The wood is very
bad; it is cottonwood, but we have no choice.
It is the only kind available.

All the walls will be of adobe.[7] These are
large Mexican bricks, made after an idea
borrowed from the houses of New Mexico.
They are made in a sort of pressed tile, half
clay, half sand, mixed with chopped hay.
These bricks are made quickly by hand in
moulds or frames of boards, and then dried
and baked in the sun, which gives them great
hardness. The same mixture of mud that
composes them serves to cement them together, and the whole makes good building
material, solid and durable summer and
winter. The brick-yard is between the landing and the camp and extends some distance
to the rear. The adobes, whose manufacture
is being actively pushed, are spread out or
piled up, according to the degree of completion that they have reached. There are already twenty to thirty thousand made and

[7] This experiment with the use of adobe or sun-dried
clay bricks was probably the first in the Northwest and
almost the last. Although not considered very successful, there is still standing a portion of one of the adobe
buildings. G. F. W.

ready for use. In two or three days they will begin the walls of the warehouse.

In fact, the building of the fort is only at its beginning, and whatever they may say, it seems to me that it will hardly be in habitable condition for this winter. The garrison is only 220 men and the civilian employees bring the number to 260. There must always be subtracted the guards on and off duty, the orderlies and men detached in the various offices of the post and district, adjutant, commissary and quartermaster, and those who are available for fatigue duty must be divided into wood-cutters, guards for the wagons, which are always under escort, brick makers and the cattle guard. These numerous labors occupy every one all the time. Whence it results that during the building of the fort, military instruction will cease. Not an hour is left for drill; no time for guard mount.

The quartermaster has pitched two wall tents which will be my temporary quarters for several days. My servant is in the rear in an 'A' tent. This is the arrangement that I had during the war. Once more I am sleeping under canvas. Come! Let us take up the life of a soldier on campaign. During two years I have had time to lose the habit, but the trick will not be hard to relearn.

* * *

Army Life in Dakota

Wednesday, August 21: An Indian employee came today from Fort Berthold.[8] Since the departure of the company that were in garrison there, he has constituted himself guardian of the grain left in storage there, and has faithfully kept the women and children from stealing anything. For this service he has come to ask for certain supplies, which will be given him, and which will be renewed each month as long as the grain is left in his charge.

* * *

The French-Canadians abound here. With one exception the traders at Fort Berthold are French. Their employees are all of French-Canadian origin. French is their language; the interpreters speak it much better than English. The building contractor and nearly all the carpenters and masons are French or Canadians. The half-breeds are all children of Canadian fathers. Certainly my native tongue will be of great assistance to me here.

[8] Fort Berthold was established as a trading post and Indian agency in 1845. In 1864 General Sully supplied it with a small garrison, as a protection against the Sioux, whom he had been engaged in chastising. For a description of the fort in 1868, see *Yellowstone Kelly* (New Haven, 1926), 25–31. The establishment of Fort Stevenson, a few miles away, in 1867, made it unnecessary to maintain a garrison at Fort Berthold, which was, accordingly, discontinued. M. M. Q.

The convoy of 110 wagons left today for Devils Lake. It is accompanied by Lieutenant Walborn who is instructed to engage a score of Red River half-breeds. Their pay will be that of a soldier, that is, $16 per month, their clothing, rations and a horse. If they do not take the clothing, they receive instead six dollars and a half more per month. If they bring their own horses, four cents additional per day. They are employed to scout about the post, to herd the cattle, and to carry the mail, on horseback during the summer and autumn, and when the snow covers the ground by dogtrain. In case of expeditions or a march over the Plains, they will act as scouts.

Thursday, August 22: Having sufficiently familiarized myself with everything, I took over today the command of the post and the district. The officers of my staff are: Captain (Brevet Major) Furey, quartermaster of the district and the post; Lieutenant Marshall, assistant adjutant-general of the district and adjutant of the regiment; Lieutenant Parsons, quartermaster of the regiment and commissary of the post; Lieutenant Norvell, assistant inspector general of the district (absent for the time); Dr. Gray, surgeon major. The post is in command of

Captain (Brevet Lieutenant Colonel) Powell. Among the officers six are married and five have their young wives with them, who, with several children enliven and brighten our military colony.

In this number I have not counted Major (Bt. Col.) Whistler, who is only here temporarily, awaiting my arrival. He is going away on leave in a few days, taking with him his wife and three children. On his return he will take command of the post at Devils Lake. Colonel Whistler is an old soldier and an excellent man. He has spent twenty-one years in the service, always in the plains of the West, except for the last year of the War, when he commanded a regiment of Volunteers in the Army of the Potomac.[9] He is waiting for the return of the *Deer Lodge* to take passage upon it.

The married officers eat at their own homes. The others, all lieutenants, mess together. As for me, I take my meals with

[9] Colonel Joseph N. G. Whistler was a grandson of Captain John Whistler, builder of Fort Dearborn, and the son of Colonel William Whistler, who also served at Fort Dearborn for many years. Colonel Whistler graduated from West Point in 1846, and served continuously until his retirement in 1886, being several times brevetted for gallant and distinguished conduct in battles of the Mexican and the Civil War. He died at Fort Wadsworth, N. Y., in 1899. M. M. Q.

Major Furey, quartermaster of the district. The provisions for the table lack variety; fresh beef (once or twice a week), ham and salt pork, beans, tomatoes and other preserved vegetables; jams or preserved fruit. Most of the families have a cow and some chickens which are great additions. The most valuable source of supply for us in the autumn is the feathered and furred game, especially the feathered. At this time there is an abundance of large snipe and teal, and later will come the ducks and wild geese, plover, prairie-chickens, all in great numbers, until the snow becomes so deep as to stop the hunting.

The heat is extreme. During the day the mercury rises to 110°F. in the shade. But I do not suffer as much as with the heat at 85° or 90° in New York. Why is that? It is not because of the gentle breeze that generally blows at the edge of the water. It is more on account of the atmospheric conditions: the air is very pure and very dry; the sky very high and deep. The weather is continually fair. Here it never rains from June to November. In revenge, from time to time there are terrible wind-storms. Last week, the entire camp just missed being blown into the river. Nearly all the tents were beaten down, furniture was upset, china broken, and a cast-iron stove was rolled by the wind right to the foot of the bench. And all in the midst of frightful whirlwinds of dust, and without a drop of rain. Yesterday the weather was stormy; one would have looked for a deluge; but everything passed in another violent wind. This time at least all the tents held.

Saturday, August 24: . . . A splendid night. What an astonishing clearness in the atmosphere! Never either in America or Europe, have I seen so many stars, nor any that seemed to blaze with such brilliancy, whether in the zenith or on the edge of the horizon. The feeling of the immensity of the heavens and the earth strikes me more forcibly here than any other place that I have been.

* * *

Monday, August 26: A party of Indians came this morning from Fort Berthold to sell vegetables and corn that they had grown and harvested. They belong to two tribes, Rees and Gros-Ventres. This name of "Gros-Ventre" was given them by the Canadians. I do not know why, for their bellies are no larger than those of the others, and to the contrary, like all Indians, they are spare and generally of a sinewy, slender build. Their true name, in their own tongue, is "Hedanza," which is decidedly more euphonic and signifies "The men from among

39

the willows," for the tribe has always lived on the banks of the river.

Some of our visitors came downstream in bullboats. A bullboat is simply a buffalo hide, sewn together in the form of a nearly round tub, with neither bow nor stern. It is kept in shape by a light frame of wood. In this skin tub, a man is seated, his shoulders here, his legs there, back of two squaws squatted beside him. These two women, as usual, do all the work, and are charged with delivering their lord and master wherever he pleases to go. Once disembarked at their destination, one of them takes the boat on her shoulders, or more often on her head, and the other carries the provisions. The Indian, like the fourth at the funeral of "Malbrook," "il ne porte rien." If the skin is in bad shape and of no value, the boat is abandoned, for in this contrivance the stream can easily be descended with the current, but never ascended. Therefore its principal use is to cross from one bank to the other of the river in front of Berthold.

* * *

Saturday, August 31: . . . The *Miner,* which, in spite of its name, carried no miners on board, took away Brevet Colonel Whistler with all his family, composed of Mrs. Whistler, two girls of ten and twelve, perhaps more, and a small boy of seven. These children have arrived at an age when it is necessary to think of their education, a thing absolutely impossible in the frontier posts where they have accompanied their father until now.

Officers without private fortunes, and therefore obliged to remain all their lives in the service, find themselves in a most difficult position in the matter of bringing up their children, especially if they are girls. If they keep them with them in the military posts scattered in the desert, any instruction is impossible and all means of education are lacking, unless the mother can devote herself to the task, and, which is rare, is capable of undertaking it. They generally have enough to do to look after the needs of the household and to clothe the children, an expensive and difficult task so far from all source of supplies. If, on the other hand, they send them away to some educational institution to be brought up, almost certainly their mother follows them, and then no matter how many economies the father may make, the expenses devour practically all his income. The entire family is under the strain, a strain under which they can not even keep up appearances.

The family thus separated, when will it be reunited again? Perhaps never. To bring girls to a frontier post is practically to ruin their chance of marrying, or to reduce their chances to the possibility of some young officer in his turn putting his head in the noose. Temporary reunions are also rare and costly, for then the officer who travels at his own expense can not go such enormous distances without considerable outlay. This is, I think, one of the reasons why so many officers quit the service after a few years, when they have the opportunity to live at home or elsewhere by any other means. Without doubt Colonel Whistler will ask for some post on detached duty that will be near Georgetown, close to Washington, where he is going to leave his family. But it is doubtful if he will obtain it as this kind of service is most sought after, and the old soldier who has passed his life on the plains far from the world of politics and the source of favor will not be able to bring to bear sufficient influence for the success of his plans. At the expiration of a leave of two months he will again have to take the trail to the frontier, and rejoin his command at Fort Totten on Devils Lake.

The departure of Colonel Whistler puts at my disposition the two large hospital tents that formed his quarters, a wall tent for my servant, and a kitchen, half-lumber and half-

canvas. My two tents are joined together,
and strengthened on the outside by a wall
of slabs. Both are floored, and a good stove
protects me in advance from the first cold.
Luckily for me, Colonel Whistler, in parting,
wished to get rid of the greater part of his
furniture; thanks to this chance I can sufficiently furnish my two rooms. I had
imagined, in my inexperience of the ways
and means of the Upper Missouri, that I
could, after my arrival at Stevenson, order
what would seem necessary either from St.
Louis or Omaha, and receive it before winter.
If I had had to depend on that source only,
I leave to the imagination the picture of my
two rooms with only my camp bed, my rocking chair and my four trunks "without accompaniment." All has turned out for the
best in the end, and without having to send
anywhere, I now have a bureau with a mirror, a wash stand, chairs, a table, a clothes
press, and even a carpet. Our dinner table
is the richer for the porcelain and glass of
Colonel Whistler.

* * *

Sunday, September 1: At sundown two Indian scouts arrived, equipped and armed like
our soldiers, except that the boots or shoes are
replaced by moccasins, though they travel on
horseback. This type of foot-gear of deer skin

is very much softer to the feet, and nothing is better for a long march. These Indians were sent to us from Fort Rice. They are bearers of a letter from Lieutenant Colonel Otis commanding the post, in which by instruction of General Stanley, commander of the Southeastern District, he informs me that a considerable band of Sioux Indians, just now camped in the neighborhood of Fort Sully, are preparing an expedition against the Ree Indians, located with the Mandans and Gros-Ventres near Fort Berthold. These three tribes are peaceful and not very strong, partly due to their small numbers, partly to their character. Nevertheless they have long been at war with the Sioux of lower Dakota, who from time to time make raids against them to run off their horses, mules, and cattle, and get as many scalps as they can lift without too much risk. As both sides are friends of the United States, we are not supposed to mix in their quarrels, and we have nothing to lose by the redskins destroying each other. Nevertheless, I have sent word immediately to the Three Tribes of the attack that threatens them, so that they may prepare for it.

Since Fort Berthold was abandoned as a military post, it has returned to the status of a trading post, where three or four traders and agents of the Northwest Fur Company hold out. Mr. Wilkinson, the United States Indian agent for the Three Tribes, and some others, also live there. Since the Indians never attack a fort, even though most of these forts are nothing but a fence of palisades surrounding the buildings, the whites are safe, even without a military garrison. Berthold is only fifteen miles from here, and if need be, I could lend a hand.

The Sioux Indians will trouble us here still less; but it is safer to be on our guard and give them no opportunity to run off some mules or cattle, a temptation that they never can resist.

A few days ago, a dozen warriors of the Three Tribes came down the river in four bullboats going on the war path to steal from the Sioux some horses, upon which they expected to return. We have heard nothing of them since, and it will be well for them, if having gone to seek wool, they themselves have not been shorn. Nevertheless, if without being discovered they reach the camp where the Sioux have left their squaws and children, they may do more damage than they had expected, and bring back more spoil and scalps than they hoped for.

* * *

Wednesday, September 4: We were not prepared to receive the reënforcement of mules that arrived yesterday. Lacking a corral into which to turn them, they are fastened, more or less satisfactorily, to a picket-line inside the camp where we keep our work animals, out of reach of the Indians. During the night eleven of them broke loose and managed to get away. Instead of staying near the camp they bolted into the prairie, and two or three squads of men on horseback, sent in different directions, have not been able to find them. I suspect that these men are afraid of the Indians, and have not dared to get out of sight of the fort. They will be beating the bushes more or less the length of several ravines, where they can not be seen, and will not venture up on the Plains for fear of getting into trouble. Only one squad has been seen on the summit of the hills, scanning the Plains beyond, and not fearing to show themselves. Many of our recruits have let themselves become frightened by the absurd stories and ridiculous reports about the Indians, until they have become accustomed to think of them as such dangerous enemies that they are rather to be avoided than attacked.

The truth is that the Indian is much less formidable than he is represented to be. If

this were not so could there be established
and maintained, isolated in the midst of the
Indian country, such weak military posts of
one or two companies, beyond reach of any
help or support, and sometimes even without
communication with the rest of the world
during the entire duration of the winter?
For the redskin, substitute the paleface, and
all these posts would be wiped out in one
season.

I have here two hundred and fifty men
camped in the open, without a shadow of
fortification, entrenchment, or defense of any
kind. A few rows of posts, making an in-
complete palisade, are planted behind the
tents where the wives of the officers live, to
persuade them that they are sheltered from
the arrows of the Indians—that is all. The
supplies piled in temporary sheds at the
landing several hundred yards from the
camp have no other protection day or night
than the rifles of three or four sentinels. The
cattle that pasture all day on the plains
under guard of three men and a corporal,
spend the night in a flimsy enclosure some
distance from there. Our sawmill is in the
open beyond the guard lines. Our buildings
under construction are five or six hundred
meters out in the wide open plain where a
band of Indians would find no more obstruc-

tion than the wind. Near there, the sutler
and ten civilians have their tents, and are
building a double log cabin. Indeed my two
companies work all day and sleep in their
tents all night without protection. Where
could a finer opportunity for attack be found
by an enemy who could unite against us
whenever he wished a thousand warriors,
tempted by the booty of our herds and
teams, to say nothing of our scalps? And
yet the hostile Indians dare not attack us.

Once—it was several days before I arrived—their war path led them into our
immediate neighborhood. There were five
or six hundred braves; that is to say, more
than double our number. During the night
they hid in some of the draws near camp, to
surprise some solitary workman or to run
off some mules, supreme object of the
warrior's ambition. The bravest took up a
position behind some piles of adobes near
the foundation of the new fort, where their
presence was discovered at daybreak, and the
men were called to arms.

Meantime, a teamster, an old cavalry
man, unafraid of the redskins, started out
with his team without waiting for his escort,
although he had received orders not to do so.
Arrived at the foundations of the new fort,
he discovered that he was surrounded by a

half-dozen Indians who cut the traces of his
animals and ran off the four mules. One of
them shot him with an arrow, almost at arm's
length, and thus he was killed by his own
fault. He was unarmed and threw himself
stupidly into the jaws of the wolf. Those
who had dealt the blow fled before the escort
had arrived or before the garrison could realize what had happened. The entire band of
warriors then began to caracole on their
horses at a distance of two thousand meters,
and to make all sorts of gesticulations in
sign of triumph. A small cannon was trained
on the principal group. A shell flew whistling to burst in their midst. One of them
had his leg carried off, another was more or
less badly wounded, and one of their horses
was disemboweled. It needed no more to
put to flight the six hundred warriors, and
the entire band, at a gallop, quickly disappeared at full speed, hastening to cross the
river twenty or thirty miles below. Since
then, nothing more has been heard from them,
and not a hostile Indian has shown himself
above the horizon.

The only real danger that is to be feared
from them is isolated murder, when they are
scattered in force on the outskirts of the
forts where woods or brush give them the
chance to hide themselves and lie in wait for

solitary workmen. But if the wood cutting is done by a detachment, they seldom risk an attack upon it.

In front of the camp, and on the other side of the river, I have a small detachment of ten men commanded by a sergeant. They have with them some ten oxen to haul to the river's edge several hundred logs that have been felled in the deep woods. Their cabins are there, and in them they stay day and night, but not an Indian has shown himself nearby. They are afraid of being discovered, and of not having a safe path or retreat, as the woods are on an alluvial plain between the river on one side, and a line of steep, bare bluffs on the other. They mistrust, too, our long-range cannon, especially since the experience they have had of them.

In order to understand the fashion in which the Indians make war—the Indians of the plains especially—it is necessary to know their ideas as to what constitutes warlike valor, and their complete failure to comprehend what we call heroism. For them, supreme merit consists in killing and robbing as much as they can with the least possible risk. Having no idea of the sentiment which makes us disregard danger, they on the contrary take it very seriously into consideration, and neither scalp nor booty will make

them gamble their lives, even when the odds
are even. They will not sit in the game unless all the good cards are in their hand. To
risk as little as possible is their fundamental
principle. Hence the system of ambush,
siege, and traps which constitute the art of
war in their eyes. To flee at first sight, without a fight, even from inferior force, is more
praise-worthy than reprehensible in their
eyes, the instant that it is justified by the
extent of risk to be avoided.

Thus they never fight in the open unless
they are at least ten to one, recognizing in
spite of themselves the superiority of the
paleface. To appear without warning, kill
some poor devil who is unarmed, stampede
a herd of cattle and run off a part of it, and
disappear before the deployment of the smallest force, are their invariable tactics.

When they find a solitary man at a distance from the fort, the first thing they do
is to cut off his retreat by galloping around
him at full speed, describing a circle that
draws closer and closer. If the man is frightened and attempts to run without thinking
of his weapons he is lost. The Indians, who
are magnificent horsemen, launch themselves headlong in pursuit; and as they are
most expert in handling the bow without
stopping or slowing down the pace of their

horse, they kill their victim by shooting him in the back; in this way have been killed almost all the men that have been lost in the Department of the River Platte, on the route of the Pacific Railroad. But if, on the other hand, they are dealing with a man cool and resolute, such a one has every chance to make good his retreat, and the danger becomes for him more apparent than real. To get out of the mess he should retire deliberately, without haste, his weapon ready, and the moment that an enemy comes within range, throw it to his shoulder. The threatened Indian drops precipitately behind the neck and flank of his horse, and gets himself out of range as quickly as possible. By this simple demonstration, and by holding his fire, he will hold the entire band at bay, be they fifteen or twenty. Even if he fires on some horseman more bold than the rest, they will not risk charging on him, for they know by experience the rapidity of fire of the new arms, and they know that our rifles are reloaded almost as soon as fired,—only the time necessary to draw a cartridge and place it in the open breech.

Experience has proved that a cool-headed man may in this way get back to the fort even from a long distance, without the Indians, who follow him with yells and gesticulations, approaching near enough to be able to discharge their arrows, the range of which is less than half of that of his rifle. If they are armed with guns their confidence would not be increased, as these would be old weapons of an inferior quality, and they would not use them with any better effect.

Last winter the hostile Indians stayed almost all winter near Fort Buford, at that time an unimportant post, guarded by only one company of my regiment. They wore out the little garrison by the necessity for increased watchfulness, and the constraint of having to stay inside the palisades; but the Indians never inflicted any loss on them, nor prevented the weak detachments that were sent after water from descending the heights, filling their casks at the river, and bringing them back intact.

The difficulty, then, is not to defend ourselves against the Indians; that is nothing. The trouble is to be able to pursue and overtake them in the desert plains, which are their natural refuge in escaping punishment for their depredations. That is a problem as yet unsolved. To better assure their subsistence, the war parties do not move in greater numbers than two or three hundred. Each warrior carries with him a piece of buffalo meat dried in the sun; he needs nothing more to live on for weeks. His horse does not eat grain; it subsists easily on the pasturage of the prairies. His forage is found everywhere and does not have to be transported. His unshod mount has no need for a forge. He has no equipment to move. There is no saddle, and the bridle is but a lasso of buffalo hide that is hardly felt. If there is a hill to climb at a gallop when being pursued, the rider runs by the side of his mount, guiding it at need with the lasso. Arrived at the top, without a pause he leaps on its back, and descends the other slope at full speed, so sure is he of the strength of his pony's legs. And then, if in spite of these advantages, the band is pressed too close, after agreeing on a distant rallying point, the red horsemen scatter in every direction, and the pursuit can attach itself to nothing more definite than a few solitary men in flight. From these facts it must be concluded:

First: The infantry is absolutely useless in pursuing Indians on the warpath, and that it must be considered only for garrison duty. The only use to which they could be put would be to send them on a long surprise attack during the winter, on stationary villages where the tribes keep their women and children,—the object being to exterminate

everyone, without which the expedition
would be of no advantage, and would only
add another embarrassment—the encum-
brance of prisoners. In such case, one should
be very certain of the position and character of these villages, for in a climate as
rigorous as this a march through the snow
and ice would be attended with such hard-
ship, such suffering, and such risks to the
soldiers, that it would be criminal to undertake it lightly without being almost certain
of results.

Second: That the cavalry is the only arm
of the service that can be employed effi-
ciently in the running down of the Indians.
Unfortunately, it amounts to nothing under
present conditions, for many reasons; the
number of recruits that are not horsemen,
and in knowledge of horsemanship are but
clumsy children compared with the redskins, who are as much at home on the backs
of their horses as they are on their own legs;
the difficulty of transporting grain, forges
for shoeing, and subsistence required in the
pursuit of an enemy that knows nothing of
such impedimenta; the inferiority of the
horses, which is scarcely less than that of
the men for this sort of service on the plains.
The Indian pony will cover, between sunrise and sunset, without a halt, a distance of

sixty to eighty miles, while most of our horses would be on their knees at the end of thirty or forty miles. The Indian pony is less laden, having no trappings. If he becomes too tired, his master will generally jump on a spare horse from among those that almost always accompany a war party, and leave him to follow along unburdened. With us, if a horse is at the end of his strength, there is a horseman without a mount. In a word, the movement of Indian horsemen is so much lighter, so much more rapid, and so much longer than that of our cavalrymen, that they always escape us. Surely General Custer is a good cavalry officer, brave, active, intelligent; he served brilliantly through the war and accomplished a great deal against the Confederate cavalry. What has he done against the Indians? Nothing. He has worn out men and horses in vain pursuit of them, and his best reports amount to only four or five of the enemy killed.

To remedy these disadvantages, what should be done? First, modify at once the system of recruiting the frontier cavalry by substituting as far as possible, perhaps by the offer of high pay as a bait, men accustomed to riding, for the recruits inexperienced in horsemanship, who now encumber the ranks; form auxiliary squadrons composed of frontiersmen acquainted with the Indian, and able to fight him after his own fashion; finally, enroll in volunteer companies the Indians themselves who are friendly to the United States, and at war with the hostile tribes, with officers chosen exclusively from among plainsmen, who are familiar with the habits, the ideas, and the language of the tribes. These red companies would render to the Government the same services that the Arabs do to France in Algeria.

This latter system has recently been inaugurated in the department of the River Platte by General Auger, and the experiment continues to show excellent results. Two companies, forming a squadron of two hundred men, have been recruited among the Pawnee Indians, and these two hundred men are more effective than any regiment of 1000 or 1200 regular cavalrymen.

The Pawnees are mounted on Indian ponies which are not shod and eat no grain. They are dressed like our men in fatigue uniform; broad-brimmed hats, blue coats, and light blue trousers. When they are engaged in the ordinary service of guard or outpost duty they retain their equipment, but the moment that they start after the Sioux the first thing they do is to throw off their saddles, their boots if they are bothersome, even their uniform if they are not entirely accustomed to it, and leap naked on their horses, upon which they can perform wonders. Thus they protect the cattle and the work animals, and have recaptured a number of these that had been stolen, and brought back some scalps with them. They are obedient, easily disciplined, sober, active, vigilant, and brave, and the unanimous opinion of those officers who have seen them at work, and of whom I have asked information, is that each one of them is worth at least three or four of our ordinary cavalrymen. They are commanded by a plainsman who can do with them anything he likes; a white man, of course. He has the rank and pay of a major. These two companies and their officers, not yet being formally recognized, are paid by the Department of the Quartermaster; the pay is the same as in the regular army.[10]

It is to be hoped that red-tape will not prevail against experience and proved facts, and that this innovation will receive every help to bring the best possible results. These

[10] The allusion is to the battalion of Pawnee Scouts recruited in Nebraska by Frank J. and Luther H. North. See George B. Grinnell, *Two Great Scouts and their Pawnee Battalion* . . . (Cleveland, 1928). M. M. Q.

results will be of the very greatest interest, especially if we are going to have a general war with the tribes of the Plains.

Thursday, September 5: The mules that escaped from the corral have been recovered. Having come upon the road to Fort Berthold, they followed it and were caught by friendly Indians in that neighborhood. Three of these, accompanied by two white traders, brought them back to camp. They received as a reward some salt pork, a barrel of crackers, some coffee, and a few small items of provisions. They went off perfectly satisfied, and in all haste, fearing to meet on the way a band of Sioux who have left the neighborhood of Fort Sully to come and attack these tribes. But it is unlikely that they will have this unfortunate meeting in the fifteen miles of road that separates us from their reservation. The Three Tribes are on their guard, and if the Sioux are not in too superior numbers, they will give their enemies a hard knot to untie. Numbers being equal, I am assured, they can fight very well; but their disadvantage lies in their great numerical inferiority. That is what paralyzes them and keeps them constantly on a prudent defensive.

* * *

Tuesday, September 10: . . . In the afternoon a band of Indians, fifty or sixty strong, appeared on the horizon down river. After coming nearer they sent one of their number to tell us who they were. They belong to a branch of the Sioux Nation, coming from Fort Rice and bound for Fort Berthold, where, it seems, they wish to establish themselves peacefully near the Three Tribes who live there already. They have camped near the river below our landing, on low ground covered with good grass for their horses. Tomorrow at daybreak they will continue their journey.

* * *

Friday, September 13: . . . The band of Medicine Bear, as this minor Indian chief is called, has returned from Fort Berthold where it appears that they have just been visiting for a few days. However, some of them must have stayed on there, as they do not seem to me to be as numerous as when they went. They camped near the buildings under construction, and during the afternoon a party of them, men and women, came to ask for some provisions, which were given them. They are accompanied by a dozen Rees who will leave them here, and return tomorrow to Fort Berthold when the travelling band takes up again the route to Fort Rice.

Sunday, September 15: During almost the entire day the wind has blown a gale and after rising in the southeast, passed into the south, then to southwest and to west, where it ended by dying down at sunset. In its impetuous course it carried dense clouds of fine sand raised from the wide sandbars that border the river above and below the camp. The atmosphere was so obscured that the rays of the sun could not penetrate. The same swirls of dust swept up into the air wherever the wind blew over the bare land, around the new constructions, in the camp and especially over the field where they make the adobes. The men were not at work; they rest on Sundays; any other day they would have been forced to suspend work. This is our simoon. Everyone remained in his carefully closed tent, but without success in saving himself from the dust which, under these conditions, filters freely in, no matter what is done to protect against it.

* * *

Saturday, September 21: I leave today for Fort Berthold where I shall visit the Indians of the Three Tribes who live there and make a hunting trip in the neighborhood, where they promise me plenty of game.

Monday, September 23: I left between one and two o'clock day before yesterday. . . . It is six leagues, fifteen miles, from Fort Stevenson to Fort Berthold: a trip of two hours. . . . The first human being that we met appeared at first in the distance like a black speck which little by little took the form of a man travelling on foot. It was a French-Canadian trapper named Beauchamp, of whom later I shall have more to say. Naturally he was armed with his rifle, and carried on cross belts his bag of bullets and his powder horn.

A little after this solitary encounter, Fort Berthold began to appear in the distance, and the proximity of the Indian village soon declared itself with strange silhouettes of odd appearance to those ignorant of their significance, the aerial tombs of the redskins, and the posts designed for the tortures that they inflict upon themselves to obtain from the Great Spirit what they desire most; success in war or the chase; exemption from sickness and accident; victory over their enemies; the chance to kill and scalp as many as possible while escaping themselves from wounds; good health, a good crop of corn, etc. Nothing has been able to force them to renounce these voluntary sacrifices, almost all of them atrocious, and in the efficacy of which they seem to have an unbreakable faith. Again and always the expiation by blood, and a far-off echo of Golgotha.

The torture posts are trunks of dead trees, forked at the top and stripped of their bark. When a young warrior has decided on self torture, he goes there accompanied by his relations and in the midst of a tribal gathering. Usually an arrow point is passed through the flesh or under the skin like a skewer. Sometimes the wound is made on the stomach. A cord is passed through this and firmly knotted, by which he is hoisted and hung suspended, chanting without intermission an improvised religious invocation. He remains there, a bloody sacrifice, hanging from the post until the rope breaks or the skin tears, or, if both hold fast, until loss of blood and suffering cause him to lose consciousness. Then if some of his family is willing to throw at the foot of the post a buffalo robe, a blanket, some corn, or any other offering to the divinity, they let him down; if not, he must die, victim of this ferocious test. I have seen some of the men who bear proudly the horrible scars of this experience. . . . The youngest train themselves to stand physical pain, considered as meritorious prayer or expiation, by cutting their flesh with the point of a sharp knife. The scars left thus on their breasts are considered as marks of distinction.

This last form of voluntary sacrifice is, with women, a sign of mourning. When their father or husband is dead, especially when killed by the enemy, they climb to the tops of their lodges and give themselves over to lamentation which they accompany by slashes of a knife on their arms, legs and all the fleshy parts of their body. This lasts generally for a year, unless before the end of the period an enemy has been killed to pay the blood price. A death for a death, and the mourning stops at once.

In battle the Indians attach enormous importance to rescuing of their dead and wounded; hence the great difficulty in estimating their losses. When one of their men falls, the others at once rush to pick him up, which is not difficult for them to do, as they only fight at long range and never in line. The body is brought back to the village, if the distance and circumstances permit; otherwise it is buried after the Indian fashion on some height whence he seems to dominate the solitude where he wandered in life.

To reach Berthold one passes through the cemetery.

* * *

Behind the field of the dead appears Fort Berthold, built originally by the Northwest Fur Company as a trading post, later occupied for two or three years by a company of infantry, and definitely abandoned by the Government to its original owners in the month of June of this year. It is merely a palisaded square of buildings constructed of squared logs, all of whose openings are on the interior court. Two high, massive gates, which close on hinges and are strongly barred on the inside, give access. To defend the outer facades, two projecting blockhouses are placed at corners opposite each other; these are pierced with loop-holes, from which the line of fire covers the outer walls, and they have an upper story which juts out over the ground floor to protect it.

* * *

The traders who live inside are the agents of the Fur Company to which the fort belongs. The factor, a Frenchman (from France) called Gustave Cagnat, received us in his dwelling which consists of four rooms.

* * *

There are no white women in Berthold, nor in any other non-military post in the country. Each white man takes an Indian woman with whom he lives and who keeps house for him, and bears him children who hardly ever speak any language but that of the mother, and who remain in the tribe if the father, which is rare, should leave the country. In a wild country, and where the customs of the Indians freely permit polygamy, the whites, like the others, may have several wives if it suits them; but this seldom happens unless they have reason to return to her family the one whom they take first. My impression is that such cases are rare. The great ambition of a young squaw is to become the wife of a white man, for she is infinitely better treated than if she were the wife of no matter what Indian. She is not subjected to the fatiguing labor, which, in Indian life, makes of the women veritable beasts of burden, cultivating the land, bearing the heavy burdens, caring for the horses, etc. With a white man she is better dressed, better cared for, better fed. The loss of all these advantages in the bettering of her condition by the choice of a white man, would make her return to a redskin a veritable disaster from every point of view. Hence they are submissive, attentive, industrious, taking good care of their children and the father of their children, and he, tranquil, well served and well cared for in his inner-man, goes about his business without feeling any necessity for a change. Perhaps, in time, he may take a second and younger companion; but without casting off the first, and the household proceeds calmly to function without internal discord to trouble the habitual peace.

The children of the whites bear the mark of their origin in the lighter color of their skins, and in the character of their faces. Some take almost entirely after their fathers. They are also much better cared for, especially the girls, who are dressed like their mothers in Indian clothes as they would be in our country. Some of the traders, more attached to their children, send them to St. Louis to some school or convent where they learn English and receive a primary education, after which they return to the desert, the girls to live like their mothers, if they can find the opportunity, the boys to serve as interpreters or to launch forth on the adventurous life of the nomad as do most of the half-breeds, sometimes in the service of the Company, sometimes engaged by the government, sometimes hunting or fighting with the Indians. It is noticeable that the French language is much more widespread in these countries than the English tongue, which is owing to the great infusion of Canadian blood among the tribes.

* * *

My visit had been announced at Fort
Berthold. A number of Indians were grouped
near the entrance gate; others were squatted
along the walls of the houses on the inside
of the court yard, while others stood erect
and silent, wrapped in their blankets or
buffalo robes, near Gustave's door, in front
of which our carriage stopped. The most
important was Crow Belly, chief of the Gros-
Ventres tribe.

* * *

I asked to visit the village at once, and
my host proposed to begin by a call on Pierre
Gareau (or Garaut), the one altogether indispensable man. So on to Pierre Gareau.

The first buildings facing the north side
of the fort are the dwellings and warehouses
of the traders who do not belong to the Fur
Company.[11] . . . Behind the houses of the
traders rises the Indian village. I can think

[11] The American Fur Company was the principal fur
concern operating on the Upper Missouri for some forty
years and had been the original builder of Fort Berthold,
Fort Union, Fort Clark, Fort Pierre and many other
posts. The company finally retired from the field in
1866 and was followed by various other smaller companies, such as those operating at the time of the
Journal. The American Fur Company operated the
first steamboats on the Upper Missouri and for many
years the only ones. Their boat, the *Chippewa*, in 1859
was the first ever to reach the head of navigation at
Fort Benton. G. F. W.

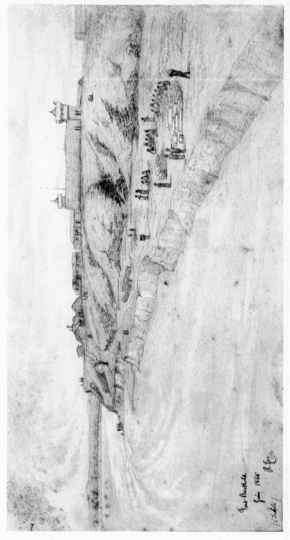

FORT BERTHOLD

of nothing to which to compare it. It is a group of great domes of earth, built without order, crowded together, and between them are light drying scaffolds laden with corn on the ear, drying in the sun. The streets are nothing but winding passages between the lodges. . . .

Here we are before the lodge of Pierre Gareau.[12] . . . Pierre was out when I entered. One of his wives, (he has, I think, two or three) immediately started out in search of him. . . . Soon Pierre Gareau came in. He is a half-breed of more than sixty

Extensive information upon the activities of the American Fur Company on the Upper Missouri is contained in Charles Larpenteur's *Forty Years a Fur Trader on the Upper Missouri*, the *Lakeside Classics* volume for 1933. M. M. Q.

[12] Pierre Gareau (Garreau) was well and favorably known to every traveller on the Upper Missouri for many years. He is said by some to have been a French half-breed. According to his own story, he was in reality a full-blood Arikara Indian. When he was a small child his Arikara father died and his mother married a French trader, Gareau, who was with the Arikaras in the Grand River village as early as 1811. Pierre was adopted by the Frenchman and received some education in St. Louis. Later he returned to his people as an employee of the American Fur Company, with which he served for many years at Fort Clark and Fort Pierre. G. F. W.

Charles Larpenteur, who knew Gareau well, described him as a half-breed. *Forty Years a Fur Trader*, 104. M. M. Q.

years, but his vigor and activity make it
hard to believe his age. Nothing about
him indicates the savage. He dresses exactly like an American, except for his moccasins, which, as far as that goes, are usually
worn by the whites in this part of the country. These soft shoes, easy on the feet, and
warm in winter, are so comfortable that one
quickly gets used to them, and in consequence hates to put on our hard footgear
again. Trousers, coat, flannel shirt, black
cravat and cloth cap, such was and always
is the garb of Gareau. His black hair, of
ordinary length, is streaked with grey. His
brick-red color might be attributed to the
sun, and can be met with anywhere among
the peasants of Europe. He is like the country men in the *midi* of France. He gives
an impression of energy, his eyes are black
and intelligent, and his large mouth, well
furnished with small regular teeth, has something the appearance of that of a bull dog.

He came to me with hand outstretched,
and an air of gladness, knowing that I was
French and that he would not have to en-
tertain me in English. His father was Canadian, and French is his native tongue. (The
French of Canada, understand). Although
he has learned English he speaks it badly,
and with difficulty; for him it is hard work;

but to speak French is a pleasure. They are all thus; the blood and the tongue cling together in them. French blood, French speech. English or American they never become.

After the compliments usual on such an occasion, I suggested that he show me around the village and serve as my guide, to which he agreed as a matter of course, and we set out together, chatting as we went. He first took me to a second lodge which belonged to him and which he called his Assembly Lodge as it was there that he received the Indians when they wished to get together. Nevertheless, there were beds there also, and he presented to me two old ladies, who are his sisters, and some younger ones, his nieces. When I asked him about his family, he told me with a sad air that he had had three sons, three warriors, who, several years before, were all three surprised and killed by the Sioux while on a hunting party in which they were taking part. But at once, as if to console himself, he enumerated the Sioux whom the Three Tribes had killed.

* * *

We returned to the fort, recalled by the dinner hour, and there the chief of the Rees, White Shield, was presented to me. . . With the grasp of the hand we exchange only the word "How" which is a general expression of welcome, salutation and approbation. He retired, as he came, in impassive dignity.[13]

The tribe of the Rees of which he is the chief is the most considerable of the three; numerically it is as strong as the other two put together. It seems to me to be also the most enterprising and warlike, which is naturally enough explained by the number of its warriors which enables it to do things that the other two can not undertake alone.

* * *

Sunday, September 22: . . . During dinner, which was served at one o'clock at Berthold as everywhere in this country, where they breakfast at seven or eight in the morning and sup at seven in the evening, I was informed that the three chiefs, accompanied by the principal personages of their tribes, would call on me presently to have a pow-wow; that is to say, a conference to discuss their affairs; what we should call in English a solemn talk. So, when the table had been

[13] White Shield's memory is still held in high esteem by his people and his grave near old Fort Berthold is marked by a large monument of concrete, set up in his memory by them. He was an hereditary chief, as the Arikara chieftainship is thus handed down and is said always to have been. Appointments that do not conform to this rule, even when made by the Indian Bureau, are disregarded by the people. G. F. W.

cleared, Crow Belly entered the room, greeted me, and proceeded to squat against the wall, or rather against a box that happened to be there. The second chief of the Gros-Ventres, Poor Wolf, followed immediately, and having said "How" also squatted in turn against the wall. The chief of the Mandans, Red Cow, was not long in doing the same. He was accompanied by his lieutenant, Eagle-Who-Hunts-Eagles.

Some time passed in waiting for the chief of the Rees; not a word was spoken on either side, and from time to time warriors dropped in singly, and silently squatted along the wall in the order of their importance. White Shield had gone to fetch the interpreter, Pierre Gareau. They arrived together, accompanied by the second chief of the Rees, Son-of-the-Star. Among the warriors were: Long Bone, so called because of his great height; Man-Chief and Four-Times-Four; Several of the warriors had flannel shirts of brilliant and variegated colors; two or three wore leggings of colored skins with fringes; all were without arms except Poor Wolf.

When everyone was squatted along the wall, the second chief of the Mandans drew from a long embroidered pouch a handful of kinnikinnick, the inner bark of a plant that takes the place of tobacco with the Indians. This bark, when dried and crumbled in a pipe, has a taste that is not disagreeable. I do not think that it is a narcotic. Then Eagle-Who-Hunts-Eagles filled his pipe, lit it, and after two or three puffs, passed it to Crow Belly, who was to be the principal spokesman of the conference. He, after having drawn several puffs, passed it to Pierre Gareau; he to his next neighbor, and the pipe, from mouth to mouth, made thus the circle of the assembly.

I remained seated at the table, having the interpreter at my right, and a little farther away, Major Furey, Lieutenant Hooton, and Doctor Matthews; but as the conference was being held in French, and promised to last a long time, my three officers were not long in losing themselves among the warriors who crowded around the door. The pipe was not offered to me, from courtesy, as I smoke only tobacco, and had just placed mine on the table. While theirs was circulating no one spoke a word, and it seemed as if we were there only to look at each other.

At last Crow Belly rose, crossed the room at a slow and dignified pace, and gave me a ceremonious clasp of the hand in token of friendship and good faith; then returned to his seat with the same measured tread, and after another silence spoke as follows:

"My Father is welcome among us; we are happy to see him visiting us here. We know that he is a great chief among the palefaces. I had wished to go down to visit him, knowing of his arrival, but I was detained in the village until today. I have wished to do it, but I have not yet been able to. But since my father is here, his Indian children wish to ask of him that he permit trade in powder, of which they have such great need to defend themselves against their enemies, and to hunt for meat and skins. For some time now we have been deprived of powder; why? What have we done to be punished by our Great Father, the great Chief of the palefaces? (The President.) It is now many years ago that our Great Father ordered us to make peace and to live at peace with the palefaces and with those redskins with whom we were at war. Lands were assigned to us, and there we have lived; and when those who made the treaty were dead, we who succeeded them have remained faithful, and have observed everything that was commanded us. We were powerful in the old days; our warriors covered the plains, and returned from the hunt with plenty of meat and skins; when they went out on the warpath, they brought back many scalps. But we have become weak and our enemies harass us and attack us. They steal our horses, and when they meet our young men out hunting, they kill them whenever they can; and as we are weak we have need of powder to defend ourselves. We cultivate the earth, and live in lodges on the land that is left to us. We trade the corn that we can spare from our own needs; but that does not suffice for all our requirements. The hunting season has come; buffalo are very scarce and very hard to kill; our bows and arrows have become useless, and we ask of our Father that he permit us to buy powder as in times past."

This discourse, delivered in an harmonious tongue that abounds in vowels, (the language of the "men of the willows") accompanied by slow gestures, was frequently interrupted by exclamations of "How!" from the assembly, sometimes singly, sometimes collectively; just as in our parliamentary debates, "very good" accompanies a fact well put by the orator.

Crow Belly was silent; the interpreter translated his speech, and taking the floor myself, I replied:

"I have come with pleasure to visit my children of the Three Tribes, because, since

my arrival in this country, I have heard
nothing but good reports concerning them,
and I am deeply interested in them as I have
nothing but praise for their good conduct,
and have nothing to reproach them with.
("How! How!") I wish to declare first to
them, that if the trade in powder has been
suspended for a time, it was not as a punishment for them, as they have not merited
any punishment; it is only a general policy
which has been applied to them at a time
when, to chastise the bad Indians, the Sioux,
the Cheyennes and other liars and thieves,
it was necessary to forbid the trade in munitions. Our Great Father in Washington is
very far away from Dakota, where flows the
Missouri; but the good conduct of his children among the willows has been reported
to him, and now he has ordered that powder
may be sold to them. ("How!") I am happy
to tell you this, and to announce to you that
I have already given the orders that will
assure for you a good hunt, and permit you
to fight your enemies under more favorable
conditions.

"I have not waited until today to inform
myself of your history, and to learn what
I can do in your behalf, to recompense you
for your good faith and your good conduct.
If you have become weak after having been

strong, it is not your fault, nor because you have been good friends of the whites and their Government. The Great Spirit has permitted a horrible malady (small pox) to spread death among you more than all your enemies could do, and as you did not know the remedies with which to fight this plague and the measures that prevent it, three-quarters of your warriors, of your women and your children have perished, and you have become weak. But because you are weak our Great Father will protect you all the more, and I will do for my part every-thing that I can for you. I know that it was the custom to trade a keg of powder (25 pounds) to each of the Three Tribes at the opening of the hunting season when you are leaving for your winter quarters in the low wooded lands. This time has now come. You may have this quantity of powder, not all together, but distributed in different por-tions according to what each individual is able to trade, provided that no man can re-ceive more than one pound at a time to start his season."

This conclusion, like the rest of the dis-course, was received with marked approval, when Pierre Gareau, delighted to be trans-lating from the French, had repeated it first in the Gros-Ventre language which the Mandans also understood, and then in the language of the Rees for the benefit of the latter. After another moment of silence, Crow Belly again took the floor:

"My Father has spoken the language of righteousness. He has been right in everything he has said. His red children thank him; but the powder that he permits us to trade will be used up before half the winter has passed. I ask him, therefore, I beg of him that we be not left without ammunition during a part of the cold moons, when the snow covers the plains, and the game comes in greater numbers down to the low lands, but to allow us two kegs to each tribe. Two kegs are indispensable to assure a good hunt, to support our families and to return with the skins that are our principal resource when the corn has not yet sprung from the ground."

I should mention here that the quantity of powder asked for by the chief on behalf of the Three Tribes was indeed well under what the existing orders permitted me to allow them. They asked for 250 pounds of powder for the winter, and that quantity might have been allowed them each month, for the Three Tribes altogether counted 250 warriors, and the limit of sale is one pound of powder per month for each of them.

Nevertheless, as I had found that the orders that had been given before my arrival, were more liberal than was necessary, I pretended to calculate and to study over the burden of their request, and addressing the chief of the Gros-Ventres: "How many warriors are there among the 'men of the willows'?" The chief considered and replied, "One hundred." Then to the chief of the Rees, "How many Ree warriors?" The chief reflected, counting on his fingers, and said "One hundred and eighty." And then to the chief of the Mandans, "How many Mandan warriors?" "Seventy," he replied with a resigned expression. I resumed my apparent meditation, and had not yet given my reply when White Shield rose in his turn, came to shake my hand, returned to his place, squatted on the floor and expressed himself as follows:

"Why does my Father hesitate to allow to his children of the Three Tribes the powder that is necessary to permit them to live? Are they not faithful friends of the whites? And has not my father himself said that he has nothing to reproach them with? Is it right that they should suffer for their good conduct and their submission to the orders of our Great Father? The Dakotas on the plains below sent messengers to us who said:

'What do you gain by remaining friends of the whites? You are weak, poor and the whites despise you. But we who steal their mules and their horses, who kill their warriors and who attack their camps on the prairie, they fear us; they ask us for peace, and to keep us quiet they give us presents and do not avenge their dead. What we have taken from them we keep, and they give us more for fear that we will take all. Do as we do, and you will have plenty of booty, and plenty of presents, and you will be richer and stronger.' That is what the Dakotas of the low country below say to us. Have we believed their words? No. Have we been tempted by their promises? No. Have we acted as they advised? No. Between the Sioux and ourselves there are no debts but the debts of blood. And that is why, not being able to persuade us to join them, they have made war upon us more wickedly than ever, and on the field of death are stretched three of our warriors upon whom the rain has not yet fallen since they were surprised and killed on our own hunting ground. Our enemies are the enemies of my father and the enemies of the white men. They are dogs who make war for the sake of booty, and make treaties only to break them. We only make war in a just cause in our own defense, and we remain faithful to the treaties that we make. Nevertheless, the presents for this year have not come, and the guns that were lent to us, and which were so useful, have been taken away from us. Why? We do not know, for we took good care of them and not one went out of our hands.

"Let my Father listen justly, and grant what is right to his red children as he would to his white children. The color of the skin makes no difference; what is good and just for one is good and just for the other, and the Great Spirit has made all men brothers. As for me, (pinching the skin of his chest where a horrible scar bore witness to the post of sacrifice) I have a red skin; but my grandfather was a white man. What matter? It is not the color of my skin that makes me bad or good. My Father, you may allow us the powder that we ask for without fear; it will not go out of the Three Tribes, and will only be used to kill the game that the Great Spirit may send us, or to defend ourselves from our enemies against whom we ask no other protection."

The discourse of the chief, accompanied by naturally eloquent gestures, had provoked numerous "Hows." Upon ceasing to speak, he resumed his impassive attitude and expression of silent gravity to listen to my response.

"The chief of the Rees has spoken well," I said in my turn. "He has recalled things that I already know, but I am glad to hear them repeated. My children of the Three Tribes have been wise in closing their ears to the lies of the Sioux; if they had listened they would have brought upon themselves the misfortune and ruin which will surely be the punishment of the bad Indians of the lower plains. For the Dakotas down there lied when they said that the whites were afraid of them. The white men people immense territories toward the rising sun, and count more warriors than there are buffalos on the prairies. What are the Sioux in comparison? Already they have been vanquished in many combats, and the blood of many of their warriors has paid for the blood of those laborers that they have killed. Very soon they will be expelled from their hunting grounds and forced themselves to beg for a peace that will not be bought by presents. And if they do not submit to the orders of our Great Father, and continue to make war on the whites, they will be destroyed; their race will be annihilated and the plains will know their name no more. And you, the faithful friends of the white man and the submissive children of our Great Father, you will become from day to day richer and stronger, cultivating your fields in peace in the summer, and freely hunting during the winter, without fear of ambush by your enemies. ("How! How!") White Shield has spoken of two things that he does not understand, so I wish to explain them to him as well as to my children of the Three Tribes: The presents for this year have not been distributed; but they have arrived and are stored here in the warehouse. Mr. Wilkinson, the agent of our Great Father for the Indians in this region, wished to begin to distribute the presents first to the tribes that are farthest away. He has gone to Fort Buford hastened by the lateness of the season, and fearing that he would not be able to get there if he stopped here first. The steamboats have scarcely enough water to get down the river now, and we have not seen one for several weeks; but the first one to arrive will probably bring Mr. Wilkinson here, where he is due to spend the winter, and the presents will immediately be distributed by him. ("How! How!")

"As for the guns that were lent, if they were taken back it was not because the Three Tribes had made bad use of them, nor because our Great Father had any less faith in them, or felt less well disposed toward them. It was simply because all the guns had to be made over so as to be loaded at the breech with cartridges of a new kind, and when we receive the new arms thus altered, we must turn in and exchange for them all the old guns that we may have so that they can be submitted to the same alteration.

"And now to conclude: The request that my children of the Three Tribes have made to me about the powder is granted them. They may trade for a quantity equal to two kegs per tribe, but in such a way that no warrior may have more than one pound at a time—and further, if, before the end of the winter, their supply is exhausted, I will permit them to renew it in just proportion to their need."

This conclusion, as one may guess, caused complete and unanimous satisfaction. There were redoubled "Hows!" and the pipe circulated more actively than ever. The chief of the Mandans who had not yet spoken, did not wish the conference to end without having expressed his sentiments. He complimented and thanked me in most flattering terms; "We have seen many great chiefs sent by our Great Father", said he.

"Many of them have talked to us, but none of them has told us such good news as my Father; none has shown us so clearly justice and reason, nor has so rejoiced the hearts of his children. We are satisfied and grateful."

When I rose to close the council, which had lasted a good two hours, the chief of the Gros-Ventres who had consulted with the others, announced to me that they would not leave for their winter quarters without coming to visit me at Fort Stevenson, in token of their respect and affection. So we shall have a solemn visitation at which, so Pierre Gareau tells me, each chief will be attended by forty warriors. This will mean some pounds of sugar and coffee, and many boxes of crackers to distribute; but the spectacle will be well worth it.

* * *

Beauchamp, who was in heaven at the chance to speak French, was full of joy. When he has to speak English, he is taciturn, contenting himself with answering questions, or translating with some difficulty, for he is in the service of the trader Gerard as interpreter. But speak to him in French, and he never stops—he yarns, and his stories lack neither interest nor originality, as we shall see. Always French blood rebels at the English tongue.

* * *

As supper time had come, I left Beauchamp, promising him to return to talk with
him in the evening, which he assured me
would give him great pleasure. I therefore
came back and taking up the conversation
where we had dropped it, I recalled his last
sentence in which he boasted that he lived
as he pleased without anyone troubling him.
But I put it in the form of an objection:

"And the Sioux?" For I wished to draw
him back to the train of his stories.

"Ah! the Sioux," he said, "That is another
matter. Between them and me the account
is to the good. It is to the death. They have
already landed three bullets in my body,
and I am none the worse for it today, although they made me pass some bad quarters of an hour. They know me and I know
them. I have not done so badly with them
in my life and, look you, it is not so very long
ago that I killed three of them in one morning."

* * *

As a corollary to this story, Beauchamp
emphasized the distinction that should be
made between good and bad Indians, and
the injustice with which, often, one is confused with the other. He himself was not
without personal grievances against the Government, by reason of a general order en-
forced throughout the entire frontier, which,

last winter, required that all white men who were living with the Indian tribes should report to the military post to which they were nearest. Whether this was mistrust of their conduct or solicitude for their safety, I do not know, but Beauchamp had obeyed it, to the satisfaction of his conscience perhaps, but certainly with great detriment to his purse—"For," he said, "during the winter months I might easily have cut and piled three hundred cords of wood on the bank of the river where we do our cutting, and in the spring I would have sold it off like white bread to the steamboats, which would have brought me in two thousand dollars, if a cent. And that is how they treat us. It is not astonishing that I like the Indians better. When one knows how things go, you see, my General, one realizes that the savages are indeed better people than the civilized. Think how everything that the Good God gave them has been taken away, and how three-quarters of the presents, or annuities, as they are called, are stolen from them by those whose duty it is to make the distribution. And if they venture to complain, they receive nothing but insults and blows. I myself have seen those who have died of hunger in this very village, and there would have been many more of them were it not

88

for a captain who took it on himself at his own risk to distribute food to the old and sick, without knowing but what he would have to pay for it out of his own pocket. And in spite of everything, you see they are without malice or revengeful thoughts, content to stand by their treaties, and grateful for the little that is done for them. Those who lose patience with injustice, and who fight to defend themselves, are despised and exterminated. The good Father De Smet[14] says that everything happens because the Good God wills it so; but as for me, I do not understand it at all."

"But," said I, in an attempt at explanation, "when these things happen, it is the fault of the bad Indians who rob and steal, like the Sioux, and unfortunately the other tribes suffer from the effects without any bad intention on the part of the Government, which, on the contrary, strives to protect them."

"Yes," he said, "when the soldiers are commanded by chiefs such as you. But most of the time, the generals and the colonels and the captains never worry

[14] For the career of Father Pierre-Jean De Smet, noted missionary to the Indians of the Northwest, see *Dictionary of American Biography*. His efforts at preserving peace with the Sioux in 1868 are alluded to in subsequent entries of the Journal. M. M. Q.

themselves about the savages. There are
some among them who get drunk, saving
your presence, more often than they should
and it needs no more than that sometimes
for a tribe to be massacred, as happened to
the Cheyennes, when a drunken colonel fell
on them without one word of warning, mas-
sacring the women and children at the very
gates of the fort where they had laid down
their arms, and where they had received rations to feed them, and even some little flags
of the United States presumably as a protection. There were some, I have been told,
that were killed with the flags in their hands.
Much trouble resulted from this in the country down river; but whose fault was it?" [15]

"Beauchamp," I said to him, "the deed to
which you refer is a crime that I do not seek
to justify nor to excuse; but you must re-
member also the massacre of the whites in
Minnesota."

"That is true"; he said, "but who caused
the massacre in Minnesota? The Sioux. And
why did others join with them? Because
they had within their hearts the injustices

[15] The allusion is to the Sand Creek Massacre, per-
petrated by soldiers of the U. S. Army under command
of Colonel J. M. Chivington near Fort Lyon, Colorado,
Nov. 29, 1864. The affair still remains "the most con-
troversial subject in Colorado history," and there is no
consensus over the question of its justification. M. M. Q.

and injuries that had been done them for a long time without their saying anything. Many of them were killed, and forty or fifty of them have been hung; but have they hung Chivington or even tried him? The relations of those whom he massacred, not being able to obtain justice or reparation, decided to avenge their dead after the Indian custom, and killed as many whites as they could. That is just the way trouble comes. They say: 'The Indians do this' or 'The Indians do that'; but one should look into the reason for these things. Nevertheless, I will leave the Sioux to you. As for them you can wipe them out as much as you please, and little harm done; but you must also protect the good Indians, such as these that are here, my General, and you will never have any trouble with them."

* * *

Wednesday, October 2: . . . A convoy arrived today from Devils Lake (Fort Totten). It is the same one that has already made one trip here. It will go back again day after tomorrow, taking the remainder of the provisions necessary for the three companies that form the garrison of that post. It is the last convoy that we shall see this season. Received newspapers up to the date of September 13. Everything is news to us.

Friday, October 4: . . . Patinaud,[16] the guide and interpreter, made me a long visit in my tent and gave me some additional information upon the Indians in this region. In coming from Fort Totten with the convoy, he met many of them; some of the chiefs came to talk with him; one or two bands, less trusting, declined to approach. Almost all were on their way to Fort Totten to surrender. More or less compromised by their participation in the Minnesota massacres four years ago, they were forced to flee from their lands near Devils Lake into the Great Plains, where they did not find the hunting grounds comparable to their own; and where they lived so miserably, and where they have undergone such privations, that they have returned in despair to put themselves

[16] Patinaud or Paquenaud was a famous character about Fort Berthold. He was a French half-breed. We find an early mention of him in *The Solitary Hunter* by John Palliser, published in London. Palliser was an Irish gentleman who in 1847 and 1848 made Fort Berthold his headquarters during some months of intensive hunting. Packineau, as the name is now spelled, accompanied him on his hunts and, though an excellent man otherwise, was known as an arrant coward. He was married to an Hidatsa woman and lived out his days among her people. He had several children one of whom, Joseph, was for long the best story-teller and interpreter on the Reservation. One of his sons and several grandsons still reside there. G. F. W.

under the protection of the Government by a treaty of peace. They will winter in the neighborhood of Devils Lake, where wood, game, and fish are to be found in abundance. We shall try to make them stay there henceforth with their families, whose presence is a sure guarantee for their good conduct in the future.

Over by Buford some hostile tribes, Uncpapas, Cheyennes, and some Blackfeet and the Spotted-Tails are gathering to procure munitions for the winter on the Little Knife, where the Red River half-breeds come to trade with them. These half-breeds, all sons of French Canadians, carried on this business with impunity and profitably last winter on White Earth River; but this time it will not be so, and we are about to put a stop to it by destroying the establishments which they have begun to build to store the munitions and Indian whiskey which they intend for the savages. If they make any resistance, an example will be made of them. Indian whiskey is nothing but alcohol mixed with water. How can anyone be surprised at the terrible effect it has on the unfortunate redskins who are poisoned by it?

* * *

Saturday, October 5: . . . The escort for the cattle that came from Fort Wadsworth left

this morning to return to its post. One of
the two officers that command it, Major
(Brevet) Hampson of the 10th Infantry,
carries a letter from me to Colonel Hayman,
an old comrade in arms of Kearny's Division
of the Army of the Potomac. I have asked
him to engage for me fifteen Indian scouts
whom we can not get here where our Three
Tribes fear to weaken their numbers, and,
the men being at war with the Sioux, deem
the detached service too dangerous. . . .

* * *

Tuesday, October 8: The Indians from
Berthold came today to say good bye to me
before leaving for their winter camp; each
tribe was represented by its chief and second
chief, as well as by four of its leading men,
with the exception of the Gros-Ventres
whose chief did not come, I do not know why.
Six of that tribe were present nevertheless,
making eighteen in all. Forewarned of their
coming, I had had my tent arranged for their
reception by placing rugs on three sides, and
seating myself at a table before them with
my officers grouped behind me in the second
tent that serves as my bedchamber. The
deputation took its place, squatting on the
rugs. The weather being cold, and the wind
blowing a gale, they were all enveloped in
their buffalo robes, the hair side in and held

together at the waist with a leather belt. Almost all of them, let these coverings fall from the upper part of the body on entering my tent, where the stove diffused considerable warmth.   *   *   *

The pow-wow was exactly like the first. I advised them strongly not to sell a single grain of powder to any other Indians, and not to permit to leave the Tribes a single thing that they had been permitted to buy from the traders, all of which they solemnly promised. There was also the question of a visit that eleven Miniconjous and three Uncpapas had just made to them to trade horses and buffalo robes for corn. These tribes are hostile. Individual bands make peace, or more often a truce of a few days in order to trade, after which they return to the Plains, and those who had visited the Tribes at Berthold do not hesitate to take up hostilities against them again if they find a favorable occasion. This is the immemorial custom of the savages, who are thus now at war, again at peace, according to what seems the most advantageous at the moment; that is, unless a permanent treaty of peace binds them by the pledges of good faith.[17]

[17] For many years the Three Tribes had been regularly visited in the fall after the harvest by various bands and tribes of the nomadic Indians in order to

I warned them never to buy horses or mules stolen from the Government and carrying the U. S. brand, nor beasts that had been shod and therefore stolen from the whites, but to confine themselves to the acquisition of Indian ponies, all of which they readily understood. Also they pledged themselves so to do without hesitation. They confirmed for me the reports already received on the trade in powder and munitions between the Red River half-breeds and the hostile Sioux and Cheyennes, protesting vigorously that they had no hand in it, which I know to be the truth, for the hostile Indians have more munitions than the Three Tribes and would be more likely to sell to them than to buy from them. The rest of the conference was devoted to denunciations of the Sioux, who make war on them, and to compliments addressed to myself and my officers. At last, to close the meeting, I announced to them that I had given orders to distribute among them some salt pork, crack-

trade skins, dried meat, etc., for corn, beans and other agricultural produce. This trade was always very profitable to the village Indians and they never hesitated to patch up a temporary peace with even their bitterest enemies during the period of the trade. Oftentimes the end of the trade was followed immediately by sudden and vicious attack on the villagers by their erstwhile friends. G. F. W.

ers, coffee, sugar and beans. Upon which, naturally, they proclaimed me a great chief, and that their Great Father in Washington had been well inspired to send them a man of mature age whose head was whitening, because 'wisdom and justice dwelt under grizzled hair, and that I was the most just and most generous of men, because the younger men had had for them nothing but indifference. And having called down the blessing of the Great Spirit on my venerable head, they departed to receive their rations, to which I had added on my own account a half pound of tobacco for each chief.

The day being already well advanced, and the sun setting, they will remain for the night outside the loghouses of the sutlers and will return tomorrow morning to Berthold, happy and content.

Wednesday, October 9: The days go by, winter approaches, and our building advances but slowly. The pleasant calculations which we made of being in our winter quarters by the first of December fade away more and more in face of the reality. The work completed gives an exact measure of the time required for the work still to be done, and the impossibility of finishing it this year has now become manifest. The work must be restricted as much as possible to what is indispensable, and we must limit ourselves to assuring sufficient protection against the extreme rigor of this climate in winter. To that end the program has been changed; of five houses forming the officers' quarters, only three will be built, and even they will not be finished in the interior. Two will receive the families of four married officers. In mine, which is double, I shall give asylum to two bachelor officers, and three more will be lodged in the second floor attic. A loghouse, with dining room and kitchen, will be built, where they will take their meals. The guardhouse and the prison will be built temporarily in the same manner, and probably the offices. This kind of building can be thrown up hurriedly, and except for its rough appearance, is just as warm and comfortable as any other. But even with these modifications, the work will not be ready until in the month of December, and meanwhile, the men, who work like beavers all day, have nothing to protect them at night from the wind, cold, and snow but A tents without fire. God grant that the months of October and November be not too rigorous.

* * *

Thursday, October 10: The Mackinaw boats, as they are called, are now coming

down the river, since the water is holding
the only two steamboats that are still in this
region between Buford and Benton. Six came
today. They stopped at the landing about
noon to buy from the commissary some supplies that the men who were on them needed;
then they started off again. They are flat-
boats carrying each six, eight, ten, and even
up to fifteen tons; the lighter have the ordinary shape, with bow and stern, and look
like any other kind of primitive craft; but
the heavier ones are merely great boxes,
square at the bow and square at the stern.
One of the latter that passed today had in
addition a sort of semicylindrical shelter or
covering of wooden planks for two-thirds of
its length. They are all propelled by rowing,
being usually furnished with two sweeps, and
sometimes, though rarely, with four. Another sweep over the stern serves as a rud-
der. In addition there is added a small mast
on which they hoist a square sail when the
wind blows from behind.[18]

[18] The Mackinaw boats, so named from the fact that
they first came into considerable use in the fur trade at
the time that Mackinaw was the headquarters for all
the fur trade of the Northwest, were until the coming
of the steamboat the principal means of transport up
and down the Missouri. They were towed by man power
from St. Louis to Fort Benton, and sailed and rowed
on the return trip. They were flat-bottomed with al-

It is in these craft that the miners from Montana return to the States at the approach of winter, when their season has not been good, and they have not the wherewithal to pay $100 or $120 for a passage on board the steamboats. Moreover this price is exorbitant when you take into consideration the way that they are packed into boxes, or temporary bunks made of planks, piled one on top of the other on the lower deck of the steamers. Those who have not been lucky in their search for gold naturally remain longer than the others in the gold-fields, prompted by the hope of finally making some rich find, and even if they do have the luck to do so, the steamboats being already gone, there remains only the Mackinaws in which to return to winter among their relatives.

most square ends, usually thirty to forty feet long and some ten feet wide, with a box-like structure built upon the single flat deck, and would carry a great many tons of freight and still draw very little water. They became the recognized vessels for the return of the Montana miners to St. Louis, and great numbers of them were built at Fort Benton and navigated downstream by them. At this period a great deal of danger accompanied such journeys and many of the miners fell beneath the fire of the hostile Indians. Boats, men, and sometimes their store of gold, were gradually drifted in and buried in the sandbars. G. F. W.

Only a few days ago eight poor devils came in this way to the Fort, not to buy but to beg for some food, which was given them, to speed them on their way. Among the eight, to use the expression of one of their number, there was not enough to be found to pay for a little glass of whiskey apiece. Those who came today were not in such circumstances, but no matter what the contents of their purses, they had more the look of brigands than of honest Christians. In general all the miners have this appearance when they return from the mines. Their clothes are worn threadbare; their heavy boots are cracked and full of holes; their trousers patched; their beards long and dirty, their hair the same; their linen—they haven't any; only heavy flannel undershirts under a common overcoat or a fringed shirt of antelope skin, everything more or less tattered. Their old hats of soft felt have a poverty-stricken air, and if they happen to be covered with a cap of buffalo or fox skin, they gain nothing as far as looks go. Probably they prefer to preserve this appearance of poverty to better hide what gains they may have made, and to reclothe themselves anew from head to foot on their arrival in civilization.

All, or nearly all, are armed with guns, rifles or revolvers; that goes without saying, for self defense demands it in their adventurous life. In the absence of law, justice, and courts, each man protects his goods and his person by force, or by a mutual association of a certain number of individuals making common cause in an association of revolvers, rifles, and bowie-knives. Thus the eight Mackinaws that made us a visit today are travelling together for mutual protection against the Indians. Such precaution is good but not always efficacious. Thus, on this side of Buford, they had to pass a camp of Sioux, who made them signs to land. Naturally they declined. Whereupon the Indians fired on them and killed a man on one of the boats. The miners returned the fire as well as they could. What the effect of it was they do not know, but they have the consolation of believing that they killed or wounded some of the redskins.

We ourselves are not immune from isolated attacks, or rather attempts to murder any of the men who may stray from their posts without arms. We had a sad example of this only today. I have said before that we have a post of a dozen men with several teams of mules and oxen, on the other side of the river, opposite the camp. The men were just returning and bringing in the teams that were employed during the day in dragging to the water's edge the logs cut for the construction of the Fort. Brevet Colonel Powell and Lieutenant Welborn, returning from a hunting party, had just crossed the river in a skiff and were hardly in their tents when shouts rang out from the opposite bank. The sentry at the landing called the corporal of the guard, and an instant later my orderly opened my tent and said: "Colonel, a man killed by the Indians." I rushed out, and could distinguish two or three men on the other side of the river, running down to the water's edge and shouting, "Send over a boat; hurry up." Some one called, "What has happened?" and the reply came to me distinctly, "A man killed or wounded by the Indians." I ran to the tent of the post commander, to have him send a detachment promptly, and a few minutes later, he himself, armed with his rifle, led fifteen men at double quick to the landing. The detachment, bending to their oars, soon reached the other bank, where the men of the post could be seen gathered in front of their log-houses. The re-enforcement of fifteen men joined them at once, and they all disappeared in the brush, except a few who were left behind to bring the victim over to the landing. This is what had happened:

No hostile Indian having shown himself near the camp for more than two months, the men had little by little relaxed their precautions against surprise attack, and often wandered some distance from their post unarmed. One of them, returning from work, stepped aside in the woods to pick some wild plums before supper. He was without arms, and was following a narrow path, when he suddenly found himself face to face with three Indians, feathers on their heads and painted black, which is their war dress. The soldier, surprised and divining their sinister intent, tried to avert the danger or at least to retard the attack by a friendly greeting. He gave them the "How" of welcome and offered them his hand; but the three bandits sprang upon him, trying to break his head with the wood of their bows. Our man at once took flight, running as fast as his legs would carry him, and shouting "murder" to give the alarm to his comrades. He had not taken twenty steps before he was pierced by three arrows; one in the shoulder, another in the arm, and the third through his neck. Nevertheless he continued to run until one of his comrades rushed out to meet him, and both regained the cabins, where the vacillating corporal did not dare pursue the murderers for fear

of falling with his men into an ambush.
When Colonel Powell got there, the Indians, who had disappeared, once the blow
had been delivered, must have had a good
start. In vain the detachment beat the
bushes in skirmish line. They found neither
the red-skins nor their tracks in the dense
underbrush, where a hundred of them might
have dispersed without a chance of being
discovered before nightfall, which was rapidly
coming on. The detachment returned as the
moon rose, having unfortunately wasted
both their time and trouble.

The wounded man was taken at once to
the hospital, where Dr. Gray proceeded to
extract the arrows. For one of them especially, the operation was difficult, the point
having struck the bone of the arm and been
bent. It had to be performed by an incision.
Arrows, it is well known, can not be ex-
tracted by the path through which they
enter; they must be forced through with
the barb in advance. The patient being
put under the influence of chloroform un-
derwent the operation without feeling the
pain. Nevertheless he has suffered much
since. The doctor, however, is not without
confidence that he will recover without
permanent disability. He had a narrow
escape.

Friday, October 11: It was noon. Superb weather and a bright sun. Upon leaving my tent a little before dinner my attention was attracted by the appearance of some mounted Indians on the crest of the bluffs which dominate the wooded bottoms whence we are still hauling logs, cut for the building of the fort, on the other side of the river. The same sight soon drew to the front of the camp other officers, some ladies, and the men returning from work. The number of redskins increased from moment to moment; they showed themselves at several points simultaneously, in pairs, in threes, in fours, and soon a dozen of them could be distinctly seen descending the slope of the bluff and entering the brush. A little later one of them appeared and galloped through the foliage right up to the edge of the river, waving in the air something which we took for a white flag, but it was really only a war shield. Mr. Marsh, the trader, long accustomed to Indian tricks, did not foresee any good from this exhibition; but the officers in whom I placed most confidence because of their experience and life in these regions were unanimously of the opinion that it was a matter of holding a peace conference with us. Being still new to Indian customs I left to Colonel Powell, commander of the post, full liberty of action to take such steps as he judged best. The result was that he took none.

The Indian began to gallop first to the right, then to the left, singing at full voice. Mr. Marsh said, shaking his head, "It is the war song." But someone else answered, "It is only to attract our attention; let someone reply." Mr. Pease, agent of the Northwest Fur Company, and trader at Forts Buford and Berthold, came up and I asked him to inquire of the Indian what he wanted. At the particular call of Mr. Pease the Indian replied with a similar one, and took up again his song of war. Mr. Pease stated that they were hostile Indians come to make an attack.

The eighteen men of the guard relieved that morning were at once recalled and ordered to cross the river in the long boat in command of Lieutenant Ward. While they were getting together all eyes were fixed on the most distant part of the woods, where a detachment of seven men was at work with six mules and two oxen. The mules, we recognized at once, were the booty which the Indians had promised themselves that they would attempt to run off. We had counted a dozen mounted Indians in the brush along the route which our men would have to travel to get back to the corral.

Three men left at the log house had climbed up the roof with their guns, and had their eyes alert for an attack. The long boat with the eighteen reinforcements left the bank at the moment when the harnessed mules, the oxen, and the escort of five men (not counting the teamsters) emerged from the woods where they were working, into an open space along the river, which they had to cross, following the open bank. Would they or would they not arrive in time? That was the question that each one asked himself, now looking at the boat crossing the river, now at the wagon train crossing the opening. The driver hurried too fast, the men had to run to keep up—a bad sign. Fear was on their heels. I should have liked to see them proceed more resolutely without rushing, the escort covering the wagons and ready to fire; but nothing could have been more the opposite.

The Indian who had appeared to make his boasts and sing his war song in our face, began to gallop back to make way for the wagon train, without getting out of the range of the guns, but not a shot was fired at him. What were the fools thinking of? We were soon to see. It should be noted that they were armed with excellent breechloading rifles, so easily and so rapidly fired in the hands of a resolute man that they would without difficulty rid him of a half-dozen Indians, especially mounted ones.

Between the corral near the cabins and the clearing was a strip of thick woods. The route traversed this at a distance of no more than twenty or thirty paces from the bank, a space filled with thick brush and some taller trees. It was along the edge of this brush, which was no more than 100 or 150 feet wide, that the Indians were in ambush. There were scarcely a dozen and only seven rushed upon the mules. At a single shot the red vermin would have disappeared; but at seeing them appear, just at seeing them, the corporal (an abominable coward named George E. Wilson) and the four men, without firing a shot, without putting up an appearance of resistance, abandoned the mules and like cowards, like a bunch of sheep, ran to hide under the river bank—the worst place, as a matter of fact, that they could have chosen to hide themselves. One of the teamsters (they were unarmed) jumped to the ground; the other urged on the mules, but they were held back by the oxen which were tied behind. The Indians burst through the brush, crying, "How! How!" to conceal their intentions. But the teamster was not deceived and when they were at twenty or thirty paces he stepped off the wagon into the brush along the river bank, where he disappeared. The thieves asked no more. In a flash we saw them vault upon the mules, cut the traces, hack away the harness and prepare to carry off their booty. One mule, however, ran toward the cabins and was saved.

All this took place before our eyes without our being able to do more than unlimber one of our cannon and throw some shells, without effect, over the woods where the action took place. Meanwhile, Lieutenant Ward, at last disembarked, took precious time to draw up his men on the bank according to the manual and to deploy them as skirmishers there, where the brush was too thick to conceal anyone, instead of rushing immediately to the aid of the wagon train and its pitiful escort. Meantime, Mr. Pease, Mr. Howell, the quartermaster's clerk, and some others who had accurate long-range rifles began to fire at the redskins across the river, and did their best. It was seen at once that to get the captured mules out of the brush they must be driven along the road which passed within twenty or thirty paces of the spot where our five poltroons were hiding. With one voice we called to them to climb the bank and shoot at the thieves.

"Fire on them! Charge them!" and similar calls, to make them blush at their cowardice.

At last they decided to climb the bank, but without spirit, and the two first into the brush fired their shots. Nothing more was needed to put the Indians into a gallop, flying pell mell through the brush. But it was too late; they had gained the edge of the woods and taken the five mules with them. By then, our men, seeing the danger past, showed themselves, and the shots which they had not dared to fire at the redskins advancing, they fired after them as they saw them in flight. To save the mules it would have needed only a little courage to shoot at the right time instead of shamefully hiding.

Our shells followed the flying Indians to the top of the bluffs and our scouts beat in vain all the low ground. When in their turn they reached the top of the ridge the Indians had disappeared in the direction of Berthold. However, they could not have gone very far if they stayed near the fires they had started, which burned on the hills at nine o'clock in the evening.

The detachment has returned; the ten men serving on the other side of the river will be withdrawn tomorrow, and the last logs which they must still haul to the banks of the river will come over on the ice when the river is frozen, if we need them. The rest of the timber which we need will be taken from this side of the river under the protection of an officer and twenty men instead of ten. Corporal Wilson will be reduced in rank for his cowardice before the enemy, and his four men will be taken out of the quartermaster's department where they were drawing higher pay. Such poltroons are good for nothing except to make mud for the adobes.

The Indians who performed this exploit are Uncpapas, a hostile tribe given to theft and brigandage. May Heaven permit that I find opportunity to repay to them the reckoning which they opened today with me.

I have just learned that four of the Indians were seen by the men when they were working in the woods. They pretended to be friends and had exchanged some "Hows" and some handshakes with them at the same time that their companions were preparing the ambush where our mules were taken. They were there to count the men, to see how they were armed, etc., and to give to the others the signal of their approach. Such are the redskins and such the confidence which can be placed in their demonstrations of friendship! It goes without saying that the three murderers of yesterday were of the same band. They came to spy out the land for the coup of today. Such is the situation in which we are placed through lack of horses and scouts. They are given to us on paper, but in reality we are still waiting for them.

Another band of Indians is reported on this side of the river at the Bad Lands, half way to Fort Berthold. This may be a part of the band which insulted us today, for this one crossed the river yesterday at that spot. The fires lighted during the day and in the evening are probably signals exchanged between them. May they only come and attack the camp!

The soldiers detached as skirmishers on the other side of the river claim to have seen the Indians carrying off on a horse the body of one of their dead or wounded. I hope with all my heart that they saw rightly. Another may have been knocked from his horse by a bullet, but nothing is less likely.

Saturday, October 12: Eight mackinaws arrived at nightfall to pass the night at the landing, where the men riding on them are now cooking their supper. They have bought various provisions and report that the season has been generally good for the gold-seekers in Montana. This company is of better appearance than the last. The men who compose it have a more prosperous manner. It is noticeable that they are all vigorous fellows, tall, with great shoulders, and generally young. They conduct themselves decently and seem in their ways very different from the insolent blusterers who come down on the steamboats.

* * *

Tuesday, October 15: ... The hostile Indians who, during the summer, have committed their depredations in the Department of Platte River are now returning north and are taking up their winter camps along the Missouri; the Cheyennes above Fort Buford near Milk River; the Arapahoes, the Uncpapas, and a part of the Blackfeet on this side of Fort Buford in the neighborhood of Knife River. The Crows are of rather doubtful intentions but have not yet committed any act of hostility against the whites, nor have the Assiniboines, although some of the latter have stolen horses from Mr. Pease, who had some provisions to deliver to them from Colonel Rankin.

The absence of any cavalry in Dakota and the lack of horses which have not yet been furnished at our posts, will force us to remain on the defensive during the winter, where with two troops we would be able to beat up all the bands wintering on the river, destroy their lodges, capture part of their stock, etc., all the things which are not possible with infantry. . . .

Wednesday, October 16: McDonald and one of the half-breeds came back from Fort Totten today, bringing the mail. The trip was not without danger. Dog Den[19] is at all times, a bad place to traverse. The ground is broken by steep hills and narrow coulees well suited to ambush. This time the danger was greatly augmented by the presence of the band of Medicine Bear, hostiles who stole five mules from us last week. It seems they have lost one of them for they now have only four. They have there ten or twelve lodges, which means about fifty redskins. It is the band of Black Moon, of Red Horn, of Four Horns, and of others who have separated themselves from the band of Bear's Ribs, to live by robbery and brigandage. Just now they are hunting in those parts on the way to their winter quarters near Fort Buford. Not far from their camp was another, of Santees, allied with the whites and from whom there is nothing to fear. Among

[19] Dog Den Butte, a landmark for many miles and part of the Coteau du Missouri, is a few miles south of the present village of Butte, N. Dak. The trail to Fort Totten passed just to the south of it. There are many Indian legends with regard to it. G. F. W.

the savages are to be found some half-breeds who sell them Indian whiskey,[20] and when, during the night, our men passed between the two camps, the Uncpapas were having a feast; that is to say, were drunk, beating their drum and shaking their rattles, dancing and singing about their fires. The occasion would have been fine had McDonald had a score of men. The Uncpapas would have paid dearly for their attack of the other day. But our two men could only profit by the night to conceal their trail from their enemies and to get away with the third horse which carried the mail, They did, however, talk with the half-breeds, and learned that the hostile Uncpapas had announced their intention of killing without distinction those whom they might find carrying the white man's mail, whether they were whites or half-breeds. This threat seems to have made an impression upon our scouts, so much so that to prepare against the dangers

[20] Indian whiskey was a lineal descendant of the high wine of the earlier fur traders, and ancestor of the cowboy's "rotgut whiskey." It was straight alcohol cut with water and sometimes flavored with anything that the caprice of the concocter might dictate. In spite of its baleful effect on them, the Indians seemed to feel that they were deeply indebted to those from whom they might obtain it. Hence part of their consideration for the Red River half-breed. G. F. W.

which threaten our communication with Devils Lake we are going to move our route more to the west. The advantages of this change are manifest, for we are able to strike the route of the mail between Forts Totten and Buford at a station established on Mouse River only some sixty miles from here. It is half of the distance which separates us from Fort Totten, and the country being frequented by hunters of our three tribes and of the Assiniboines, is much safer than the defiles of Dog Den.

The plan was, for the winter, to send from here at a fixed day and from Totten also, two dog trains which should meet halfway and exchange dispatches. In adopting the new route, we shall send from here one train only to the station, and the dogs at Fort Totten with their drivers will be transferred here to relieve the tired teams and to replace the animals which may be lacking here for one cause or another.

Next Monday, McDonald will leave with the three half-breeds to explore the new route, assure himself of the location of the station, and go from there to Devils Lake, whence he will carry the mail once more by the route followed up to now. The Yanktonais, the Santees, and the Cut Heads are around Totten, camped near the lake, and on good terms with the garrison, who have no complaint to make against them.

In the afternoon two Indian chiefs came to pay me a call. One, well known in this region through his unvarying attachment to the whites, was Running Antelope; the other, who has not yet won a name for himself, is the youngest son of Bear's Ribs and chief of the friendly Uncpapas. Running Antelope is this man's uncle.

* * *

Bear's Ribs has left a great reputation on the Upper Missouri. He was a man of great courage and of implacable resolution, faithful to his word, and one to be counted upon in any circumstance. Old General Harney had brought him over to the side of the whites and after that time no test ever altered his devotion, which ended by costing him his life. He separated early from one part of his tribe (the Uncpapas), which refused to follow the same line of conduct, and persisted in its hostility toward the Government. Among those who followed him he showed himself to the end a strict and terrible judge. A gradation of punishment did not exist for him, and a violation of his orders was uniformly punished by death, with himself acting as executioner by means of a revolver which he carried always in his belt.

They tell some odd examples of this summary justice in the contacts of the undisciplined young men of his band with the military posts, which at that time scarcely extended north of Nebraska. There was then at Fort Pierre a bell to sound the alarm. One of his men, received with him into the fort, got the idea of striking the bell, and took a shot at it. Old Bear's Ribs marched up to the delinquent and, drawing his revolver, stretched him dead at his feet. The repression of all theft was no less energetic, so much so that the loss of this resource so dear to all Indians, among whom rapine is an honor, caused to rise against him in the hearts of some of his warriors a hatred that only the fear which he inspired prevented them from manifesting.

The chief was not ignorant of this feeling and recognized well the danger which he ran among his own people, so that his wives watched always around the lodge, relieving each other like sentries. He never went out without his revolver and a short double-barreled gun; but nothing could change his inflexible will to make respected the word which he had given to the whites, who indeed treated him generously, giving him provisions, blankets, and ammunition. When his young men dealt with the traders one

often saw him come and sit down near the
transaction, his legs crossed, his head resting in his hands, speaking no word to anyone
and enveloping himself in a meditative silence. Then there would be neither any
complaint nor any dispute. Trade was easily
and promptly made under the black eyes of
the old chief, whose anger no one dared to
provoke. He had killed eight or nine men
when at last he fell a victim of the vengeance
which he had kindled against himself. It
seems that the officers' table was about to
be served when eight or ten of his warriors,
bursting into the room, threw themselves
upon the food and began to dine on the
spoils. Bear's Ribs ran up, and jumping
into the midst of the pillagers stretched one
of them out on the floor. The rest then all
jumped on him and killed him; not, however,
until he had killed a second one of them and
wounded several others.

Such was the end of Bear's Ribs. His
murderers escaped, I believe, and went to
join the hostile portion of their tribe. He
was buried with military honors and his
band, having left to the commander of the
fort the choice of his successor, his eldest son
was named and exercised for a time the
authority, contrary to Indian custom, which
makes the choice of a chief the result of an

election. The eldest son of Bear's Ribs died of a disease, and it was then that his younger brother was called to rule. It is this young chief who has just paid me a visit today with his uncle, Running Antelope, who exercises over the band an authority similar to that of a regent, though his nephew is 25 years old. But the Indians consider age as a guaranty of wisdom and ability; for them, youth is fiery and thoughtless and that is why the training of a young chief is prolonged into maturity.

Beauchamp, who is still here, knew Bear's Ribs well. He told me a story which shows the character of the chief before he had made such a reputation for terrible justice.

Beauchamp had had two horses stolen on the prairie while he was on a trapping expedition and busy tending the traps along a stream frequented by beaver. He soon learned without any doubt that they were at a hunting camp of Uncpapas not far from there. He was much attached to his horses and, too, their loss was for him one of considerable material importance. So in spite of the evident danger which he ran in going to reclaim them, in spite of the urgent pleas of the Rees to keep him from going, he resolved to take the risk and venture among the Uncpapas. He entered the camp without trouble and was not long in noticing his two horses tied at the door of a lodge. His first care was to put the saddle which lay upon the ground nearby on the better of the two horses. The bridle, you know, consists for Indian horses of only a long thong of leather ending in a buckle. During these preparations the thief watched and gave several loud yells. Beauchamp, resolved to repossess his property at all hazards, mounted the animal and unslung his rifle. Some other Indians ran up, naturally taking the part of the thief and working themselves up to kill the white man on the spot. Probably this would have been done had not Bear's Ribs, attracted by the noise, come up to find the cause of the uproar. Beauchamp claimed his horses; the Indian did not want to be despoiled of them; but the dispute concentrated particularly on the second horse, which the chief then took and tied at his own door until the facts could be made clear. The thief took his knife, cut the bridle, and led the horse back where he had previously put it. The chief, calm but threatening, untied the animal a second time and led it back to his lodge. "Take care," said he to the young Indian. "Do not touch this horse again."

But the thief paid no heed to this injunction, and a second time cut the bridle. Then

Bear's Ribs, raising his gun, killed the poor beast, innocent cause of the dispute, to put an end to the argument. Then running after the undisciplined warrior, he half killed him with a blow of his tomahawk while Beauchamp, profiting by the confusion, fled at full speed, glad enough to get back his best horse and his own skin from the squabble.

Such was the man whose youngest son came today to sit under my tent. He is a big youth with a face more melancholy than warlike, and with a soft voice which is quite in contrast with his great height and broad shoulders. His uncle, Running Antelope, spoke first in approximately the following words:

"Father, we came today from the village of the Three Tribes to visit the great white chief of whom we have heard on the banks of the Missouri, to listen to his words and to give him our hand as a sign of submission and fidelity. It makes my heart glad to see in this region a great chief who commands other chiefs to the east and to the west, and to take to him words of peace and friendship, as the other chiefs before him since the time of White Beard (General Harney) have heard them from me. These words are not deceitful; everyone who has passed along the banks of the Missouri knows this. My

mouth has never uttered lies; my hands
have never been dirty. Since the day when
we first allied ourselves with the whites I
have always been faithful to them at all
times and in all places. The skin of my body
is red but my flesh is white, since for many
years I have eaten the bread of the whites.
I have received my food from them and I
have accustomed myself to live as they do.
Others have made treaties and violated them;
one day they have been whites in order to
receive presents, and the next day they have
stolen their horses or have soiled their hands
with the blood of white travellers on the
prairies. As for me, my tongue is straight
and my hands are clean. And what I say
for myself I say also for this young son of
my brother, Bear's Ribs, who lost his life
in the white man's cause. All the services
which I was able to render to the great chiefs
whom our Great Father has sent among us,
I have rendered them, since the day when
White Beard, after having taken me with
him high and low through the country, said
to me, 'Go among the redskins, and carry
to them my words or go among the soldiers
and carry to them my writings.' To the
bluecoats I have faithfully carried the writings. To the redskins I have spoken as my
father ordered. Some have made peace and

have kept it; others have remained on the Plains and did not care to listen to my advice; but I shall continue to speak to them if my father wishes it, to lead them to the right and incline them to keep peace."

Running Antelope is highly intelligent, as his countenance bears witness, and he expresses himself clearly, accompanying his words with eloquent gestures, as do the greater part of the Indians.

I replied with some eulogies of his past conduct, which was already known to me (which was true), for I had heard him talked about ever since my arrival on the Missouri, and I received his visit with the more pleasure since I already knew him by reputation. In a few words I was able to make him understand my sentiments: "I wish what is just, and reason will always rule my conduct; constant protection and encouragement to all friendly Indians who keep their word and live in peace and friendship with us; war to a finish and exemplary punishment to those who attack us and who try to fool us with lies and betrayals. For them punishment may be delayed. It may not reach them in a week, in a month, in a year; but they will not escape it and I shall infallibly settle my account with them, when the fort is built and when the moment has come. The good and honest men, on the contrary, whether they have white skins or red, can count on me to do everything for them that I am able, for such is the wish of our Great Father and such is my own wish."

It goes without saying that my remarks were well received with some approving "Hows" several times repeated. Immediately I gave the conference a turn to a dialogue, asking a series of questions about the hostile portion of the Uncpapas, on the plans for wintering of the other band, the number of their lodges (90), and the approach of the Cheyennes, the Arapaho, and the Blackfeet toward Fort Buford.

When this part of the conference had been completed the young chief, who up to then had remained silent and motionless, rose in his turn, came and shook hands with me, and presented to me in turn as his uncle had done, the papers which he carried and which are certificates of loyalty to the whites, recommendations to the commanders of military posts, and even orders sent to Bear's Ribs by different generals. When I had gone over these various documents the young chief addressed me in his turn:

"My father will hear my words with indulgence for I am young and without experience; I have not yet taken my place in

the councils among those whom age has
given wisdom or valor has made illustrious.
But I have in my heart the same sentiments
that my father, Bear's Ribs, put there, and
I have in my head the words which he often
repeated to me when I was young. He said
to me, 'Whether I live or whether I die, be
always a friend to the whites; protect the
traveller across the prairie and our Great
Father will protect you. The Great Spirit
who has made the white men as many toward the rising sun as the stars in the sky at
night has wished that they spread out over
the plains to live with his red children. Such
is his wish; we must obey him for he is the father of all men, whatever may be the color
of their skin. The white men will have pity
on the red men who shall live in peace with
them. They will be generous for your father
and for all those who, like him, have allied
themselves with them. They will be generous to thee and thy brother and to the tribe
if you remain faithful to them.' My father
died, acting as he had spoken; my brother
died without changing in feeling and conduct. And as for me, I have never had
any other thought. What Bear's Ribs has
taught me I shall practice, following always the example which he set me. I have
wished to assure you, my Father, of this, to

hear your good words and feel my heart strong again when the great chief has spoken."

One can divine in advance my reply. It was stereotyped. A eulogy on the memory of Bear's Ribs, the honest and brave man, faithful to his word and devoted to the whites. His merits flower again in his son and all the things which could not be done to recompense him during his life, so soon cut off, is a debt which will be paid to his son, who may always count on our friendship and protection according to the wish of our Great Father.

After fresh thanks from the two Indians and new assurances from me, I terminated the conference with something more substantial, sending out for the commissary. Lieutenant Parsons was an old acquaintance of Running Antelope and there was a cordial exchange of "Hows" and handclasps. I announced to my visitors that the lieutenant had an order to give them provisions and that they might follow him to go and receive them, and since the young chief had asked Patinaud, the interpreter, in an undertone, if he might have instead some pipesful of tobacco, I had added to the provisions two plugs of tobacco which I had got for myself from the sutler. My two red children retired, enchanted with their new Father, that goes without saying, and resolved to try new schemes through the winter to bring him the submission of the hostile tribes to whom they will relay his words. At the conclusion of the conference they set out for Berthold with Gustave Cagnat and Patinaud, who had come here with them.

* * *

Friday, October 18: The band of Medicine Bear passed the camp on their way to Berthold. This is the band that McDonald and the scout saw near Dog Den, and which they took for one of Uncpapas. These simpletons of savages have had a good hunt. They had got a number of buffalo hides and quantities of meat, when bad luck made them meet the half-breeds and their horrible whiskey. They did not fail to get drunk and had a night of orgy; during their drunkenness their furs had passed into the hands of the half-breeds, to whom they had sold them for some bottles of poison. So they have very little left and they are going to Berthold with their ears back, to get ammunition and take up the hunt again.

Up there, there are at the moment some hostile Indians come to trade horses for corn and probably for powder, if they find an opportunity to get any. They came in great numbers, crossing the river by swimming on their horses, or in bullboats. Mr. Pease has sent us warning that they intend to cross the river in force to make an attack on us. Let them come and they will be well received. We are on our guard and we are watching the teams sent out to haul lumber; for an Indian attack means an attempt to steal mules or cattle. As for attacking the camp, that would be the greatest favor they could do us; but unless they have completely lost their heads they will not be such fools. They must have robbed most successfully during the summer, for from the reports coming from Berthold, they are well armed with guns, rifles, munitions, and abundantly provided with horses and mules.

The wagon escort is reinforced each day with men relieved from guard at eight in the morning, which makes the total escort force more than fifty men.

Saturday, October 19: A day of fog. A cold and penetrating wind from the northeast. Mr. Wilkinson, the government Agent among the friendly Indians of this district, has returned from Buford, where he had gone to begin the distribution of the annual presents to the tribes. Steamboats are no longer coming down and it was necessary to travel on a mackinaw to return to Berthold, his residence. There he has made the distribution to the Three Tribes, who, having received their presents, leave now for their winter camps.

One would suppose that they would leave their supplies of corn in a warehouse under a guard of their men. Nothing of the sort. Their way of preserving the grain which they intend for trade is much more original and altogether Indian. Each family having harvested and prepared its crop, its male members go outside the village by night to dig a cache, the location for which has been chosen with care. This cache, it goes without saying, is generally in thick brush and always in a dry spot where the flow of water and the rain can not damage the contents. The opening is round and as narrow as possible. The inside capacity is measured by the amount of grain which must be stored there; the walls are clean and smooth and covered, as is the bottom, with mats of twisted hay. There, as secretly as possible, they go and store their provisions unobserved. They close the opening tightly and cover it with earth, leaves, and grass, with such skill and cunning that nothing betrays the location to the view. When they quit the village for their winter camps they leave the corn in these caches, which are extremely difficult to locate.[21]

Meanwhile, it often happens that they discover by accident the location of each other's caches and this may result in mutual stealing. If the thief is caught in the act, though the thefts are undertaken in such cases only at night, he runs grave risk of being killed on the spot by the owner; but if the theft is discovered later the family arranges to recompense amply the victims, with both damages and interest. Among the Indians there are but two punishments: death and payment of damages. The alternative of damages is offered in all cases, and consists of death. The degree consists only in the importance of the injury. Such is the penalty for the stealing of grain; the same for the theft or injury of a horse; the same for the killing of a man. Only in the latter case the damages go, not to the victim, but to his family.

[21] The practice of concealing food supplies, goods, and other property in caches was widespread among the Indians, and from them was adopted by white hunters, trappers, and explorers. Numerous references to it have occurred in earlier volumes of the *Lakeside Classics* Series. See, for example, Zenas Leonard's *Narrative*, 258–59; Josiah Gregg, *Commerce of the Prairies*, 56–58; *Kit Carson's Autobiography*, 28–29; Alexander Ross's *Adventures on the Oregon or Columbia River*, 196. M. M. Q.

When Running Antelope saved the life of
Gerard, Patinaud, and two other white men,
there was a fight among the Indians who
wanted to kill them and those who wanted
to protect them. The latter were the stronger.
killing two or three of their adversaries.
Upon which it was deemed proper that Gerard should give two good American horses,
not to those who had saved him, but to those
who had attacked him, to pay for the lives
of those who had died. Their blood being
thus ransomed, all idea of vengeance was
removed and there was no longer any cause
for trouble with the survivors.

* * *

Tuesday, October 22: . . . Three Rees from
Berthold came down today by bullboat.
They have again had horses stolen by the
Sioux, so these three are going on the warpath to get even with their enemies and steal
from them what horses they can, not by
open force, but at night and by stealth. It
goes without saying that they will lose their
skins, or rather their scalps, if they are discovered. They are armed with two guns
and a bow and arrows, without counting
their knives. I had some provisions given
them and in the night they re-embarked
in their buffalo hide, to continue their de-
scent of the river until they reach the hunt-

ing grounds where the Sioux bands are likely to be found. If they succeed, they will return, mounted, over the prairie where large game will not be wanting. If they fail it is more than likely that they will never return.

* * *

Friday, November 1: Beauchamp has come from Berthold to bring me two beaver skins which I ordered from him; I have learned from him that the Indians of the Three Tribes have been shamefully robbed by the agent charged with the distribution of their annual presents. This thing is nothing out of the ordinary; one might even say that it is the general custom on the frontiers. If one went to the bottom of the matter one would find that the hostilities of most of the tribes and the troubles which result from the n are merely the consequences of the shameful bad faith with which the agents steal from them the greater part of the annuities which the Government sends them. As to the affair of the Three Tribes, here is what Beauchamp told me:

The agent, Wilkinson, had held in the warehouse for several months the presents to be distributed, and it was difficult for the poor redskins, who had no access to the warehouse, to assure themselves that the merchandise remained intact. However, they

134

mounted guard on the outside during the nights and several times their sentinels were sure that they heard the noise of hammers and boxes being broken open at an hour when one would expect the whole village to be asleep. When thereafter several employes of the traders at the fort appeared with new flannel shirts, "See," they said, "some shirts to deduct from our annuities." Perhaps they were mistaken, but it is little likely.

As a last evidence, one of the steamboats, the *Deer Lodge*, brought to Berthold the full complement of the annuities, consisting of provisions, dried meat, hams, sacks of flour, blankets, cutlery. The merchandise was unloaded under the eyes of the Indians watching from the bank. They were able for themselves to determine the number of boxes or sacks of different items and decided that the distribution should be made to them on the spot. Nothing would have been easier; but despite their insistence and protestations the Agent ordered that all the merchandise be first moved to the fort and there put in the warehouse where he kept it two nights and a day. When at last the moment came for the distribution, the boxes had been opened and many were only partly full. The boxes of plain knives, full on arrival, had lost one layer of their contents. Some blue shirts with red facing had disappeared; some sacks of flour marked U.S. with the government seal had been replaced by unmarked sacks of condemned flour, leavings from the trader's warehouse, The quantity of blankets had much diminished. Under the circumstances White Shield, chief of the Rees, refused to sign or recognize a receipt in full for the presents sent by the Great Father at Washington. The Agent, furious, declared him, on his own authority, deposed from the dignity of chief, and replaced him by a young man of the tribe without even paying him his annuity, which was above two hundred dollars.

Hence, should one ask me what has become of the merchandise stolen from the Indians I can only answer: yesterday there left Berthold a convoy of eight or ten wagons loaded for Devils Lake, where the merchandise which they contain is destined to be sold to the Indians who frequent that post.

Question: whence does this merchandise come? And if it belongs legitimately to the Berthold traders, agents of the Northwest Fur Company, why this transfer to Totten? Are there not at Berthold tribes with which one can trade as well as anywhere? Above all, consider that Mr. Pease, one of them, has just taken a convoy of merchandise to Totten from St. Paul, where he went for the purpose of getting it. All that looks very transparent to me and confirms fully what has been repeatedly told me everywhere upon the frontier, by Indians and otherwise; that is that the Agents of the Indian Bureau are nothing but members of a vast association of thieves who make their fortune at the expense of the redskins and to the detriment of the Government. They accept an annual salary of $1500 and, at the end of a few years, they return to the States, having made their fortunes. That fact calls for no further comment.

For this evil there is but one remedy; to transfer the whole administration of Indian affairs to the War Department, replace the Agents by the quartermasters of the frontier posts under the control of their superior authorities. Then the Government would save millions and would live without difficulty in peace with the Indians. But when will this remedy be adopted? It has been proposed and strongly recommended and urged in Congress and elsewhere. But the whole interested association of robbers was united, and put up a lobby, using every means, both legal and illegal; thus it has been able up to now to keep itself in power despite all efforts and all the accumulated proofs of its misdeeds. Living in corruption, the Indian Bureau maintains itself through corruption and God knows when Congress will free itself from its venal influence and put an end to its career of spoilation.

Saturday, November 2: Toward noon snow began to fall; it has fallen without interruption all the rest of the day; it is still falling while I write these lines just before going to bed.

* * *

Thursday, November 7: The cold has decreased considerably but not enough to spoil the skating, which is excellent, and to which those of us who practice that exercise gave up the whole morning.

In the afternoon Gustave Cagnat came to see me. Yesterday Gerard also paid me a visit. Both are traders at Fort Berthold, it will be remembered. Yesterday Gerard confirmed for me, in general, Beauchamp's report, though with marked variation in the details. Now Gustave, questioned by me, affirms that there are gross exaggerations in the report. He states that in his presence Agent Wilkinson demanded explicitly and several times of the old Ree chief, not a receipt in full, but a receipt according to the count of the merchandise which he received, taking care to have explained to him the difference through an interpreter, Pierre Gareau. He explained thus the loss of a part of the presents: the first steamboat upon which they were loaded in the spring sank by accident in the river; the sugar melted; the provisions were broken up; some were lost. The agent had a new requisition made to replace them. This was refilled only in part, as was proved by the invoice which Wilkinson has shown to Cagnat. Thus, in place of two cases of hunting knives, only one came; the same with the blankets. The old chief, badly counselled and urged (according to Cagnat) by some whites who exercise a bad influence over him (Beauchamp and Gerard, I suppose) has obstinately refused even to give a receipt for the goods received, and consented by himself to yield his office to the second chief, the Son of a Star, who has been replaced by the chief of the warriors, Iron Bear. The following dialogue occurred between the agent and White Shield:

The agent: "My friend, you are getting too old; age troubles your brain and you talk and act like an old fool."

The chief: "I am old, it is true; but not so old as not to see things as they are. And even if, as you say, I were only an old fool,

I would prefer a hundred times to be an honest red fool than a stealing white rascal like you."

Not bad for a savage.

However, in his anger old White Shield seems to have declared that the chieftainship gave him more trouble and fatigue than satisfaction, and that he would willingly consent to be relieved of it; or something approaching that, upon which Wilkinson took him at his word.

All this seemed to me to be rather confused, and I can see clearly just two things: first, owing to commercial competition Gerard and Cagnat do not get along together, the first having the Rees as his special customers, the second, the Gros Ventres and Mandans; second, Cagnat makes common cause with Agent Wilkinson, and Gerard has for employe Beauchamp, who, being a son-in-law of the Ree chief, follows along the road of his interests and prejudices.

However it may be, the affair is not one under military jurisdiction. A report has been sent in the name of the Rees to Father De Smet, a Catholic priest very influential among these tribes; among whom he has long resided. The Father is now in Washington and in process of placing the report before the eyes of the Secretary of the Interior, who is in charge of the Indian Bureau, and even perhaps under the eyes of the President. I am very curious to see what the result will be.

The northwest wind which rose in the afternoon has increased more and more in the evening. Mixed with it are gusts of sleet, of snow and rain through part of the night.

Friday, November 8: This morning the weather was clear, but the wind continued to blow a gale. Its violence rather increased than diminished toward mid-day; a new lowering of temperature resulted, the sky clouded and soon the air became filled with fine snow carried violently by the wind; the small flakes became thicker and the storm continued to rage during the rest of the day.

* * *

Monday, November 11: A part of the band of the Black Catfish, of the tribe of the Yanktonais, has arrived here. They come from Fort Rice, where game has become scarce, which decided them to go farther north to winter where the buffalos are more plentiful. They have with them their women and children, and for two or three days they have pitched their lodges on Douglas Creek near the edge of the timber. There are altogether no more than 25 or 30 of them.

Tuesday, November 12: . . . Yesterday morning, according to orders of the evening before, a group of six soldiers in charge of a sergeant with four half-breed scouts, left with two wagons filled with rations, forage, and the necessary tools to build, at previously chosen points, log cabins for shelters during the night, or in case of snowstorms during the day, for the mail carriers between Totten and Stevenson. They will build these cabins, first at Cold Water; second at Dog Den; third at Bass Island. This last station will be the half-way station. There will meet the evening of the day after their departure from the two points at the opposite ends of the line, the mail carriers, who will be sent out on a regular schedule the first, tenth, and twentieth of each month, While my six men and six scouts begin building the first station, the other two scouts, carrying the mail, will continue on their way to Fort Totten, where they will carry my orders. The day after the receipt of my orders the commander of the fort there will send out a party of ten men and a sergeant, who, with the scouts from the fort, will construct an intermediate station, two perhaps, between Bass Island and Totten. The work will be finished before the end of the month, and regular service will commence the first of December, which will bring us mail and papers three times a month.

Thursday, November 14: The Yanktonais want to winter near the fort, on the bank of Douglas Creek, offering to scout the neighborhood, thus paying their way, and inform us of the approach of any hostile band. Their hunting trips will cause them to beat the country in every direction, and they can be of some service to us. In exchange they hope only for some provisions from time to time, which it is easy to grant them in view of their number. Two of them have been engaged to go to Fort Rice to bring back the letters and papers which must have come for us there since the passage of the last steamboat, by way of Forts Abercrombie and Wadsworth, or by that of Sioux City, Randall, and Sully. They left this morning with a mule to carry their provisions and the letters.

The plan for the officers to take regular possession of their quarters this winter is definitely abandoned. It would take too long to make the two unfinished houses habitable; of the others, nothing is done but the stone foundations. So we are going to build some log houses as temporary lodgings for the officers and for offices for the different branches of the service, as well as for quar-

ters for the musicians. The two company
barracks, the hospital, and the warehouse
are only far enough along so that they may
be occupied next month.

Wednesday, November 20: . . . Monday,
day before yesterday, a band of Yanktonais
arrived here. It is the band of Black Eyes, a
chief noted for his fidelity to the whites and
for the services which he has done for some
of them under different circumstances. For
example, some time ago, some years I believe, a number of whites were captured by
a party of hostile Santees when Black Eyes,
being in the neighborhood, with his warriors
attacked the Santees, defeated them, and
freed the prisoners, perhaps saving their
lives. He even furnished a horse for one of
them, that they might get back to St. Paul
and find there the necessary help.

Black Eyes is accompanied by a score of
braves and some ten women and children.
On approaching the camp he formed them
in line of battle on the plain, all on horseback, and advanced with the whole line facing forward, singing in chorus a song of
peace. Then they filed off one by one behind
the tents, to go and camp on Douglas Creek
near the lodges of the little band of Big Hand,
who also belongs to the same tribe. There

is nothing more picturesque on the prairies
than these bands of mounted Indians.

* * *

Yesterday, Tuesday, having gone into the
sutler's cabin for some small errand, I found
assembled there some fifteen Indians, among
them Black Eyes, his brother Howkah, and
the soldier chief whose name signifies He
Who Wears Beautiful Things. . . . When I
addressed some remarks to the sutler, Black
Eyes asked of someone who understood Sioux
who I might be, and upon the answer that
I was the great chief who commanded all
the other chiefs, there was a stir among the
Indians and Black Eyes, advancing, extended his hand to me with the indispensable "How." Howkah did the same and
The Man Who Wears Beautiful Things, also
called the Black Cat, saluted me in his turn
after the same fashion. There followed a
short choppy conversation, badly enough
interpreted by one of the employees of the
quartermaster, named Le Blanc, a young
Canadian who understands and speaks Sioux,
but hardly enough to fill the office of interpreter. Nevertheless the three Indians presented to me in turn their papers, commis-
sions and certificates, as evidence of their
qualities and their character of faithful
allies. No business was discussed between

us; but the chief, Black Eyes, announced to me his intention of paying me a call with his warriors as soon as we could get a satisfactory interpreter. Pierre Gareau, well known to all of them, is expected here in a few days; besides two half-breeds who speak Sioux came in a few hours later, bringing the mail from Fort Totten. But we have not needed to have recourse to them yet.

This morning after breakfast McDonald, the guide for the half-breed mail carriers, came to tell me that the Yanktonais, having found among the Canadians employed by the quartermaster one named Martin who spoke very good Sioux, desired to pay me a visit and have a pow-wow with me. Having nothing better to do for the moment I sent word that I was ready to receive them. They at once presented themselves, Black Eyes (in Sioux Yah-psa-tapsah), Howkah, and the Black Cat at their head, to the number of about a score, all braves and warriors, in their ordinary dress, the greater part in checked flannel shirts, each wrapped in a buffalo robe or a brown blanket. Among them, although not belonging to the same band, was old Big Hand, with his hatchet of a peculiar shape and a bouquet of white and red feathers on his occiput.

* * *

Everyone sat down, the chiefs on chairs, the rest on the floor, the last comers outside the open door; they lit their pipes, I lighted my pipe, and silence reigned for some minutes, the pipes circulating from mouth to mouth. Then the ceremony of papers and certificates was repeated, though I had already read them the day before, but of which for further assurance they begged me to read to them the contents. That done, another pause preceded the opening of the conference, after which Black Eyes, having exchanged a preliminary handclasp with me, then with Martin, the interpreter, opened his address.

In such circumstances the exordium by insinuation seems to be the proper form:

"I am a great chief; I command many warriors, and the Indians of the Plains, having learned that our Great Father in Washington had sent you to us, have joyful hearts. That is why the Yanktonais of the Upper Missouri have said to themselves, 'We will go to visit our Father, the great chief, who has not before come among us, and we shall be happy to know him, for his fame is great among the whites, and already has spread afar among the tribes of the Dakota.' How!"

I responded as follows: "After the great war between the white men, in which we, the men of the North, conquered the men of the South and took back their immense territory which they had hoped to take away from us, our Great Father in Washington has sent me among his children of the Dakota, no longer to make war, but to preserve peace. As for me, that which I wish is equal justice for all. In my eyes all men are sons of the Great Spirit, whatever may be the color of their skins, and in my rule I shall do what is just and right for all, for the redskins as well as for the palefaces. ("How!" in chorus). So the Indians who are honest and faithful friends of the whites will always find in me a man always ready to defend and protect them with all my power; as for the Indians of bad faith and hostile to the whites, those who steal and kill, they will have in Dakota no enemy more determined and persevering in fighting and punishing them." (Prolonged applause.)

"When I was a child," replied the chief with the black eyes, "the Indians freely traversed the plains which belonged to them, without ever meeting a white man there; but today the pale faces appear everywhere just as if at home, and their soldiers are established along the whole course of the great Missouri from the countries where it rises to those where it loses its name."

(A pause. The chief regarded me with his half-closed eyes. I had attentively listened to his assertion as to the property rights to the Plains; but I remained still and silent, waiting with an impassive countenance to see what the wily Indian was leading up to.)

"And since my Father occupies with his warriors a part of our hunting grounds, I wanted to come here to welcome him and to visit him with the feelings and sentiments of a friend." (How!)

But it did not suit me to be thus placed in the position of a guest among the Yanktonais and I hastened to reverse the roles.

"Many things have happened since the chief was a child," I replied in turn, with a voice somewhat more animated and watching him a little more fixedly. "If he had so good a memory as to recall the time when the pale faces did not appear on the plains, he could also recall without doubt that there were formerly toward the rising sun other Indian tribes, numerous and good warriors, who undertook to fight the pale faces and who have been so completely destroyed that neither plain nor mountain any longer knows their names today." (Profound silence. One hears often of the impassivity and dissimulation of the Indians; but Black Eyes and Howkah alone remained impassive. All the others, their eyes fixed on me, their heads slightly inclined forward, testified without reserve a deep attention and almost an eager interest in each of the phrases which Martin translated into their language.) I continued:

"And why have those tribes been destroyed or dispersed? Because after having made treaties with the white men, they have violated them; because after selling great expanses of hunting ground to the pale faces, they wanted to keep them from taking possession; because after having promised them alliances and friendship, instead of living in peace with those who first came to till the soil, those tribes stole from them their stock, burned their farms, killed and maltreated them, and took their women away as prisoners. That is why the Great Spirit, seeing that they were liars, thieves and murderers, has permitted that their tribes be destroyed, and not only did they fail to regain the territory sold, but they have lost forever what they had left. Thus the white men who are so numerous on the earth that no Indian could count them have advanced toward the setting sun, and have come to the Missouri. But the Indians who have kept faith and have remained friends of the whites have received payment for the lands sold and have kept those which they wanted, and today they till the soil, are rich and happy and live in peace and friendship with the whites around them. The bad Indians who have broken their word during the great war of the whites, and who, being at peace with the pale faces, have surprised and massacred those whom they were able to reach in Minnesota, those have lost all property rights in their lands. Many have been killed in battle; others have been hung in ignominy; others have left their lands, which now belong to the Great Father, and when they surrender and ask for peace it will be to obtain the protection of the whites, and their assistance to prevent death from famine when the game fails."

The chief hastened to assure me that he and his band were entirely innocent of everything that had happened in Minnesota; that none of them had taken part in the massacre and that as for him he had never been able to break any treaty since he had never made any nor sold any lands.

"If you have made no treaties and sold no lands," I replied, addressing him directly in the singular as is invariably the usage in the Indian languages, where one never addresses a single person in the plural, "at least the great chiefs of the Yanktonais have done so and have sold wide lands between the Minnesota and the Missouri."

"It is true," said he, "but these are the lower Yanktonais, and the lands of the upper Yanktonais extend (making a circular gesture with his hand) everywhere around here and far to the north."

"No," I answered. "The lands of the Yanktonais do not extend so far; you have told me that I am standing here on land which belongs to them; you are mistaken. This land has never belonged to them. Before belonging to us, it belonged to the Panani (the Rees), to the Hidatsa (Gros Ventres), and to the Mandans whose hunts took in all this part of the Plains. It is they who live now at Fort Berthold where they live peacefully and raise corn in good faith and friendship with the whites."

The chief smiled and gave a negative nod.

"If you have made no treaty," I pursued, "why do you stay at Fort Rice in the summer, under the protection of the whites? If you have sold no lands why do you receive from the Great Father annual presents for you and yours? Who gave you the shirt which you wear? And those of your warriors, and the clothes with buttons like those of our soldiers? And the blankets which I see here on their shoulders? You have sold no lands and yet you receive payment for them."

For some moments the warriors had evidenced a strong distaste for the turn that the conference had taken. They exchanged remarks in a low voice, of which I divined the sense from the way in which they looked at the chief, embarked on a poor way of achieving the principal object of their visit. At length Howkah, acting as their spokesman, addressed some words to his brother and, extending his hand to me:

"We think," he said, "that enough words have been said on this subject, and we want to talk about other things which the chief wants to tell you."

"Let him speak!" I answered briefly. The chief of the black eyes well understood that he was on dangerous ground, and girded himself to get out of it, repeating his protestations of devotion to the whites, and invoking his rights to their friendship from his past conduct, which were proved by the papers which he had shown me. Then, abandoning all pretence of receiving me on their lands, he humbly begged for permission to establish his winter camp in our vicinity, at whatever place I should indicate. I made no objection and let him make his choice, reserving only the immediate vicinity of the fort and the wooded lands whence our men hauled the timber for building. He then proposed the woods bordering the river at six or seven miles from here near Snake Creek. "For," he said, "the chief at Fort Rice has told me to go toward the north where I would find a chief more powerful than he who would receive me well for my good conduct and faithfulness to the whites. He said I would be your friend, you would protect me and give me provisions for me and mine." (The real purpose of the conference was out.) "The buffalo are scarce and other game at a distance," he added, "but my Father, who is a great chief, will come to our aid."

I had been warned that Black Eyes was an inveterate beggar, even among the Indians, whose favorite vice is begging. So I did not hasten to accede to his requests, although my instructions from General Sherman were to be liberal in such matters with friendly Indians. I asked how many tipis or lodges the chief counted in his band. He had 150 tipis, which indicates at least five or six hundred persons and includes the women and children. He told me that the band, which he had preceded by two days with a party of warriors, would arrive today, and asked if I would not give him some pro-

visions before its arrival. I refused but said
I would give him some when the band arrived.

Then, to assure the most possible, he said
that what I should grant would be received
with thankfulness, convinced as he was that
I would give enough so that each one might
have his own little part so as not to create
jealousies. And when I remained silent he
counted over on his fingers what he asked of
me: sugar, coffee, crackers, salt pork and
corn. I promised only to see what I could
give him at this time. "For," I told him,
"when the end of the winter comes, if game
has not been abundant, you and yours will
have nothing to eat, and I must take care
to keep enough to help you then because
you will have greater need of it than
today."

Then there were other things; he asked me
for hats for his warriors and whatever I
might be able to give them in the way of
clothing. At the finish I sent him politely
to take a walk, recalling to him that he had
received his presents at Fort Rice and that
the Indian agents and not the officers were
charged with the duty of giving clothing to
the redskins; I was going to adjourn the
sitting when he interrupted with one last
request.

"Would I not give him permission to buy some powder?" To buy, he emphasized. He and his warriors were ready to pay. I promised him permission for a moderate quantity based on the number of warriors, estimated at about a hundred, and at last my visitors rose and took their departure with fervent thanks, coming in turn to shake my hand. How!

In the afternoon the rest of the band has indeed appeared, filing along the crests seven or eight miles from here. The number has not been exaggerated, judging from the count we have made with the telescopes. They are camping tonight on the bank of the river near the place where they want to winter.

Thursday, November 21: The distribution of the provisions to the Indians of Black Eyes' band took place today. . . . The Indians, under the direction of the chief and the principal people among them, themselves made the distribution, and now the whole band has taken the back trail to their camp in groups and this time without order or ceremony.

While I was assisting at this picturesque spectacle, two mail carriers arrived as couriers from Fort Buford. In going to Buford by the way of Knife River they were captured by a band of Indians and taken to a camp of hostile Sissetons and Yanktonais.[22] They passed themselves off there for Red River half-breeds, thanks to their half-Indian costume, although they were white and English. They understood enough Sioux to get the sense of a deliberation in council, at which their fate was under discussion. The Yanktonais wished to put them to death. It was the band of a chief called Two Dogs. The Sissetons, on the contrary, insisted that their lives be spared. Their chief, whose name escapes me, spoke long and eloquently, it seemed to them, in favor of the captives, and in the end his advice was taken. They were set free after their Henry rifles and ammunition had been taken from them with the following warning: "We are letting you go," said the savages to them, "and you will be able to return to Fort Buford. But once there, go back home at once, and do not again carry the papers of the Americans. If the Americans wish to communicate with each other let them carry their own letters for then we shall know whom we should

[22] This route by way of Fort Berthold and the Knife River again refers to the Little Knife and was the route which crossed over to the southerly point of the great loop of Mouse River. G. F. W.

kill." This was explained to them by a Sisseton who spoke passable English.

The courier whom I questioned was of the
opinion that it will be impossible to maintain communications between Buford and
Totten by the route followed up to now. Not
only is it infested with hostile Indians, but
it is also without protection against winter
storms over a great part of the route. It
passes through the Plains and in such a
region it goes a hundred miles without sight-
ing a single tree. It is therefore just about
decided that the future service will go by
way of Fort Stevenson, since between Stevenson and Buford the road skirts the river
and consequently the wooded lands, which
offer some shelter against the storms, refuge
from Indians, and fuel.

Even by the latter route communications
will still be exposed to grave dangers. The
courier has counted six Indian camps between Buford and Berthold, mostly hostiles,
and a considerable number of others are said
to be in the region. Coming from Buford
the two couriers have travelled only at night,
resting and sleeping during the day, hidden
in the brush with their horses. If they are
captured that ends their lives.

At Fort Buford a wagon sent out to cut
wood has been attacked within two miles

of the fort. There were only five men in the escort. One of them was killed; his body was found horribly mutilated, report says. Another was seriously wounded with an arrow in his body. The four mules were driven off. It is not reported that any savage was either killed or wounded.

Friday, November 22: An unusual mail arrived today from Fort Rice, brought by five men, a sergeant and four Indian scouts, accompanied by the two Yanktonais whom we sent out. For my share I received two letters from France and three from the United States, of dates some time since, and papers for the month of October.

Lieutenant Colonel Otis, who commands at Fort Rice, proposes that we exchange papers and dispatches twice a month, sending on the day fixed from each post a party of several men who shall meet half-way. The arrangement, which we are accepting with pleasure, will begin on the first Monday of December, and continue each fifteen days. Thus we are now assured of two ways for regular communication: one by Fort Totten, Fort Ransom, and Fort Abercrombie, the other by Fort Rice, Fort Sully and Fort Randall. . . . I am advised that scouts can not be recruited for me at Fort Wadsworth because they are at war with several tribes in our region so that none of their young men wish to engage to serve on the Missouri. We are going to try to find our scouts among the Yanktonais of the chief with the black eyes.

Saturday, November 23: The last smile of autumn was extinguished yesterday with the last rays of the setting sun. After twelve days of wonderful weather during which we have had only white frosts at night, disappearing early each morning, the sky clouded up toward evening and the temperature fell, under the influence of a northwest breeze. This morning we have had a light fall of snow, after which the thermometer has continued to fall more rapidly. Toward noon it stood at 20 degrees Fahrenheit. At four it had dropped to 16 degrees. It is now (8 o'clock in the evening) at 14 degrees (10 degrees below zero Centigrade) and everything portends a glacial night.

We have used the twelve days of good weather to advantage in finishing the roofs of the two company quarters; but the log-houses intended to serve as lodgings for the officers were commenced only day before yesterday and if the cold is not relieved the work will suffer from the new delays which will follow. We can only hope.

Tuesday, November 26: The thermometer continues to float between 20 and 25 degrees Fahrenheit. Snow has fallen without interruption since morning. Yesterday evening around 8 o'clock, in a black night, several shots on the other side of the river brought everyone out. It was Indian marauders who had come under cover of darkness to try to steal the mules employed to haul logs. But a sentry is posted there night and day in a sentry box in the form of a turret on the roof of the log house. The sentry, having seen the marauders, fired a shot, and the men, rushing out, pursued them to the thickets where the redskins disappeared, not to be seen again. The beasts are in a palisaded corral adjoining the cabin. Thus the thieves scarcely have a chance to get them out. Besides, it must be believed that the reception which they received yesterday evening will henceforth dissuade them from further attempts.

* * *

Wednesday, November 27: Snow last night; snow all day and nothing to indicate any cessation during the night, although it has not stopped falling for 36 hours.

* * *

Thursday, November 28: Prisoner in my cabin. Always the snow, always the north

wind and the thermometer below zero Fahrenheit.

* * *

Thursday, December 5: The band of Black
Eyes remained only a few days in its camp.
Perhaps the buffalo were scarcer than they
expected, in the vicinity, perhaps the wandering nature of the Indians took the upper
hand; they wasted no time in filing before
the camp and, crossing Douglas Creek, in
going to camp below us in the woods whence
we have cut a great deal of building timber.
They then came to announce that their halt
at that place was only for a few days, waiting until the ice on the river should be solid
enough for them to cross with their animals
and baggage. (Since Sunday, December 1,
several of our men have crossed from one
side to the other.) Tuesday (day before yesterday) their musical organization, composed
of three drums and 24 singers, to which were
added 5 or 6 squaws, came on horseback with
great pomp and in full regalia to give me a
farewell performance; that is, under pretext of
dancing and singing, to get more provisions
from us. Nevertheless, I do not complain,
for the sight was certainly worth seeing.

* * *

Wednesday (yesterday) the band had not
yet left; they were packing the baggage, so

they said. The departure was to be this
morning. But this morning the wind blew a
gale, and in such weather they could not
think of starting. I had already surmised
that they would come again to beg before
starting, and I was quite justified. At first
Black Eyes came alone to ask an audience
to find out if I had received an answer to a
letter which he had asked me to send to
Lieutenant Colonel Otis, commander at Fort
Rice, on the subject of some provisions received there for him since his departure. The
answer had arrived and was very satisfactory. Then he asked that some provisions
which he had left deposited in the warehouse
should be delivered for himself and his
family. Nothing could be more proper. But
I profited by the occasion to make a strong
complaint over some thefts attempted by his
young men and their wives, to our disadvantage. To say "Indian" is to say "thief."
These same redskins who are truly friends
of the whites, who receive annual presents
at Fort Rice, and occasional provisions at
the different posts which they visit in their
excursions, never fail when they are near a
fort or post, to hunt for opportunities on
every occasion to steal there whatever they
can. Here the temptation for them is irre-
sistible for, the fort not being finished, all

the provisions are in the commissary tents; the grain, above all the corn, of which they are especially fond, is piled in sacks under shelters and the harness is still hung these days on pegs inside a temporary corral which is very easy to enter, nothing in the camp being enclosed within palisades. The result has been that during these last few nights the sentries have on several occasions fired on the Indian marauders who profited by the darkness to come to commit theft. Although they knew from experience that the guards were watching and that they risked the chance of being killed by a rifle shot, they have nonetheless succeeded in getting away with several sacks of corn, in cutting up some harness to get the leather straps, and lastly in carrying off entirely two saddles.

During the day they sent their women and children, though they did not themselves come, to loiter around the warehouses and find out just how they might steal in the easiest way, and after this scouting they made, or attempted to make, their foray in the night, unless the challenge of the sentry, followed by a shot, put them to flight for a few hours or until the next night. One of the quartermaster's men, Martin, who acted as my interpreter, even surprised one of the

squaws cutting up a harness in broad daylight. Familiar with Indian usage, as with
their tongue, he beat the woman concerned
and drove her beyond the limits of the camp
with kicks in the rear. But since we can not
adopt this Sioux method as a rule, it has been
necessary to forbid to all the Indians without
distinction entry into camp or approach to
the warehouses or corrals, but particularly
to the women who swarmed around the camp.
Since snow covers the ground and also, for
three nights, we have had the first quarter of
the moon, one would think that the difficulty of escaping the observation of the
sentries would have kept the Indians at a
distance; but it availed nothing, for the
temptation to steal is among them greater
than the fear of danger.

The chief appeared very humiliated under
the reproaches which I addressed to him on
this subject. He protested ignorance concerning these misdeeds and in fact I believe
that the principal dignitaries have nothing
to do with them. He expressed his great
regret over the evil conduct of some of his
young men for whom, he said, he felt much
ashamed. And he retired, promising to make
a search through the lodges and return to us
everything that he should find there which
might belong to us.

Toward noon I went to call on the sutler, Mr. Marsh, having had word that yesterday a hostile Indian had come in to the band of Yanktonais under Black Eyes. He had even gone into the sutler's warehouses where his conduct had inspired such suspicions that one of the employes put him out, revolver in hand. The suspicions were confirmed by Black Eyes who, questioned on the subject, by Captain Powell, had revealed that he had indeed received as a visitor at his camp a warrior of the unsurrendered Uncpapas, named Red Horn, who is reported to us from Fort Rice to be an incorrigible thief, a murderer on occasion, whom we suspect of having taken part in the theft of mules here and at Fort Buford. Jack and Junot, the two employes of the sutler, gave me an account of the details which had excited their suspicions; how they had seen this unknown Indian pilfering crackers while a soldier was buying some, and how the passive attitude and withdrawal of Black Eyes, who was present, had made them conclude that the fellow could not belong to his band. During this time Howkah (He about Whom They Sing), the chief of the band's soldiers, He Who Wears Beautiful Things, (and who to-day certainly did not wear any of them) and two or three others came in. Then I learned that Red Horn had left yesterday evening for Fort Berthold on the way back to his camp, where he was trying to draw the Yanktonais to join the hostile bands. The subject being exhausted, Howkah stretched out his hand to me and since one of the half-breeds was there he began his little request, as usual with the customary exordium: As a friend of the whites, obedient to the Great Father, faithful to his word, he was ashamed and his heart cast down to learn that some wicked little deeds had been done during the night by his young men. The expected conclusion: He was going to leave tomorrow with all the others and his family was without anything to eat. He would like to have just a few provisions, only enough for one family of five people. I refused. We have already given too much to people who will steal from us. Not that I accused Howkah of it directly, but, as second chief, he should have had more authority over his young men and, since they acted badly, I should give nothing to any of them.

I was curious to see if, after that, they would return to the charge after another fashion in order to subtract some provisions from us. Only a short time elapsed before my curiosity was satisfied.

Toward four o'clock I was reading in my cabin when some Indian songs burst forth noisily from the direction of the fort. I enquired the cause, and the reply was that a score of Indians approached singing, bringing back the two saddles stolen the other night. It was all that the search made by Black Eyes served to produce. Naturally the corn could no longer be identified and the bits of harness were too easy to hide. Always singing, the Indians, under the leadership of Howkah and the soldier chief, filed through the camp, carrying the two saddles which they finally placed before my door, taking care to squat about them in a circle to await my good pleasure. And what could be my good pleasure except to take the saddles and have some provisions distributed to those who brought them back, in order to recompense them for the restitution and encourage them in the path of virtue? Thus once again, willy nilly, those red devils succeeded in wresting some provisions from our hands.

Between 8 and 9 o'clock in the evening three shots from the post on the other side of the river advised us that the crazy thieves, in spite of the snow, in spite of the moonlight, were still skulking about the post, in order to steal something and thus put to profit their last night in our neighborhood. A quarter of an hour later Captain Powell brought the sergeant of the post to me. He had crossed on the ice to report that all day the Indians had swarmed incessantly about the post, in spite of every effort to drive them away. This evening many of them came again to plunder and succeeded in stealing two sacks of corn from the little corral attached to the log house. Our men shot over the heads of the thieves, knowing that they belonged to a friendly band; and they fled for the moment, but impunity probably would encourage them to return in the night. The sergeant asked if he should confine himself again to merely frightening them.

"Are they armed?" I asked him.

"Yes, their bows and quivers can be seen."

"Well, if they come back tell the sentry to aim carefully; try to kill one of them; it is the only way of having peace with these wild thieves."

The sergeant retired, evidently satisfied with the order he had received. We shall see tomorrow what it will produce. If the marauders do not return, it will have no effect; if they do, so much the worse for them. Patience has its limits beyond which it degenerates into weakness, and particularly in dealing with Indians, one must guard against appearing weak, for they despise the weak and respect only the strong.

At any rate I hope by tomorrow to be relieved of these friends, the most importunate that we could have in the neighborhood.

Friday, December 6: Disappointment. I have not yet finished with the Indians. First, the Yanktonais have not yet gone. I was assured that they were packing their baggage and that part of the band had started. But I can see at a distance on the prairie a bunch of horses which proves that a large part of them are still there.

Furthermore, the old Ree chief, White Shield, the same one whom the Indian Agent Wilkinson deposed, arrived yesterday evening with a score of his warriors. He spent the night in Trader Gerard's log house and has asked me for an audience through Beauchamp, who came with him to serve as interpreter. Toward 10 o'clock I gave an audience to the old chief and three of his principal warriors, but as they opened the door whom should I see but Black Eyes, Howkah, and the soldier chief. I thought that by asking in the Rees without the Sioux, the latter would remain outside, but with the mannerlessness of the man of nature, stranger to all that civilized man calls discretion, my three intruders entered along with the three or four other Indians. I made them understand through Beauchamp, who speaks a little Sioux, that I had business to discuss with the Rees. "How!" they answered in unison. That was fine! And without imagining that they might be in the way they all sat down. It was necessary either to tolerate their presence or throw them out. As I did not know whether, according to their ideas, this might not have been an injury for which they might seek vengeance on the Rees, in order not to disturb the peace concluded between the two tribes, and reflecting besides that, since they spoke different tongues, they would not be able to understand what transpired, I decided to let them sit at the conference. Then the calumet passed from lip to lip between the Sioux and the Pahlanis, and I smoked my pipe, everyone preserving absolute silence. This pause, which invariably precedes the pow-wows, is without doubt intended to give to the one who is to speak time to meditate on his words, and everyone holds himself respectful to these meditations or meditates himself, but I have no great doubts that the second chiefs and the assistants are interested chiefly in enjoying themselves when it comes their turn to smoke the kinnikinnick and the rest of the time do not think about anything. The silence lasted longer than usual and took a good quarter of an hour. The Ree chief, I presume, was disturbed and grumpy at having to present his business before strangers; but at last, collecting himself, he decided to break the silence. The conference lasted two hours and taught me more than any others of the character and customs of the Indians. The chief had come to complain of having been deposed and of not having received the sum total of his presents sent for him and his band by the Great Father at Washington; and during two hours, as explicit and pressing as I might be in my direct questions, I was not able to obtain a single answer of "Yes" or "No," to no matter what. He confined himself with circumspect prudence and cunning care to generalities, refusing to say anything definite. He supposed, he thought, he believed, but never did he affirm a fact, even an undeniable one. For instance: was the merchandise, yes or no, at the departure of the steamboat, placed on the river bank? The answer: a long story of the steamboat going up river to Fort Buford with the agent on board. What were the missing articles? The answer: the boxes had been broken open and some articles of clothing similar to those of the Indians have been worn by some of the whites at the fort.

It was impossible to find out from him whether or not he has consented to his replacement as chief by his son, who was the second in line. It was impossible to make him say why he refused to sign the receipt for the merchandise delivered. "The Red Man raises his hand toward the heavens and calls upon the Great Spirit as his witness." At last this question: what is it that the chief asks to have done for him? Phrases about the joy with which his heart is filled at seeing me, for I am good and just to my red children. A definite question: does the chief wish that I report his words to Washington? This time I thought I had him. I told Beauchamp to ask him, yes or no. Neither yes nor no; I might do it if I wished; if not, he would be perfectly content!

Then I explained to him that a report would be useless because he had not cared to state any actual facts such as how the whites act among themselves when sending and receiving merchandise. I even stated to him that our Great Father and we chiefs of the soldiers think that the Indians do not receive all which is given to them and that often someone steals a part of it; but that if our Great Father could not do justice, it was the direct fault of the Indians themselves, who did not try to keep track of what was sent them and so were unable to prove that something was missing, even though they knew that it was. The chief listened to me religiously, but evidently was more impressed by the friendly spirit which my words breathed than by the practical sense which they might make. He retired with a cordial hand-shake, declaring to me that his heart was satisfied and that he was leaving content.

When the Rees had gone, the three Sioux remained seated as if nothing had happened. This time my patience was at an end. I opened the door and, calling them from inside, I made them understand by signs and a few words of Sioux that the night before some of their people had gone to steal grain from the post located on the other side of the river and that I have given orders to shoot to kill at any thieves. Upon which Howkah answered me very intelligently that I had done well and that it was so much the worse for the thieves. Black Eyes assured me that it was some Uncpapas, which was not true. Upon which I turned my back on him, returning to lunch. And there were my three mendicants marching along behind me in the hope of still getting hold of something. I then turned and, indicating the direction in which I was going, I said to Black Eyes, combining gesture with words, "I am going that way," then, putting my thumb on his chest and pointing with my other arm in the direction of his camp, "You go that way." He was unable to equivocate any longer and at last my three bores took the path to their lodges with empty hands.

I must mention here in passing that today I took up the study of the Sioux language. Evenings Martin will come now and again to spend an hour in my cabin and will give me a lesson in the following fashion; I shall ask him the names of objects commonly in use among the Indians, and I shall write the word as he pronounces it, in French spelling. Thus with the adjectives, adverbs, and verbs. The Indian language having no grammar, it is a matter of memory. When I have words enough in my head the construction will come very easily, for it is most elementary. The verbs have no tense. Thus: "I have come today" is "me come today"; "whence do you come?" is "from where you come?" Thus: "you would go if I wished," "you go if me wish." Whence I conclude that I may be able to speak Sioux fluently by next summer if I apply myself to it with some regularity during the winter.[23]

Saturday, December 7: This morning on leaving my cabin to go to breakfast my first care was to cast a glance over the plain toward Douglas Creek to assure myself that the Yanktonais had gone. The plain was empty. There appeared there only a few horses belonging, without doubt, to the nine lodges of Uncpapas camped on this side at the edge of the woods. I was still rejoicing after breakfast when, to my great stupefaction, on looking through the window at the back of my cabin, I saw once more my intolerable beggar, Black Eyes, with his inseparable Howkah and four or five of his warriors heading for my door.

---

[23] The author is somewhat in error in his disquisition on the Dakota language. Naturally it was difficult to distinguish grammatical construction in view of the method by which his study was carried on. Nevertheless, the language contains nouns, pronouns, adverbs, adjectives and verbs; it recognizes singular and plural, tense and, to some extent, moods. It is, however, a simple and easy language to learn in comparison with the Mandan and the Arikara, which are much more grammatically complete. Much of the variation of meaning in the Indian languages is achieved through the use of modifying syllables prefixed, affixed, or incorporated in the words. G. F. W.

"What do you want now?" I asked him in a tone calculated to show him that I was tired of his visits.

"To speak to you and give you some news."

I sent for the interpreter and resigned myself to hear the news, which consisted merely of information that the band had left; that part had gone to rejoin the Rees and the other part were going north to hunt between Little Knife River and Devils Lake. Very good, but—six lodges remained here and in these six lodges the present company and their families. Thereafter interminable words about their friendship for the whites, and their past history which I already knew by heart; the whole thing, let it be known, in order to arrive at a request for provisions. I refused flatly; but I took the trouble to explain to them that I still had to feed my soldiers for six moons before a steamboat would bring more provisions; that I must manage the little surplus that I might have in order to be able to assist my Indian children during the rest of the winter and into the spring, if game should fail them; also if they were hungry the Yanktonais belonged to Fort Rice whence they drew clothing and provisions, and that I had already done enough for them in giving them a feast and in adding thereto on two occasions some provisions for a certain number of them; that I must think first of the Three Tribes, our always faithful friends, who, although living the greater part of the time in our neighborhood, were not always coming to bother me with their demands like Black Eyes and his people; that I was tired of it; and that instead of trying to live at the expense of the whites during the winter without doing anything it would be very much better to show a little pride and activity, and to hunt with their young men to get themselves some meat; that besides, I was disgusted with the conduct of their young men who, after having been well received and well treated by us, responded by stealing from us or having their women steal.

The pipe passed from mouth to mouth, and soon Black Eyes, then Howkah, took up the word to repeat what they had already said ten times. At last, seeing that my determination was unshakable, they solicited humbly that their women be allowed to pick up the grains of corn scattered on the ground and lost when filling or emptying the sacks to feed the cattle; promising that they would always be directly watched by one of them who would see that they would do nothing wrong. To get rid of them after two hours of conversation, I granted the permission on condition that the women should be at all times under the surveillance of the first soldier of the band whom the chief pointed out to me. And can you guess the consequence? They came this afternoon to pick up the spilled grain, and at sunset the wagon master reports 12 sacks of grain cut open with knives, and it goes without saying, well lightened of their contents. Such are the Indians, and above all the Sioux. Black Eyes, his band and his women, may be taken as typical. I need not add that the concession granted this morning was withdrawn this evening. The camp was entirely forbidden to them, and they are welcome to go hang themselves.[24]

[24] That the Sioux are much more given to thieving than the Three Tribes is without doubt true. However, stealing in all the tribes was governed much by circumstances and conditions and by the attitude of the Indians toward those with whom they were thrown in contact. In many weeks spent among the Indians of the Three Tribes, often leaving all my possessions in an open tent, I have never had a single article taken. It is very doubtful if a similar experience could have occurred even once in a civilized white community. On the other hand, had I been a stranger, on the reservation without permission, and overbearing towards the Indians, it is conceivable that my property might not have been so safe. G. F. W.

Sunday, December 8: Today I received my promotion to Brevet Brigadier General in the regular army to date from March 2 last (1867), a time when I was still at Brest. Had I known of it I would have spared myself the expense of a complete colonel's outfit; however, one can understand that I am not regretful.

* * *

Wednesday, December 11: Two prisoners have just escaped and deserted between 6 and 8 o'clock in the evening. One of them wore a ball and chain on his foot, of which he has probably been able to rid himself with a file. To get away they entered one of the stables and took out two mules upon which they fled, in spite of the cold, in spite of the snow which has fallen all afternoon, and in spite of the deserts which they will have to traverse. The full moon will favor them on their way but where will they find the way? They must have necessarily got together some provisions, but without feed their mounts will be able to carry them neither quickly nor far. Tomorrow morning we shall be able to go look for their tracks. If they have gone toward Berthold there is a good chance that they will be retaken. If they have gone toward Devils Lake—before reaching the British possessions, they have the triple chance of dying of hunger or cold, of being killed by the Indians, or of being re-taken at Fort Totten. A hard prospect! But nevertheless, they are gone.

* * *

Saturday, December 14: . . . Black Eyes has once again reappeared. This morning he asked for an audience for himself alone, and presented himself in full feather with his crown of eagle plumes, his shirt embroidered with quills of red and yellow, little rings of horsehair scattered all over his breast and shoulders, and, to complete the costume, his eyes hidden by a pair of spectacles, dec-orated with cloth, and the forehead covered with little strips of rabbit skin ending in bits of black fur to simulate the ermine's tail. In this solemn regalia, he had come to make his farewell, that is, to look for some more provisions. But first it was necessary to get me into a favorable frame of mind. Hence he commenced his speech by assuring me that I was a great chief whose name was al-ready well known among the Indians of the Plains. I cut short this exordium by asking him directly for what he had come and what he wanted this time. Alas! He and his family had nothing to eat. His son-in-law had accidentally broken his gun. He was the only one who could hunt of those who were

still with the chief, the others had only bows
and arrows and there were no buffalo. Would
I let them die of hunger? A strong and per-
emptory refusal on my part to give them
anything more. Why did he not return to
Fort Rice, which was his residence, and
where he has some reserve provisions? He
asked nothing better than to go, but how
could he travel without something to eat?
The prospect of getting rid of him once and
for all modified some little my first resolve.
I am sure that the sly redskin had counted
on that. I asked him if I gave him some provisions for the journey how soon he could
leave. "I am ready now," he answered.
"I would have gone today, but I can get on
the road tomorrow morning." It was then
expressly agreed that I should give him
something to eat for himself and his family
on condition that they would return at once
to Fort Rice and I should have no more of
them. So it was settled. They soon returned
to their own camp, after getting some salt
pork and condemned rice, and this time I
hope to be rid of Black Eyes and his band at
least until next year.

The mail has just arrived. Our communications are from now on regular and assured
with both Totten and Rice.

Monday, December 16: The weather is

frightful, the exact word to the letter. All day yesterday snow fell without cessation. The sky has never lightened and it continued to snow last night. But the worst thing is the wind, which has risen to a tempest and scatters the fine, icy snow in whirls and clouds. Drifts of snow have formed before our cabins, and this morning we were blockaded so well that it was necessary to use picks and shovels to open a passage for us.

For scarcely half an hour the sun appeared toward 9 o'clock, but soon the gale began again to blow from the northwest; the air is again filled with clouds of snow, the sun has disappeared behind their opaque veil, and since then we know not whether it has snowed, that is, whether the hard little flakes like diamond dust come from the sky or the plain. We have had to give up digging paths in the camp, for hardly are they opened when they disappear under snowdrifts piled up by the wind. Here the snow is three feet deep; there scarcely three inches. These heaps which the storm piles up, it levels again according to its caprice, carrying it elsewhere as the Missouri does with its sand-bars; but it takes only a few minutes to accomplish the work for which the river requires days and weeks. And all the time one can hardly see one's hand before one's face. At intervals the view opens up, and again closes, and at times the eye can see only the nearest objects within a radius of twenty paces. Everyone has read the description of the simoons in the great deserts of Africa. For the Sahara substitute the prairie; for sand, snow; for the caravan, the garrison of the camp, and you have the same effect under other conditions. The detachment sent to cut wood was scarcely able to get back with a small portion of the daily provision. There have come back instead three men with ears and noses frozen. Happily we have some coal to help out until tomorrow. But it must be remembered that, since the mine was discovered after the starting of the fort, our stoves are not made for coal and we can use it only by burning it with equal quantities of wood. What if the wood gives out! Let us hope at least that after two days and three nights of snow and storm the weather will be better tomorrow and will permit us to preserve our fires under our canvas roofs against the polar temperature. Useless to mention with what ardor we want to take possession as quickly as possible of our log houses.

Tuesday, December 17: And indeed the wind has fallen! The weather is calm and the sun shines, but without warmth. The thermometer yesterday was −3 degrees; this morning at seven, − 10 degrees, at ten o-clock, − 5 degrees.

* * *

Today the pale, cold Dakota sun has given us a very curious spectacle. As if, in his weakness, he forced himself to give us quantity instead of quality, he has presented to us three suns at once, himself and his double image at equal distances apart, one to the east, the other to the west of himself. It is the phenomenon which the astronomers designate by the name of parhelion. It seems that it is produced only in high latitudes to the north. It is an effect of refraction, the explanation of which at the moment I cannot find. For the rest, the actual observation is enough. It goes without saying that the two false suns were much less bright than the true sun. Nevertheless each one formed a glow of white light shining with a very pretty effect. The sky, or the atmosphere, to speak more exactly, was slightly hazy, without cloud, but not without light fog or haze. Everything being covered with snow, the brightness of the true sun was overpowering but by shielding the eyes from him with the hand or any other opaque object, his counterparts shone with their full brightness and one could easily look directly at them with the naked eye. The phenomenon occurred between noon and one o'clock, and for us the day has a right to the truthful designation, day of the three suns.

Wednesday, December 18: And the thermometer descends again! Yesterday evening at nine it was −22 degrees Fahrenheit, and this morning at seven −26 degrees, that is, 58 degrees below the freezing point. . . .

Thursday, December 19: We have come back to the torment of the snow. The day has been terrible. A repetition of Monday.

* * *

Tuesday, December 24: The mail arrived today from Buford; probably the last we shall receive during the winter from that post. It was brought by three men with four horses. The small detachment was led by a Red River half-breed named Gardepie. The name proves that his father was a Canadian. The mother is of the Cree Indian tribe which lives in the British possessions. Gardepie came here himself from Berthold to bring the packet of letters for Fort Stevenson and in order to inform me of the incidents of his trip. Like Brown, one of the couriers who preceded him, he was captured by hostile

Indians a day's march this side of the Yellowstone. The band which captured him counted no more than 20 or 25 lodges set up on the banks of the river. The chief is called, as he understood, Marhpiaskat, which signifies White Cloud. Most of the savages were more or less drunk, which proves that there was among them a half-breed trader with a certain quantity of Indian whiskey (alcohol cut with water) and some ammunition. They again declared to Gardepie that they had decided to stop all mail from Fort Buford and to kill all the American couriers. "Do not complain," the chief said to him, "and consider yourself lucky to escape with your life. We let you go because we all know you, but do not come back or we shall treat you like another American. For what difference is there between you and the Long Knives if you carry their writings and if you are paid by them to serve them? Do you know what you are doing? You are not working for our life but for our death, for the destruction of the redskins, of our warriors, of our women and our children. Everywhere the whites become established the buffalo go, and when the buffalo are gone the red hunters of the prairie must die of hunger. Only a few years ago the buffalo grazed on the banks of the Missouri in unnumbered herds; the prairie was often black with them, and life was easy for the Indian and his family for they always had meat to eat, and robes to trade. But the white men advanced as far as the great river and their soldiers built many forts beside the water. They traversed the prairies to the north and to the west and all the game retired before them. This side of the fork of the Missouri (the mouth of the Yellowstone) it is doubtful if there are enough buffalo to feed even part of us and we must depend on deer and antelope, having nothing to eat if they fail us. That is why the whites must go before all the game disappears. As for you, to get some new pants, you help them and you are their friend; so for some new pants you want us to die. See how well covered and warmly clothed you are! I am a chief; nevertheless you see that I have barely enough to keep me from the cold with an old used coat. The white men are the cause of this; if they had not come here we would have plenty to eat and plenty to wear. We can not live on our own lands until they are gone."[25]

Gardepie used all his eloquence but was only able to save this time the packet of

[25] Perhaps the most detailed and vivid narrative of the extinction of the buffalo, here accurately foretold by the red spokesman, is John R. Cook's *The Border*

dispatches and three of his horses. The fourth had to be given to the savages, but they allowed the two men who accompanied him to go with him. The result is that probably all communication with Fort Buford will continue to be intercepted until spring, at least unless hunger obliges the hostiles to leave their present camps to go and seek better fortune on the other side of the Yellowstone.

* * *

Thursday, December 26: At last, at last, I have taken possession of my log house. . . . This morning the dismantling began immediately after breakfast. A wagon came to take first the kitchen equipment and the cook to make it certain that we should dine in our new lodgings; then another wagon took my trunks and furniture. The same with Major Furey, Dr. and Mrs. Gray, and Lieutenant Norvell. We are the only tenants whose apartments have been finished, for we live in the same building. This building consists of seven rooms, all, of course, on the ground floor; it is entirely built of logs of 8 or 10 inches in diameter, placed one upon the other and chinked with mud and long shavings, the whole forming the wall. The roof

and the Buffalo, reprinted in *The Lakeside Classics* series in 1938. M. M. Q.

consists of poles sawed lengthwise into slabs and resting in the center on a large log for a roof-tree, and at the sides on the walls, since there are walls. On top of these half poles a bed of hay; above the hay a bed of ordinary dirt, and on top of the dirt the frozen snow. The roof is nearly flat; seven logs make the height of the facade, which has in consequence a height of about 8 feet, and includes a last and smaller log which runs along the edge of the roof as a sort of support to hold the slabs, the hay, and the dirt. Each room is 15 feet square, having a door, two little windows with six panes each, of real glass, a floor of pine wood, and a monumental stove furnished with a drum which almost doubles the heat. The rooms are separated by walls of logs and mud like the outside walls. They are broken by a door between the kitchen of each apartment and the room which serves at the same time as parlor, dining room, and bedroom, unless one prefers to eat in the kitchen.

When these log houses, humble homes in all the clearings in the wildernesses of North America, are built in the summer so that the mud which is an integral part of them has time to dry before freezing, one may brave at his ease there the most rigorous winters. But it must be remembered that ours were only commenced after the coming of winter and that the construction was continued through polar temperatures, through snow storms and freezes sufficient to break stones. To plaster on the mud it was necessary to keep up great fires to heat the water for mixing with the dirt. The primitive mortar being scarcely in place, the cold seized upon it, penetrated it and transformed it into a hard mass, part earth and part ice. When then the blasts of snow came before the doors and windows were in place the snow drifted inside, whirled about there, penetrated into the cracks in the roof and stuck to all the rough places of the bark. It was swept out as much as possible and, the stoves having been placed this morning, we entered rejoicing.

The interior of my room was like a chapel of the Virgin in the month of May, lacking the altar and the statue. For the snow and ice flourished everywhere in arabesques, in froth of alabaster, in fantastic tracery, all of it a glistening white but not very warming. The stove was lighted, but the door remained open at a temperature below zero Fahrenheit to permit the entrance of trunks and furniture, so that in this first struggle between fire and ice the fire was defeated. It soon had its revenge. The door once closed, the

temperature began to mount with a re-
actionary violence, and the stove with its
drum displayed its power in a most in-
contestable fashion. Upon which the ice
and snow, recognizing themselves decisively
vanquished, began to dissolve in tears. The
thaw worked to put the mud back into its
condition when the cold had seized it; it
made it more tender, softened it, dissolved
it, and this interior revolution went through
the following phases: First, the mud came
away in chunks from the walls and roofs; it
dropped down and soiled with an incessant
dripping everything which was exposed to
this new kind of stippling. Second, a hail of
little pebbles, which, warmed in the pockets
of mud which held them captive, hastened
to profit by their independence in obeying
the laws of gravity. Third, cracks, at first
unnoticed, revealed themselves; fissures
opened and the outside wind pushed in
streams of snow which burst in sheaves and
powdered my floor. It snows in my room.
Fourth, the heat reaches the snow and ice in
roughnesses of the walls, in the cracks of the
roof, and then to the depths of the little
grottoes where they were hidden. They
come out in the form of cascades which run
on all sides. It rains in my new lodgings;
with the rain, the snow, the drafts, the little

avalanches of dirt, they bid me welcome.
Will all this last long?

Thompson, my orderly, a Yankeeized
Englishman, has passed his afternoon in
stuffing up the openings, ditches, fissures
and cracks as fast as they were discovered
or produced, going out, coming in, working
outside, plastering inside, climbing on the
roof, and he has hardly been able to keep
up with the work. George, my negro
domestic, is astounded. He leaves the
broom only to take a mop rag, and never
stops mopping except to sweep, finding
scarcely any time to put my things in order;
to make my bed, to shake out my bed-
clothes. I asked him if he had ever heard of
the rock of Sisyphus. "Never." I could not
therefore make him understand the resemblance between his unceasing and always
recommencing labors and those of Sisyphus
or of the daughters of Danae of whose
history he was just as completely ignorant.
At last the evening has come. The holes
are mudded up; the snow no longer enters
my home and the brooks are changed to
more and more languishing drippings. The
source of them, it seems, has been nearly
exhausted. But the little avalanches persist
here and there at intervals; the silence of
my hearth is brusquely interrupted by the

dry sound of little pebbles falling in a cascade and bouncing on my floor. My table, my commode, my chairs, my bed, are spotted with little muddy blobs which make me regard my roof with a mistrustful eye. One must, however, go to bed. Let us retire then, and above all let us cover the head with a buffalo robe whose thick fur will serve both as a covering and a shield. After all one must not forget that the temperature of the room is easily kept at the most comfortable point, and that in the lodging of boards and canvas which I quitted this morning it was only by means of unlimited fuel that one obtained a much less satisfactory result. When the fire was out there the cold reigned without opposition and in the most tyrannical fashion. At night one could feel one's nose freeze at the edge of the cover, and were it necessary to get out of bed before the stove had been going for a quarter of an hour one would shiver as though in the open air. There also were cracks produced by the contraction of the porous cottonwood boards. To defend oneself from the chilly winds and needles of snow it was necessary to caulk the seams with tarred cloth, like an old ship which leaks water at every seam. Thus, everything considered, in spite of the first trying day, I remain convinced that my new shell, though being of an appearance more primitive and less pleasant than the first, will be nevertheless infinitely more comfortable for enduring the rigors of a long winter, of a winter such as the heavens inflict on the icy plains of Dakota.

* * *

Sunday, December 29: . . . On December 16, Bismorin, called La Bombarde (a Canadian half-breed) left here with two Yanktonais Indians engaged to transport our letters to Fort Rice. They should have met on the seventeenth, half way, another party from Fort Rice, at the station recently built for this purpose, where they should have exchanged dispatches and both parties should have been back by the evening of the third day, or the fourth at the latest. The fourth day and the rest have passed without bringing us any news of them and it was not until the twenty-seventh that La Bombarde reappeared, alone and without letters. The history of his journey is a complete Odyssey. Although the snow had fallen frequently and abundantly during the month they had not expected to find it so deep on the Plains. Having no dog teams with them, they met from the start with very great difficulties. Not only was the snow deep everywhere and reaching a depth of four or five feet in crossing the ravines, but the excessive cold had frozen the surface in an icy crust, which, breaking under the feet of the horses, wounded their legs, cut their skin, and very sensibly weakened them. Nevertheless they arrived at the rendezvous. The other party had arrived there first, had waited in the cabin constructed for that purpose, and seeing nothing of our party coming, had taken the back trail without pushing on farther, in spite of strict orders which they had received. The fire which they had built was not yet out when our men arrived and discovered that they would have to go on to Fort Rice. During the night two of the horses took fright, probably at the appearance of some wolves. One broke his halter, the other succeeded in slipping his over his ears, and both disappeared in the brush, the station being on the bank of the river. In the morning they had to hunt for them in the snow. One of the two Indians froze his feet and the other, being the only one that still had a horse, took up the route with the letters to Fort Rice.

"I shall wait for you four days," La Bombarde told him. "Then I shall have recovered my horse, and, leaving your companion with some of your people, we shall return together without losing any more time." The Indian gone, the half-breed succeeded, after unheard-of hardships, in finding the two horses in the hands of Black Eyes, who had found them on his way back with the band to Fort Rice. He made no difficulty over returning them at once, and hastened with his people to the station to find their man with the frozen legs. They took him with them and it is probable that they succeeded by their empiric treatment in returning to him the use of both legs.

La Bombarde, left alone, waited in vain for his other companion the duration of the time set. His matches were either lost or wet; he no longer had any fire. His provisions were exhausted owing to all these delays; he no longer had anything to eat. In scouting around he learned from some Indians who were hunting in the thickets that the one whom he awaited had got to Fort Rice and started back and that they had met him on the way. The half-breed got from them a little food to give him enough strength to get back to Stevenson as quickly as possible. He started back, leading the horse of the injured Indian and his own (both were government property). In spite of cold and hunger which urged him on, he was unable to get back in less than three days —three days more of misery, of fatigue, and of suffering. As for the Indian, he failed to meet him and up to now we have no news of him.

Such is the story of our last postal expedition to Fort Rice, which will not prevent another one starting tomorrow, Monday; this one will consist of a soldier, of a teamster employed by the quartermaster (Martin, my professor of Sioux), and of the invincible La Bombarde. This La Bombarde is astonishing. He takes these diabolic trials with a stoic sangfroid and I should say with almost a philosophy which nothing can discourage. It must be that he has seen many similar ones to have reached the point of considering his last trip as the usual thing, and to start it all over again after three days.

Monday, December 30: All of our communications are more or less disarranged. The men with the mail from Buford to Totten who left day before yesterday for Devils Lake, have come back, discouraged by the obstacles, although they had a sledge drawn by four dogs. They are going to get a reënforcement to their outfit at Fort Berthold, where they are stationed since two of their stations by the way of Mouse River have been abandoned. Then they will start out again tomorrow or the day after to try their luck again. We ourselves sent out a courier in the same direction on December 20. Between Stevenson and Totten, it will be recalled, there are five stations or shacks where our men may at least find a shelter each night. At the half-way station (the third) they should have met the courier from Totten the evening of the third day, that is to say, the 22d., and should have got back here the evening of the 25th. Today, the 30th., at ten o'clock in the evening, they have not yet reappeared. They are therefore already five full days late. If they do not arrive tomorrow our new courier will leave the day after without our having received the letters and papers which the one who left on the 20th. should have brought. Such are the little graces of a Dakota winter.

* * *

JOURNAL FOR 1868

Thursday, January 2: . . . No news from Fort Rice and no news from Fort Totten. Another mail was sent out for Rice on December 30 (last Monday) and another for Totten yesterday (January 1). Let us hope that these will have better fortune than the two preceding ones.

Friday, January 3: At last we have a courier from Fort Rice; the three men sent

out December 30 met punctually those from
Fort Rice the same day. Our two Indians
went with them—the one who had his feet
frozen was almost completely well.[26]

Very few letters come to us by this route.
I did, however, receive two from France but
of a date earlier than the last I received three
weeks ago by way of Fort Totten. It is particularly the journals which come to us by
way of Fort Rice. By those which we received today we see that all the regiments of
infantry and artillery are going to be gradually reduced to a minimum of fifty men per
company according as events shall work to
clear out their ranks. The consequence will
be, if peace is not concluded next spring with
the hostile Indians of Dakota, that the
Government will have to increase the num-

---

[26] The distance from Fort Rice to Fort Stevenson was
between 90 and 100 miles in a direction between south
and southeast, there being two considerable bends to
the east by the river in that distance. The mail road
in milder weather angled across these bends to save
considerable distance, but in winter the carriers followed the bottom lands of the river most of the way.
The trail passed through the present site of Washburn,
N. Dak., followed down along the Painted Woods,
crossed the present site of Bismarck, and thence proceeded to the southeast to a point on the east bank
opposite Fort Rice. The half-way station was probably
in the vicinity of the Painted Woods, still a well-known
locality in the region. G. F. W.

ber of regiments on the Upper Missouri. It
is fortunate for us that this regulation will
not be in operation here until the forts in my
command are finished. Reading the papers,
I consider myself fortunate to be far from
the spheres where politics are busy; what
goes on down there is disheartening, and in
the South, among the states formerly in
rebellion, the military commanders might
say to each other like the Inca chief to his
minister, both on the grill, "And I, am I
then on a bed of roses?"

Sunday, January 5: . . . The day has been
the most horrible imaginable. The wind has
not stopped blowing with violence from the
north, and drifting the thick clouds of snow
and ice. Does it come also from the sky or
rather has the blast gathered it up from the
Plains to fill the air with these whirls, aerial
clouds which rush about as though lost, like
clouds on the ocean under the furious whip
of the tempests? We do not know. What
we do know is that one can scarcely discern
objects at the shortest distances, not, at
least, when facing the wind, for the snow
then scarcely permits one to open one's eyes
at all and lashes the face as if an invisible
hand had whipped it with sharp thongs.
Imagine if you can what such weather is
with a temperature of 14 degrees below zero

Fahrenheit. Indeed, no one has stuck his nose outside. Each has remained prisoner in his cabin. We must get used to this. It is henceforth our destiny for most of the winter days.

* * *

This evening the storm seems to augment rather than decrease. The wind sings a melancholy song, roaring in the chimney of the stove and on the roof of the cabin, which it actually vibrates. Our couriers will have undoubtedly spent the day at one of the stations. It is a still further delay in the arrival of the letters that we await so impatiently from Fort Totten.

* * *

Monday, January 6: If yesterday was, as I have written above, "the most horrible that one could imagine," today surpassed anything imaginable, for incontestably the weather has found means to become worse. I should have believed it impossible had I not had visible proof. Yesterday evening after I had gone to bed the wind howled in the chimney of my stove of which it made for itself an organ pipe. This morning when I woke it was like a furious concert of whistles and shrieks keyed to the loudest possible tone. The tempest did not cease during the night, I thought. Soon my servant opened the door as reveille had just sounded. Only he jumped in rather than entered, and closed the door behind him with evident haste. I opened my eyes to find the cause of this abrupt invasion, and to my great surprise, I beheld a man entirely white from head to foot, a veritable statue of snow, since the frost gave to his outer garments a sculptured stiffness. "Where the devil did you come from?" I asked him. "From my room." Let it be known that George's room is separated from mine only by the dining room forming the angle of the building and the kitchen around the turn, a distance of 25 or 30 feet at the most. "And I thought I should never find the door; the building is half buried under the snow, and it is impossible to see before oneself." "The continuation of yesterday," I thought to myself, and dozed off again while George, who has the great merit of not speaking unless spoken to, lit the fire and brushed my clothes without further explanation. When he left I rose without haste and loafed into my clothes waiting for the hour of breakfast. The hour of breakfast passed, then another hour, without George coming to announce that it was served. Surprised at this unusual delay, I resolved to go and find out the reason, and I opened the door. At the same instant the air from outside rolled in in the form of a thick vapor; a whirlwind of snow struck me full in the face and powdered me with white from head to foot. Somewhat overwhelmed, I hesitated on the door-sill and looked out; nothing was visible but an opaque white veil which the wind bore in a solid piece without a tear in it, and beyond which hid the buildings, although they are only a few steps from my door.

I looked down and the imprint of the door panels seemed to be engraved on the side of a snow-drift three feet high, resting at one side against the door casing, and dropping on the other side to about two feet, where George had dug a path and where the draft of air continued to scoop out a sort of valley. I wanted to see more, and closing the door, not without difficulty, I reached in two or three jumps the entrance to the dining room. It was open; I leaped inside. The snow had smothered everything; the floor, table, chairs and other furniture, even to the walls, which it had decorated with white festoons. To produce this result in one night, a crack the width of a thumb, left carelessly at the top of the door which did not fit very tightly there, had been sufficient. Through it the snow, driven by the storm, had rushed in in a sheet to break up

and fall everywhere in an icy powder. My
orderly and my servant, as well as Major
Furey's, strove diligently all three with
shovel and broom, but with scarcely any effect. To throw the snow outside, the door
must be opened; when it was opened as much
snow came in as was thrown out. The three
looked like three snow-men and finished by
giving up the undertaking, confining themselves to clearing the door-sill so that the
door might be closed again.

But how were we to breakfast? I looked
into the kitchen through the open shutter
in the wall, for convenience in serving. The
kitchen looked like a decorated opera house
in miniature. The needles of snow which
hung from the ceiling gave it the appearance
of a grotto hung with stalactites, which the
whims of the snow, in clusters, in streamers
and in waves, had given a truly fantastic
character. In the midst of these strange surroundings the imprisoned cook watched
over the cooking of a beefsteak which was
soon brought half-frozen to me in my room.
The cook we could not liberate from his surroundings all day. He is blockaded in his
kitchen by a compact drift of snow under
which the door, because of its location, is
completely buried. But he has utilized his
imprisonment by busily stopping up all the

cracks, holes and vents which he had hereto-
fore neglected. For some purposes misfortune is useful. I am imagining the surprise
of the culinary artist when this morning, on
emerging from under his blankets where he
had slept soundly, he had found his lodging
so metamorphosed. He must have thought
that he was still dreaming.

The whole day has passed without the
least change in the storm. Always the thermometer has been at 22 or 23 degrees below zero; always the snow whipped by the
storm through the dim air; always the wind
whistling and howling from the north, and
always the mournful song in my chimney.
The wood and coal service has ceased. Fortunate those who, like myself, have a sufficient supply of them for two full days. But
how shall we keep warm tomorrow if the
storm does not abate tonight?

It goes without saying that all day I have
seen no one but my servant. To open the door
was a serious business, for if the wall of snow
fell inside it must of necessity all be cleared
or the door would not close again. And meanwhile the air would rush in, in clouds of
vapor, and the snow would roll in, in billows.

It was, however, necessary to open the
door for dinner; a second beefsteak, a second
cup of coffee; but there was a dessert, too, a

THE BLIZZARD AT FORT STEVENSON

slice of peach pie. After which I was re-barricaded and set to reading, to writing and as a relaxation to study in all its phases the problem of the knight in chess. The hours passed with the same speed as if it had been the finest weather in the world; nothing will hasten, nothing retard them, although it pleases us sometimes to reproach them for their too rapid or too slow flight, as measured by our pleasures or our pains, by our fears or our desires.

This evening again I go to sleep with the song of the wind which pursues its tune without failing. One of my windows is completely under the snow. I hope that at least the other one will permit me to see the light of day if not the sun when I awake. Forty-eight hours of such a storm is more than enough to fully appreciate the savage rigors of a winter sky in Dakota.

Tuesday, January 7: On awaking this morning from a dream, very clear, very perfect, in which I was conversing with some souls no longer of this world, I saw the reflection of the first light of day on the red calico curtain of my window. At least that one was not yet under the snow. I pricked up my ears. The song of the wind was no longer more than an almost imperceptible murmur, and I concluded from that that good weather had at last returned. However, a profound silence continued to reign outside, which caused me to wonder. The hour passed, George did not appear. The best thing seemed to be to rise without waiting for him. I lighted the fire in my stove with some twigs fixed for that purpose; I made a leisurely toilet and waited until 9 o'clock without seeing or hearing anyone come. George must be blocked in his room and unable to get out until someone should come to his aid. Whereupon I decided to open my door, risking the difficulties which I might encounter in closing it again. I found myself faced with a wall of snow 4 feet high, beyond which I could see only the same white veil. The upper part of the entrance, acting like a transom, gave passage to the same cloud of vapor and the same billows of snow struck me in the face. It was a continuation without change of the day before, except that for some cause or other the wind had ceased its concert in my chimney. This glance outside was enough to dislodge a small mass of snow. My door refused to close. I had to resort to my large-bladed hunting knife hurriedly, to scrape clear the casing and sill, clean the grooves, and when the latch went into its seat again, a fine carpet of snow extended

in diminuendo from the door to the center
of the room.

* * *

Wednesday, January 8: When I woke up
light entered my room only through a little
more than a pane and a half of glass. All the
rest was under the snow. In following the
line of the drift I thought I could see that it
must have entirely covered my door, but I
was mistaken. Dupont advised me soon
from outside that it was no more than four
feet deep in the trench. When he had given
me light by clearing my window, and liberty
by clearing my door, I discovered with
pleasure that the sun was shining and the
storm seemed over. However, the air was
still charged with that terrible diamond dust,
the form which the snow takes when buf-
feted about at very low temperatures. The
thermometer had risen a little. It was still at
18 degrees below zero. During the night it
had dropped to −24 degrees.

* * *

Returned to my quarters, I have had from
Lieutenant Colonel Powell some details of
their misadventures. Mr. Marshall and his
young wife have not opened their door since
Sunday. Their only communication with
the outside is by the door of their kitchen.
Even that had to be opened by shoveling

through a mass of snow which blocked it completely. Last night their last window was buried like the others, and they have had to use lights until such time as a trench might be opened to let daylight in to them. The worst of it was that the snow had gotten in in quantities between the roof and the canvas ceiling and even in the chimney and the drum of the stove, all of which had to be cleared out before they could light a fire. Then the heat produced on all sides cataracts from which they had to flee for refuge to their kitchen.

That is one disagreeable thing from which all except myself have suffered. This fortunate exception in my favor is due to the circumstance that I alone have properly looked after my lodging, that I had all the cracks and holes mudded up and dry before I had the walls covered with canvas. From having neglected these precautions all the other officers have suffered double all the inconveniences of which I blindly complained when I took possession of my new quarters. Pure ingratitude, of which I plead guilty.

To Lieutenant Walborn came a still worse experience. In the room where he lives with his wife and two young children the door, which someone had undoubtedly tried by force to close without clearing away the snow in its way broke loose and fell back into the room. An avalanche engulfed the conjugal domicile, the snow spread everywhere; the family took refuge in the kitchen and when at last the mess was cleared up and the exterior opening closed again, then began the streaming of snowy walls thawing. The tribulations of Lieutenant Marshall are not very great and little different from those of Lieutenant Parsons, who also has his young wife with him, and a piano besides.

Those whom I admire in all this, as much indeed as I pity, are these young women who brave all these mishaps—I might say for them all this suffering—with courage and a heroic gaiety. If they complain, it is with a gently resigned air which clearly indicates that they had foreseen it all and do not regret being so exposed. But most of the time they have the high spirit to be the first to laugh at their misadventures and to prefer the comic to the tragic side of it all. The American women have indeed true breeding; courage in danger, constancy in sacrifices, resignation under privations, abnegation in their devotion, seem to be inherent virtues in their character. No one could adapt oneself more resolutely to circumstances, accommodate oneself better to adventures, nor brave with such humor the harshness of military life upon the frontier.

* * *

Friday, January 17: It is eight days today since the great storm was over. Since then the weather has been clear and cold except for one cloudy day during which the wind was not very threatening. The thermometer has stayed between −20 degrees and −22 degrees until yesterday, when under the influence of a breeze from the south it rose to −14 degrees. Today this higher temperature has become much more noticeable through a bright sun, and at two in the afternoon the mercury mounted to +20 degrees, that is to say only 12 degrees below the freezing point. For us it is comparatively almost a spring day. And in the meanwhile, in spite of these eight days of fine weather, we remain without news of the four couriers sent out, two on December 20, and two January 1. It is therefore to be feared that all have perished, lost in the snow. Their journey going and returning is of six or seven days at the most, and here it is seventeen and twenty-seven days since they left. No mail was sent out for Totten on the tenth of this month; but if the weather continues favorable we shall send another day after tomorrow, or on the twentieth, under con-

duct of La Bombarde, the last half-breed
still with us.

Monday, January 20: La Bombarde came
back yesterday with his two Indians from
his expedition toward Fort Rice. It is plain
that the dangers, the sufferings, and the
privations of their first trip have not discouraged them. They met the couriers from
Fort Rice at the halfway station, exchanged
their dispatches and correspondence, and
have returned here with no other incident
except that one of their horses gave out,
probably from fatigue and the cold. The
mail which they brought consisted only of a
dozen miscellaneous newspapers and a few
letters, all our correspondence having been
directed through Fort Totten. It was another
encouragement for trying to open again our
communications in that direction, and, encouraged by the success of the couriers for
Fort Rice, we have sent out this morning
for Devils Lake five men, four on horses
and one with a sledge. Among them are La
Bombarde and Martin. They left at break
of day and came back three hours after noon,
after having tried in vain to scale the barriers of snow drifted on their route. The
drifts at the foot of the hills and in the
coulees are fifteen or twenty feet deep. Their

surface is crusted but breaks under the weight of the horses, who are at once buried to the belly and unable to proceed. Several times the men had to dig away the snow to get their horses out. They have tried for the ridges without being able to reach them, and the plain without being able to cross the coulees. One obstacle overcome or avoided with great difficulty, another immediately presented itself a little farther along. In brief, after six or eight hours of useless efforts, thinking that the country was about all in the same condition, they felt compelled to retrace their steps.

* * *

Saturday, January 25: We are trying again. Yesterday morning we again sent out La Bombarde and Martin for Fort Totten, alone this time and without accompaniment of soldiers, who are for them rather an embarrassment than an assistance. The soldiers do not know the country as the half-breeds do. They can not endure the same fatigues nor the same privations. The two couriers left on horseback, for the sledge dogs are, God knows where, since the last month. It is doubtful if their mounts will carry them to their destination, but if they are compelled to abandon them, our men will pursue their way on foot even should they, as Martin said to me, take fifteen or twenty days to get there. That is fine, but at that rate when can we expect them back? Not before the commencement of March and then the time will be near for communication by water to be opened. However, it will be a full two months before the arrival of the first steamboat, and if our letters reach us even then we shall have a fine pile of correspondence to peruse.

While waiting, we are continuing to communicate with Fort Rice every fifteen days, and day after tomorrow morning two Indians are carrying our letters in that direction.

* * *

Sunday, January 26: Our two savages have left this morning with our correspondence for Fort Rice. Before leaving, one of them came to me to show me that he was really without any other clothing than a buffalo robe in which he wrapped himself and an old flannel shirt and two leggings stopping just above the knees. I had a pair of trousers given to each one, a jacket, and a military overcoat, and they left, enchanted with their fine appearance and above all with the comfort which they enjoyed. But up to now they have endured the rigors of the winter without other protection than their buffalo robes. And this morning when

215

one of them showed me his bare legs and old shirt the thermometer stood at −20°. And in that condition without having a cold!

* * *

Monday, January 27: Two half-breeds have arrived from Fort Buford, bringing dispatches of no great importance. They have succeeded in completing their journey without interference on the part of the Indians. Since they knew the place where Brown and Gardepie had been stopped before, they avoided it with care and made a detour on the prairie in place of following the river banks. Besides, it is not certain that the people of Lafaille (Snow Bird) are still there. Hunger may have dislodged them and sent them to join the assembled bands on the Yellowstone River, where there are, it seems, buffalo in abundance.

Brevet Major Clarke, who now commands Fort Buford, has made a raid on the Red River half-breeds who traffic in ammunition and whisky with the hostile Indians. He has broken up their establishment and seized their goods, furs, and provisions and keeps all of it for disposition by the Government. The reports and official papers prove that everything is much improved at that post under the authority of the new commander. It could hardly be otherwise.

The wind blows a gale again. The thermometer stays below zero Fahrenheit. Bad weather for our couriers to Rice and Totten.

Tuesday, January 28: At sunset a few black spots seen on the edge of the snowy horizon apprized us that a party of several men were coming in our direction. At once everyone was hoping that they might be couriers from Fort Totten who had succeeded in getting through in spite of the obstacles. Before night, with the aid of telescopes, we had distinguished two men and four horses. The two men were La Bombarde and Martin bringing with them, beside their own mounts, the horses of the two couriers who left January first, under the following circumstances, the report of which was at once made to me by Martin himself.

The two half-breeds left on horseback, as I have previously noted, on the twenty-fourth of this month, last Friday. The first night they had to camp in the open plain. With their shovels they built a sort of snow cabin and passed a tolerable night in it. The horses were already very tired although the distance gone was no more than ten miles. But they had to work their passage through the snow where the animals at times sank in up to their necks. The icy crust had already cut their pasterns deeply and they had left behind them a trail marked with long streaks of blood. Nevertheless, on the twenty-fifth they took up the journey. The obstacles seemed to become worse and more complicated, for the ravines were so filled in some places that there was no sign of them and in others the drifts had taken on such proportions that they resembled hills and threw our two couriers into continual perplexity over the road to follow. It must be remembered that these men of the Plains, to whom the country is familiar, orient themselves by natural objects, landmarks such as hills of a certain form, chains of hills, lakes, or ravines recognizable by certain signs. But under the unusual heaps of snow this winter these means of orientation have failed them. The large hill had completely changed its appearance at a distance, the chain of hills was almost effaced by the drifts piled up on its flanks; the ice-covered lake had disappeared and merged under the snow with the valley; the ravine no longer existed. Thus put off their route, but not yet discouraged, they arrived the second day in the locality where they should find the first station cabin. They searched in vain for it with their eyes. No sign nor indication of it was apparent in the vast and silent expanse. Certain, however, that they were not mistaken, they left their mounts and set out on foot in search of the station. After a laborious and painful hunt they saw at last, at some distance, a horse which seemed to have come out of the ground, but which in reality had emerged from an invisible coulee onto a hill whose shape had merged with the drifts about it.

Under this hill lay buried the station. Our men ran (metaphorically) to the place and, to their great surprise, found themselves face to face with two horses in a most pitiable state, being no more than skin and bone, with their legs literally hacked to pieces— horses which in spite of their appearance they at once recognized as those on which our couriers had been mounted on leaving the fort on January 1. How these poor beasts were able to live for twenty-five days there on the snow without shelter and without feed through the great storm is an enigma which seems difficult to resolve. One must believe that by pawing the snow with their hooves in the more exposed places where it was the thinnest they were able to get to the dried grass which prevented them from dying of hunger. As to the cold, the only remark to make is that they must have tremendously thick coats and great tenacity of life. At any rate there they were, alive and undoubtedly well content with the help which had come to them.

Our two men had at first considerable difficulty in finding the exact location of the cabin; it was indicated to them by a depression in the snow over the opening in the roof left for passage of the smoke. It was absolutely full of snow. They set to, with the shovel, with as much haste as possible, since they feared to find the bodies of their two friends buried in some corner. They enlarged the opening and cleared the interior; but they found only the saddles and bridles of the two abandoned horses. There they passed the night about the fire, and the next day at daybreak their first care was to start a search for some indication of the fate of their predecessors. If they had perished in the snow the wolves would have dug out and devoured their remains or those of the dogs which they had with them. But their exploration, though pushed to a distance of five or six miles around, succeeded in discovering nothing. Whence they concluded, and it is certainly most likely, that in the impossibility of getting their horses any farther, the two couriers had abandoned them there to pursue their journey with the dog train of three dogs, for the fourth had gotten loose and returned to the fort the day after their departure. What then has become of them? We shall know later; but one does not like to recall that on the day following their departure from this station they had to struggle against the fearful blizzard which turned the plains upside down for some six days.

La Bombarde and Martin had no dogs. During their search, more than once their horses had foundered in the snow where they lay, refusing to go farther. Then they had to pursue their search on foot and became more and more convinced of the impossibility of bringing their enterprise to a satisfactory termination. On top of these conclusions the wind commenced to blow a gale, the air filled with whirling snow; all objects at any distance disappeared from view behind a thick veil, and the two half-breeds had no other alternative than to abandon, in turn, their horses to continue on foot, an impractical attempt, or to return to the fort with the four horses, and that without loss of time. They decided wisely on returning and, not without new fatigues and new perils during the storm, they have got back this evening to Fort Stevenson.

From all of which it is more than ever conclusively evident that no mail is likely

to come for us from Fort Totten until in the
month of April. It is terribly vexing, but
what can one do? With inevitable disap-
pointments it is wisest to be resigned and
have patience.

Thursday, January 30: A day to be marked
with a white cross. In spite of our foreseeing
to the contrary, there has at last arrived
today a mail from Fort Totten. Our men
who left on December 20 and January 1
have at last returned. Not one has perished,
that is the big thing. After that the story of
their privations, of their fatigues, their suffering, becomes a secondary matter. It is
too long to recount. I will confine myself to
stating that they reached Fort Totten more
or less frozen, and that naturally it took them
some time to thaw out their feet and hands
and noses and ears before starting out again.
One of the men from Fort Totten, more
dangerously frozen, is still in such a state
that it is doubtful if he will recover. The
six-day storm having held them captive at
one of the stations, their provisions became
exhausted. They had already been compelled to leave their two horses, as has been
related above. There remained to them a
mule which served as food for the dogs; and
two dogs (the youngest and most affectionate,

poor beasts) in their turn served as food for the men. When they met the men from Devils Lake who had started out from there at the same time, they were in no state to return to Stevenson, and in consequence they pursued their journey to Totten, from which they were less distant, and they reached there whole.

* * *

Tuesday, February 4: . . . The old chief of the Rees, White Shield, has come with several warriors to ask for some provisions. I have had him address himself to the commander of the post in order to relieve myself of Indian mendicancy. The reports from Fort Berthold are bad. Those Indians who have returned there are literally dying of hunger, having exhausted their stores of corn. Those who are still in the winter camps or who rove the Plains are in no more favorable condition. The emigration of the buffalo toward the east side of the Yellowstone River leaves them almost without game, and consequently without food, for the deer and the antelope are very difficult to hunt and kill. Against them, bows and arrows are useless and only those armed with guns are able to take them by surprise. The rapidity of these animals in flight forbids all pursuit, while on the other hand the buffalo are easily come up with by a horse of ordinary speed. It is this fact which causes it to be said with truth that the Indian lives on buffalo meat and that wherever the buffalo fails the Indian must disappear.

The compassion which one feels for the periodic hunger, which, almost every winter, destroys a part of the Indians, is considerably lessened when one comes to reflect that it is only due to their incorrigible laziness and to their incurable repugnance for all labor. The roughest conditions seem to teach them no lesson. At Berthold they have consented to grow corn because they themselves do not have to take a hand in the work. The women, those work animals on two feet, do all the work of cultivation, plant, hoe, gather, husk, and store the grain, while their lords and masters, wrapped in their robes, warm themselves in the sun, smoke, and gaze about. In vain has the Government offered them all sorts of seeds, animals, implements, as free gifts. No! They prefer provisions to eat and clothing to wear, and refuse to raise any kind of stock or to cultivate any crop which would impose on them the slightest labor. According to their ideas, to render themselves independent by putting their hands to the hoe or the plough would be a dishonor, a degradation; but to

humbly and importunately beg their subsistence from the whites, and to steal at
need, is nothing to wound their pretended
dignity, so far have they gone in the loss of
all moral sense.

The trader Gerard tells us that four redskins have literally died of starvation at
Berthold. Others will undoubtedly suffer
the same fate before the end of winter. As
remedy, the others can think of nothing except to beg for help at Fort Stevenson.

* * *

But the American Indian race appears to
have run its course and fulfilled its transi-
tory mission in the march of humanity. Its
resistance to all assimilation with the white
race is an active element toward the destruction which it carries within itself and which
forwards the eventuation with great rapidity.

* * *

Saturday, February 8: Last night was the
coldest night of the winter. This morning
at seven the thermometer stood at $-30°$ F.
The mercury has not before gone so low.
Fortunately the air is perfectly calm, which
makes the temperature more endurable.[27]

[27] This reference to thirty degrees below zero Fahrenheit as the coldest of the winter would lead to the belief
that, in spite of the storms, this was not one of the very
cold winters. Since 1872 the coldest recorded tempera-

Wednesday, February 19: . . . The Mandans, back again at Fort Berthold on account of the absence of big game and the consequent famine, came yesterday to visit and to ask for some help in the way of provisions. Today we have had distributed among them some boxes of crackers more or less moldy, some hominy, and some barrels of salt pork more or less damaged. These provisions, condemned by a commission on sustenance, could not in consequence be given to the troops as rations, and thus found their most natural and useful destiny. They were distributed to the Indians, who appreciated them just as much as if they were of good quality, and they ate them very willingly.

These Mandans are certainly peaceable and easy people to deal with. I was present today at the distribution among them of the provisions which had been given to them in bulk. The chiefs and the warriors on one side and the old women on the other completed an inner circle around the provisions. The young women with their children and

ture is fifty degrees below zero, and the temperature usually descends for a day or so during most winters to a low of from thirty-five degrees to forty-five degrees below zero. Periods of forty days have occurred several times when the mercury was below zero every day. Such a period is often followed by one of daily temperature above freezing for a week or two. G. F. W.

the young girls formed an outer circle at a distance of six or eight feet from the inner one. All the men and women were seated on the ground. Three or four warriors chosen for the purpose went to and fro distributing to the circle, to each one his portion of every article. All of this was done with perfect order and in silence. No one thought of complaining or asking for anything more, no one showed the least discontent, nor seemed to compare his share with that of someone else. It must be said that the distributors acquitted themselves of their duties with quickness but perfect justice and absolute impartiality, only the two chiefs being somewhat favored. Each one sat in silence as they waited for what was still to come, and the women did not scold. The horses—poor hacks—bearing the too-evident marks of their winter sufferings, fed at liberty on the spears of grass which pierced the snow, or lay down in the sun with a tranquil resignation. The dogs, harnessed to their travois, rested their pointed muzzles on the shoulders of their mistresses, in the uncertain hope of also obtaining some portion of the feast.

When the distribution was finished each returned to his horse, passed around its jaw the long thong which serves as bridle, placed on its back the double sack of provisions, and all the band descended onto the ice again and took in a long file the road to Fort Berthold going up along the river.

* * *

Sunday, March 1: My but I am tired of this interminable winter! Of this eternal snow which, for more than three months, has not let us even see the ground and blurs our eyes with its unchanging white; of this steady cold which released its hold for some eight days only to return with that much more severity, as severe on the last of February as at the last of December; of these monotonous days which follow one after the other and all alike, without variety, without incident, like great drops of ennui falling one by one into the dead sea of the past; of this isolation from the rest of the world with which we can scarcely keep a few uncertain communications at intervals of 20 to 46 days, which leave us for entire months without news of our kin, without reports of our friends; of these privations of all sorts, natural consequence of our place in these deserts; lack of exercise on the ground which the snow makes impractical on foot, and the cold on horseback; privations at meals where the absence of fresh vegetables, of eggs, of small game, of veal, of mutton, and even of large game reduces us to a regimen which produces scurvy among the soldiers, and destroys all appetite among the officers; lack of active occupation for the mind in this daily forced captivity where we must struggle with the hours, by exhausting in reading everything that can be found in the way of books, good and bad, among us, where study is limited for lack of materials, where the hours of sleep become hours of deliverance just as they are for a prisoner; of this absence of any social distraction which keeps me in my miserable hut of logs fifteen feet square, alone during the day and alone during the evening for when sometimes on Sunday I have made a visit or two on some of the officers I usually have enough of that for two or three weeks.

Indeed I am then tired of all of it! But what to do? Duty has drawn the line, it must be followed to the end. Next winter I shall be in possession of my house, I shall have my crayons and pencils, I shall have means for serious study, books on geology, a microscope, books on astronomy, on mathematics, I shall then be able to turn to profit this tiresome leisure against which, lacking experience, I did not sufficiently fortify myself last summer.

After all there is barely a month left to endure these conditions. April will certainly bring some change and May will consummate our deliverance.

Today I received the first news of the publication of my *Four Years with the Army of the Potomac*. The work must have appeared in Paris during the month of November and have been in New York in December, but our postal communications are such that I had not yet received word of it. The news was communicated to me by Dr. Gray, who found a mention of it in a paper from Missouri brought the other day by the courier from Fort Rice.

* * *

Tuesday, March 3: For several days the rumor has been current here, coming from Fort Berthold, that a courier from Fort Buford had been stopped and severely maltreated by the Indians; that the dispatches of which he was the bearer have been destroyed, his dogs killed, and he himself, despoiled of his arms and nearly all of his clothing, had arrived with frozen feet and in a most pitiable state at the winter camp of the Gros Ventres. As the Indians are constitutionally the greatest liars that I know, I had hoped that this was merely a story such as they are always telling. Unfortunately it is nothing of the sort; and this time the report is confirmed by the following extract from a letter from Gustave Cagnat, brought this morning from Fort Berthold: "Some Gros Ventres have come here and with them Joseph L'Espagnol, who was robbed and beaten by the Sioux while carrying the mail from Fort Buford. All the mail is entirely lost, and the man had great difficulty in even saving his life. He arrived here with his feet still somewhat frozen. Hunger and suffering have rendered him almost out of his head and I am not able to learn just how the accident happened, but as soon as I get the complete details I shall hasten to communicate them to you." From some of the Gros Ventres it is known only that the guilty ones belong to the Santee tribe, hostile Sioux who played a very active role, a few years ago, in the Minnesota Massacre. They have beaten the courier horribly, have hit him on the head with the butt of his gun, have partly torn out his hair and beard, and left him in the snow with no other clothing than a pair of trousers and a cotton shirt. That they did not kill him on the spot was due to the fact that they took him for a half-breed; but they must have believed that the state in which they left him could result only in the prolongation of the agony. The fact is that it is well nigh a miracle for him to have reached alive the camp of the Gros

Ventres, who thawed out his feet and got him in shape to be moved to Fort Berthold, where, it seems, his mind is still affected by the terrible sufferings which he has undergone. In two or three days he will probably be in a condition to complete the story.

* * *

Friday, March 6: The courier taken and maltreated by the Indians was brought to me this morning by Gustave Cagnat. He is a poor devil of a Mexican known under the name of Joe the Spaniard. He has been for seven months in the service of the mail contractor Ruffee, and during these seven months has not received a cent of his wages, and no more than the others, does he expect ever to get a cent. He was located at Fort Buford when, the service being interrupted, Major Clarke proposed to reopen communication with Fort Stevenson at government expense. But the threats of the hostile Indians made to the two couriers who were stopped during the winter, and the fear of being killed by them, prevented the half-breeds from accepting the proposition. The Mexican alone, driven by his wretchedness, concluded with the commander of the post an agreement by virtue of which he engaged to make two trips (going and coming) to Stevenson with the papers which

might be entrusted to him. What is most
surprising is that he undertook to make the
journey alone and on foot with a single dog
dragging the sort of frame which I have described elsewhere and which goes under the
name of travois. Having placed the mail
and the necessary food for himself and the
dog on the netting he started on February
13. All went well as far as Little Knife
River, nearly two-thirds of the way. He
avoided three camps of Indians by leaving
the river and following the ravines of the
prairie in such a way that he could not be
seen. This success unfortunately inspired
him with too much confidence, and knowing
that there was left between him and his goal
only a camp of Gros Ventres he stopped at
the mouth of the Little Knife in a log cabin
which during the previous summer had served
as a station for the carriers of dispatches
and which must have been abandoned at the
commencement of winter. Deciding to rest
there, he lighted a fire and set about break-
fasting with a cup of hot coffee. It was a
grave imprudence, as the result proved. The
smoke rising from the chimney attracted the
attention of a party of hostile Indians who
were wandering about or hunting in the vicinity, and they directed their way toward
the cabin, surrounding it. There were thir-

teen of them, but three in advance of the others appeared at the door of the cabin. Our man was deceived.

After exchanging a few words one of the Indians, addressing the Mexican, and pointing out to him the packet attached to the travois, asked him to whom it belonged. The man answered that it was the property of Mr. Ruffee.

"You lie," said the Indian, "It is the soldiers' mail from the Yellowstone."

And as he spoke he took his knife, cut the bindings, slashed open the sack and exposed the dispatches. It seems that then Joe the Spaniard, believing that he dealt with only three Indians and hoping to get rid of them, put his hand on his revolver. Upon which they leaped upon him, tore the gun from his hand, beat him with repeated blows, and threw him on the ground. He tried then to seize his knife but it, too, was wrested from him and the blade made deep cuts on the inner side of his finger tips. Then one of his adversaries struck him a violent blow with the butt of the gun on the back of his head, which put an end to the struggle. Joe lost consciousness and lay on the ground bathed in the blood which poured from his two wounds. A frightful pain in his face at length brought him back. The savages, to bring him out of his faint, were amusing themselves by pulling out bits of his beard and mustache and his face was torn and bleeding like his right hand and his head. In this condition the amiable redskins (there were thirteen now) forced the poor half-dead devil to cook for them the little coffee and few provisions that he had with him, beating him without mercy when he faltered. They killed his dog before his eyes, chopped up the travois, and threw the letters into the fire, burning them to the last scrap of paper. They had taken his arms, they had eaten his provisions. Now they despoiled him of his clothing, pulled off his moccasins, his woolen socks, his drawers, his flannel shirt, his overcoat, his fur cap and his blanket, leaving literally nothing on his body but an old pair of trousers and an old shirt of antelope hide with the hair taken off.

When the Mexican understood their intention of leaving him in the midst of the snow-covered plain without shoes, without food, without head-covering and almost without clothing, preferring a quick death to the long agony which lay before him, he begged them to finish him at once and to kill him before they went away. Upon which one of them took an arrow, adjusted it to the bow and was going to transfix him with it when another one, stretching out his arm, prevented the completion of the murder and they all went off without even a backward glance toward their victim. Since Joe has the complexion of a Mexican and could easily pass for an Indian with his thick, straight and long black hair, it must be believed that the savages took him for a half-breed, otherwise they would undoubtedly have dispatched him altogether.

When he was alone the instinct of self-preservation became energetically aroused. If he must die it should at least not be without having made a supreme effort to save his life. And although weak, bleeding, wounded, bare-headed, and barefooted, he set out to try to make Fort Berthold. The man must have been vigorously tempered both physically and in morale for, in the state which I have just described, he walked all evening and all night. He still walked the next day and both feet were frozen and bleeding. To complete his misfortune the wind rose and increased the intensity of the cold. Soon there was a blizzard; the snow rose in thick clouds, filling the air and obscuring the horizon. No longer any way to orient himself. Dying of cold, of hunger, of exhaustion, the unfortunate man knew not which way to turn; his reason, clouded, ceased to be of any assistance to him, but so long as the power to move remained in him he wandered, lost in the snow. When at last all strength left him he laid down to die. It was in this state that a party of Gros Ventres found him about to expire, farther up than the old station whence he had started. The poor fellow had walked all day in the opposite direction along the trail which he had made during the night.

The Indians have certain remedies very efficacious for the ills to which they are most exposed. They picked up the dying man, made him take some nourishment, dressed his wounds and his frozen feet, wrapped him in a buffalo robe, and reanimated him sufficiently to be able to set him on a horse. After having kept him for some days with them, since they were going to leave the camp and return to Fort Berthold, they took him there on the third and, as we have seen, he promptly completed his recovery. Gustave Cagnat gave him a vest of knitted wear, a flannel shirt and a pair of furred moccasins, and this morning he has come to make his report to me.

Joe the Spaniard (so named because he is Mexican) is of short build but sturdy and vigorous. His face is the color of burned Sienna earth, his hair black as jet and like a

mane surrounds his face in which his brown
and squinting eyes give him an expression
a little fierce. He promises faithfully that
his tormentors will pay him for his treatment
if he finds them again and he has taken care-
ful note of their peculiarities—one especially with a little beard on his chin and a
scar at the corner of his right eye which
special marks make him apparently rather a
half-breed than an Indian. But Joe is very
reticent in this respect, as if he were jealous
of his vengeance and as if he feared that
someone would take that pleasure from him.
I am convinced that should he happen to
meet the man with the scar he would not
fail to settle the score with him.

The most extraordinary feature is that,
far from being discouraged by the terrible
experience which he has undergone, he
thinks of nothing now except to set out on
the road to Buford, and he has already set
his departure for tomorrow. "If you wish
to furnish me with a horse," he said to me,
"I shall take the mail with me and this time
I shall take care of myself in such a way that
the Indians will not catch me again. Otherwise I will charge myself with a certain number of letters which I shall sew in the lining
of my overcoat and I shall make the trip
on foot." All this as all the rest of his story

given with perfect tranquillity and with a calm voice in a composite language where Spanish is mixed in equal parts with a semblance of English of the worst sort.

"How is it," I said to him, "that you are not disgusted with carrying the letters?"

"No," he answered, "I have engaged to make two trips for which I am to receive $200 and I am determined that I shall have my $200 or I shall leave my bones on the road."

My faith! It shall not be said that I have allowed a gallant of his stripe to leave on foot. I have given the requisite order for mail for Buford to be turned over to him and that a horse be furnished him to carry it. I have made him a present of a blanket; Major Furey has done the same, and tomorrow Joe the Spaniard, warmly clad and fortified with the necessary provisions, will set out for Fort Buford, charged with the dispatches and correspondence. Will he arrive this time in good order? I hope so, and I dare even to state that I have a presentiment of it, the result will prove if—"This oracle is surer than that of Colchas."

Saturday, March 7: The Gros Ventres on their return from winter quarters have come to pay me a visit. Already the Mandans

and Rees have received provisions from us.
It is their turn. I have made them address
themselves to the commander of the post,
who is more particularly charged with these
distributions. But before leaving they have
insisted on having a conference with me and
I have received the four principal personages with Pierre Gareau, their interpreter.
They were: Crow Belly, first chief; Poor
Wolf, second chief; and the leader of the
warriors, with his second in command. All
four were in full dress; shirts of buck or
antelope skin covered with quill work and
with fringes made in part of leather strips,
in part of locks from a horse's tail or from a
human scalp. The chief wore some necklaces with pendants on his breast and ear-
rings of pearl shell, also rings passed through
the upper part of the edge of his ear. All
four had a bunch of feathers on top of their
heads.

I have already described in detail the customary ceremonial, the preparatory silence,
the pipe passing from mouth to mouth, the
hand shake before the harangue. I shall not
go over it again. The discourse had for its
principal purpose to establish the fact that
most of the provisions which had been distributed to them were stolen (which I already very well knew.) But the Indian could

not limit himself to this detail and there was a discussion between us of a quantity of other matters. For example, to get to the matter in hand, like Petit Jean and Intimé in getting to the stealing of the capon, the speaker started from the egg, or rather "before the beginning of the world," thence to the appearance of the first whites on the banks of the Upper Missouri. "The Great Spirit," said he, "has given to the white man great foresightedness; he sees everything at a distance, and his mind invents and makes the most extraordinary things; but the red man has been made short-sighted, he sees only what is close around him and knows nothing except what his fathers knew, aside from the things that the white men have taught him. It is they who have brought the horse to the plains and who have taught us to make the corn grow. They have given us the crockery pots and the pots of iron to cook our food, and they have furnished us with the guns and powder to kill our game." Then came the distinction between the good and the bad savages; those who have always been the friends of the whites, who have never betrayed their word, and who have always made good use of the presents which they have received; and those who have only made treaties to break them, who have soiled their hands by stealing from and killing the whites, and who have used their guns and powder not against the game but against those from whom they have received them. Among the first are the Gros Ventres, and among the latter the Sioux. "What then is the outcome of these two behaviors? The Sioux, liars, thieves, and murderers, have received presents in abundance, and guns which they use to kill us, and they are rich in horses and all other things while we have remained poor from not having received all that our Great Father has sent us, and we have scarcely anything with which to cover us and at times nothing to eat. And this even though when the Great Chief (General Curtis) came to see us some years ago he said to us: 'My children, be faithful to the whites, obey your Great Father, keep the peace and hold to your word, and the smoke of your fires will rise straight to the sky.' We have done as our Great Father has ordered and, in spite of all, the smoke of our fires instead of rising straight toward the heavens is thrown down on the ground and has been chased by all the winds. The Sioux enemies are rich, powerful, numerous—the Gros Ventre friends, formerly as strong as and more brave than the Sioux, are now poor, weak, and few in number."

All this, let it be understood, is an adroit mixture of truth and falsehood, combined to stir the generosity of the Government. It was not very difficult for me to answer. The chief told again how, at the time when a company of soldiers was stationed at Fort Berthold among them, the Sioux frequently came to attack the village. The Gros Ventres bravely fought them, and, although inferior in numbers, had always driven them away; but the white soldiers had never assisted and helped them. They were simply drawn up under arms before the fort and had remained distant and inactive spectators of the fight. After several repetitions the discourse of Crow Belly ended with a recital of the care taken of Joe the Spaniard, whose life his men had saved.

The object of my response was less to extend myself into the past and follow thus Crow Belly, but rather to show him the road into the future and to try to clarify for him and his people their true interests and the needs of their present condition. So, after having recalled to him that, according to his own statement, the whites had annually furnished presents of everything which they needed for a living: household utensils, arms, ammunition, clothing, blankets and food of all kinds—this generously paying for

243

the friendship of the Gros Ventres and the
cession of their land in a strip fifteen miles
long and two or three miles wide where Fort
Stevenson was even then rising; after having
recalled to him again that when they were
short of food we gave them some freely and
several times a year; and further, that the
differences between the Sioux and the Gros
Ventres, far from being in any way the work
of the whites, were the result of horrible
diseases (smallpox and cholera) which had
almost exterminated, by the will of the Great
Spirit, the Three Tribes, formerly powerful
and always brave, even in their reduced condition, I came to what seemed to me to be
much more important: "There was a time,"
I said to them, "(it was a long time ago
for the fathers of your fathers were not
yet born), when all the vast lands which
extend from one sea to the other, to the
north, to the south, to the east, to the west
and the setting sun belonged entirely to
red men. One day some men who had
crossed the great sea toward the rising sun
arrived in the country of the red men, they
were only a few warriors, not more than you
can hold of kernels of corn in one hand, and
the nations along the sea shore thousands
and still more thousands. However, the
white men established themselves on the

lands where their ships touched; they spread all about, always more and more came, either living in friendship with the friendly tribes, or fighting and exterminating the enemy tribes. Now they are the complete masters of lands so vast that by comparison all the hunting grounds of my children are like a handful of dirt, and they have become so numerous that even with their notched stick my children would never be able to count them. And the red nations which have gone to war against them have disappeared and even their names are forgotten. How has this come about and why have the white men so increased and become so powerful while the red men have grown fewer and lost their strength? I am going to tell you truly. The cause is this (listen well); the white man works all the time, the red man never. The white man cultivates the ground and the red man hunts. The white man builds houses and lives without changing about, in big cities or in the midst of fields of which each one owns a part; the red man lives in his tipi which he carries with him over the Plains, where he is ceaselessly wandering."

And having insisted thus simply but still as emphatically as I was able, on the advantages of labor to which the whites owed all their riches, all their inventions, all their power, I endeavored to make them understand the absolute and immediate necessity for the Three Tribes of Berthold to turn to labor. "When the Indians alone occupied all the hunting grounds and the prairie was black with herds of buffalo, when game was abundant at every season, hunting sufficed to feed and clothe the red man; but that time has passed. The buffalo grows fewer and fewer. He goes toward the sunset, and during the winter not one has been seen between the big lake (Rice), and Medicine Water (Totten), between this post and the Yellowstone (Buford); all are on the other side of that river. So my children who were camped on the banks of the Missouri have suffered cruelly. They can collect no skins to sell except a few of the elk; they have scarcely anything to eat, and to procure food many among them have been forced to sell even their horses. And what is it that has enabled them to live during this time? It is the corn which they harvested last summer. How many would have died of hunger if they had had only hunting on which to depend? So what has saved the lives of many of you, especially the old people and the children, is the fact that you have cultivated the ground a little as the whites have taught you. And nearly all the trade that you have made this year is again in the corn which has furnished you the resources for trade.

"In spite of that you are poor and you suffer from hunger because you plant too little, and you plant too little because only your women work while you men who are strong and vigorous disdain to work, and you pass your days smoking in the sun when you are not hunting. It would be quite otherwise if you would change your habits and if you yourselves would cultivate the soil for the harvest of crops of all sorts which you do not even know; if you would, like the whites, raise some beeves and some hogs; if you had poultry and cows.

"I say to you; your Great Father would like to furnish you all necessary seed, animals and tools, if you decide to use them. Listen to the voice of the Great Spirit. It is he who wants his red children to live differently than their fathers have lived. That is why he has destroyed more and more the large game, and has led to the Missouri the white men to show the red men how to be happy, to become rich in horses, in cattle, in grain, to be warmly clothed in winter, never to lack food, and always to have something to sell to the traders or among the Three Tribes. All that you shall have if you obey the wishes of the Great Spirit; otherwise you will live in misery and want and you will die, too—not from any fault of the whites but through your own fault."

Such is, in substance, the little sermon which I preached to them upon the necessity of labor. Incidentally, and apropos of the neutral attitude of the soldiers as spectators of their fights against the Sioux, I told them the fable of the horse that wanted to avenge himself on the deer.

"So," I told them, "nations formerly warlike and powerful have been exterminated for having invited the white warriors to mix in their quarrels."

After which I recounted to them the fate of the Iroquois, the Hurons, the Delawares, and many others, at the time of the wars between France and England on the frontiers of Canada. Then I added: "Our Great Father, who does not want his red children to perish, but wants them to live in peace and to be happy, forbids his soldiers to help the Indian warriors to destroy each other. For if he sent them to fight with one tribe against another, all would ask for aid, and many would be killed while those who survived would be weaker and more dependent than ever. It is, then, only in the interest of his red children that the Great Father does not want his soldiers to mix in their quarrels."

All this was heard by my Gros Ventres with the most serious attention and the appearance of great interest. The conclusion was that they were going to ask their agent for new seed and tilling instruments, and that they would ask Father De Smet, for whom they have a great veneration, to send them a missionary to teach their children the tongue of the Long Knives, to cultivate the ground like them, and to live and work like the white men. Will they keep their word and will they fulfill these good resolutions? That is the question. That will depend, I believe, on circumstances. If the buffalo come back this year and game is abundant—farewell to agriculture. But if the hunt fails, faced with famine and misery, at least a partial conversion is possible, the more so since the first step for the Three Tribes has already been taken by the building of a village and the cultivation of corn.

In any case I have advised them, as well as Pierre Gareau, their interpreter, to repeat my words to the men of their tribe and to the Rees and Mandans as well, which they have promised. This promise will be much easier to keep than the other. So I hope that

it will not altogether be forgotten on their
way back to Berthold.

* * *

Sunday, March 15: . . . The other day one
of the Rees was at Fort Rice in the camp of
some Sioux friends. They had given or sold
to him four horses and he was smoking the
peace pipe in one of the lodges, when all at
once with no quarrel, no provocation, no
warning, and no threat he fell transfixed
by an arrow. He who had done the deed
was a Brulé who was in the camp on a visit.
He leaped on his horse and fled at a gallop.
It was evening. I know not if he was pursued, but he escaped. The most curious
thing is that this cowardly assassination is
regarded by the Indians as an act of bravery.
The guilty one will glory in his deed and will
count the murder among his great exploits.
If any disfavor attaches to the business it
will be not against the assassin but against
the band which did not protect the victim
and whose hospitality has been violated with
impunity.

In announcing the misfortune which had
occurred they have requested of the Rees
that they send some of their young men to
get a dozen horses, which they were offering
as a sort of reparation. The blood shed will
then henceforth be a matter between the

Rees and the Brulés. If the two bands meet,
the relatives of the young warrior assassinated will paint themselves white (sign of
mourning) and will go to howl and sing their
lamentations for the victim in front of the
companions of his murderer. Then the latter
will pay for the misdeed by offering buffalo
robes, horses, or other presents, each one
giving what is convenient. The blood will
then be washed away; the Rees in their turn
will make some presents and peace will
reign between them until the next assassination, individual or collective. But if the
Brulés do not wish to pay for the blood the
Rees will look for and find an occasion to
avenge themselves and will without fail kill
those of the enemy band who may fall into
their hands. In the meanwhile seven of
them left this morning for Rice to get the
twelve horses. * * *

Tuesday, March 24: . . . Yesterday a letter
arrived at Berthold for one of the traders,
brought by chance, for no courier was expected. It was from Father De Smet, who
writes to Mr. Gerard to announce to him his
arrival soon, and his plan to put himself in
communication with the hostile Indians to
prepare the way for the commission charged
with concluding a general treaty of peace.
After having treated at length of Indian

affairs Father De Smet ended with a few lines announcing that the greatest confusion reigned at Washington on account of the impeachment of the President. "But," he added, "you receive the papers, and politics are no affair of mine." In consequence of which he included no details.

* * *

Wednesday, March 25: . . . During the afternoon and night a considerable rise was evident on the river. The water, increased by the melting of snow of the past days and by the storm, raised the vast bed of ice which held it prisoner and gradually detached it from both banks. Toward noon a moment came when the river, overflowing its lower banks, spread out impetuously on the lower bottoms, flat lands formed by alluvial deposits, thus doubling at certain points the width of its bed. Immediately the immense shell of ice started moving and the breakup was here. At first the ice floated adrift in enormous sheets. One of them was not less than a half-mile long. Soon long fissures appeared with prolonged cracking noises; the sheets divided, broke up, crashing against each other, more and more crowded, drifted down to the sharp elbow which the river forms at less than a mile below the fort. There its course is much restricted between the abrupt curve of the left bank and the vast elevated point of sand which forms almost a parallel line. It was upon this point that the breakup presented its most stirring spectacle and showed all its power. The great cakes of ice, constricted between the two banks and pressed by those which followed, sub-divided and broke into heavy chunks. These blocks, pressed against the others in front of them, ground together, piled upon each other, broke up, heaped in piles on those below, and soon this part of the gorged river became a vast chaos of ice. At some places the cakes piled up on the bank to a height of twelve or fifteen feet. Many of these ice cakes, which were not less than 1 or 1½ feet thick, must surely have weighed several tons. But such was the force of the current and such the pressure of the huge blocks of ice that these great masses were lifted up, stirred together, and carried one upon the other like so many pebbles. Their piling up ended by blocking the river and forming across it a formidable barrier. The ice cakes which followed pounded against it with a sonorous roaring and became under the eye, as we watched, new heaps of ice. The forced arrest of the river extended little by little over a greater and greater area and between four and five in the afternoon the river presented for over a mile of its length the appearance of a tremendous but motionless confusion. All the lower ground covered with willows through which Douglas Creek flows into the river presented, on the contrary, the appearance of a tranquil lake where were reflected in a luminous serenity the colors of the setting sun. There, indeed, the ice had not drifted; the water only spread through the obstacles of brush and trees and once the high point was reached, being out of the current, it became quiet as a mirror in which the willows and dogwood whose roots it bathed were complacently reflected. The breakup, stopped this evening, will doubtless resume its course during the night.

It is to be noted that the breakup came this year three weeks earlier than last year. Its usual time is during the first half of April and it occurs only occasionally in March. As I remarked before, the spring of 1868 is early. The melting of the snow is the determining cause of the breaking up of the ice, for without the rise the sheet of ice, which is more than a foot thick, would still hold for a week or two in spite of the sun. However it may be, we have assisted today at a tremendous and gripping spectacle.

* * *

Tuesday, March 31: . . . The Indians who
have quitted their winter camps on the Yellowstone are on the trail to the posts where
they live during the summer. Day before yesterday there arrived the first detachment of
forty lodges. Part are of the Yanktonais,
belonging to the band of Black Eyes. It is
the part which went toward Fort Buford.
With them were some Sissetons of the old
band of Wontanahan. The band of Medicine Bear came to join with them today. All
have set up their lodges (skin tents) on that
part of the prairie which extends back from
the landing. Their horses pasture at liberty
along the foot of the hills, their women go
and come, gathering wood, carrying water,
leading the horses, etc., and all this movement gives to the prairie an altogether un-
accustomed animation. Tomorrow they will
take up their route to Fort Rice and will be
followed from here in a few days by the
band of Bear's Ribs, and that of Running
Antelope (Uncpapas). We have distributed
some provisions to them, and this evening
there is a feast, singing and dances in their
camp, in rejoicing over their good fortune.
The poor devils have suffered cruelly this
winter, they, their families, and their horses.
The latter bear the marks of it. They are so
weak that until they are fed up the Indians

will not be able to hunt the buffalo with any success. And meanwhile this game of their choice is also mixed in this general return of animated life to our vicinity. The great herds of buffalo which had emigrated to the other side of the Yellowstone at the beginning of winter are coming back to us with the spring. Several herds have already reappeared in our neighborhood. The Gros Ventres and Rees, whose horses are in better condition, have already killed some; but the Yanktonais have pursued them without success, their horses playing them false. It is well known that the buffalo does not run very fast and that an ordinary horse will surpass him in speed.

The Sioux, camped near us today, bring good news of the hostile bands with whom they have wintered. At the beginning of the winter they were in very bad humor. They talked of nothing but continuing the war, attacking the soldiers, and stealing their horses and mules as soon as spring should come back. Some great discussions took place on the subject, the tribe of the Uncpapa and that of the Yanktonais being divided into hostile bands and friendly bands. The Santees are nearly all hostile, but at the conclusion of the Minnesota massacres, in which they played the principal role, they were pursued and chastised so severely (some hung, others shot) that they have very little power in themselves. The friendly chiefs, Medicine Bear, Running Antelope, the son of Bear's Ribs, have insisted on the advantages of the peace which they enjoyed, and the misfortunes which the others would bring upon themselves by taking up hostilities again. A noticeable portion of the hostile bands was already tired of war and disposed to put an end to it. The partisans of peace, therefore, found themselves in the majority, and misery aiding them, they came to this conclusion, that they would abstain from new hostilities and await the arrival of the government commissioners to conclude a general treaty of peace and friendship if the conditions offered were acceptable to them.

I am sending by yesterday's courier this information to General Terry since it will particularly interest him, as he is a member of the commission charged with treating with the hostile Indians.

* * *

Wednesday, April 1: The information brought by Medicine Bear has not been slow of confirmation. This morning there arrived a chief of the Cut Heads (Sissetons) called Red Horse (Ta-shunka-donta) with

257

forty lodges.[28] This chief has never surrendered to the military authorities. In 1862 or 1863, after the Minnesota massacres, he left his hunting grounds situated around Dog Den Butte toward Devils Lake.

Since then the band has wandered over the Plains, especially toward the north near the frontier of the British possessions, where they passed last winter with a party of Assiniboines. Long privation, miserable hardships, the scarcity of game, hunger, now influence them to listen to the voice of their Great Father and to submit themselves to his orders. They have lost many horses during the winter, and those which are left to them are not strong enough to follow buffalo. They are going to Fort Rice and from there will return to the Santee reserve below Fort Randall, where, probably, they will settle to plant some corn for the summer. Their tribe is so dispersed that Red Horse does not know how many lodges there are left of them, nor where they now are.

[28] Red Horse was a well-known chief of the Cut Head band. This band is here described as Sisseton. Red Fish, a very old Dakota, who recently died, claimed to be a member of the band and described it as being a division of the Yanktonais. He stated that the name was given them after a raid on the Chippewas in Minnesota when they cut off a number of heads of slain Chippewas and brought them home as trophies. G. F. W.

But for himself and his warriors he is making absolute submission, and will present himself at the place fixed by the commissioners to conclude there solemnly a lasting peace. The conclusion of this information, you may divine, has been a distribution of provisions, of which they had great need, and tomorrow they will take the trail, more satisfied, probably, than they have been for a long time.

Toward noon there arrived in their turn the Three Tribes from Fort Berthold, sent to receive also a certain amount of provisions. The chiefs, the warriors, and the women were of the party. The distribution was made on the prairie back of the post, after which they all went to camp on Douglas Creek, where they will pass the night, and tomorrow morning they will return to Berthold.

With them came Running Antelope. He informs me of the coming soon of different bands, some to make submission, others to renew their friendly relations.

* * *

Thursday, April 2: This morning I had a long talk with Running Antelope. He furnished me all the most precise details as to the bands which wintered on the Yellowstone. Nearly all the chiefs will be present

at the peace conference, when the definite
time and place are set. While waiting, they
will come and make a preliminary submission to the different forts nearest to their
residence. The most doubtful are the formerly hostile Uncpapas under the leadership
of Black Moon, Red Horn, Four Horns, and
Sitting Bull.[29]   Those with whom peace
seems assured are the Sans Arcs commanded
by One Horn (about 400 lodges); the Minneconjous, who have not yet made any
treaties with the whites (600 to 700 lodges);
the Brulés, and different small bands of the
Santee Sioux, or Sioux of the Mississippi; and
the Assiniboines. This is very good news, and
if, as everything seems to foretell, a general
peace is concluded, our residence in the military posts of the Upper Missouri will certainly be much more agreeable than formerly.

[29] This is the first mention of Sitting Bull, who, as
the Journal very definitely tells us, was at that time
known as a chief of the hostiles and a leader in battle.
The myth that he was a cowardly medicine man seems
to be a later product of his feud with the Indian Department, after his final surrender. The Uncpapas, now
on the Standing Rock Reservation, as well as the Sans
Arcs, the Minneconjous, and the Brulés were all of the
great western Dakota division, the Teton. The Assiniboines, though not of the Dakota nation, seem to be
close relatives of the Yanktonais and their language
very closely resembles that dialect. G. F. W.

Running Antelope was charged by the chiefs, whom he has named to me, to bring these messages of peace to me personally, and he has not failed to let me know that the fact of my French birth is for them a source of particular confidence. For one cause or another the Indians of these regions have always entertained friendly relations with the French of Canada. No one else, I believe, has so well understood the character of the savages or has known as well how to keep on friendly terms with them. The Anglo-Saxon or American race, on the contrary, has hardly had any transactions with them except through brute force, demoralization and oppression. Hence the difference with which the redskins regard the Canadians and the Americans. The more I live among these children of the desert, the more I read the official documents relative to Indian affairs, the more the ideas which I brought with me are modified. The mass of iniquities of which the poor redskins have been the victims on the part of the whites surpasses the imagination; it must be seen to be believed.

Running Antelope had his whole body slashed transversely, his arms too, with long red lines, scars of gashes which he had inflicted on himself as a sign of mourning for

the death of a 19-year-old son whom he lost
by sickness last winter. Fifty or sixty gashes,
and in the heart of winter!

Friday, April 3: . . . Mantoouakan, Medicine Bear, arrived this morning with 40 lodges.
A fresh conference, and another distribution
of provisions. How monotonous it becomes;
I left the carrying out of it to Brevet Lieutenant Colonel Powell. One of the hostile
chiefs who wintered on the Yellowstone has
been killed by accident. In a fall from his
horse a knife which he wore at his belt penetrated his flank and the wound was mortal.
The name of the chief was Ishetan-Otanka,
the Buzzard.

* * *

Tuesday, April 7: Howkah, the brother
(or uncle) of Black Eyes, arrived in his turn
this morning on his way to Fort Rice after
an excursion on the prairie in the direction
of Devils Lake. I have had some provisions
distributed for himself and the little band
with him, which amounts to but ten lodges.
Medicine Bear, who has remained in camp
on Douglas Creek, has had, at the same time,
his share of our largess. He warns us to look
out for a band of incorrigible Uncpapas, that
of Red Horn, Black Moon, Sitting Bull and
Four Horns. They are the same ones who
have committed the depredations of last

fall, and are the only ones who still persevere in their hostile designs, and announce that they intend to stay on the warpath. Some of Medicine Bear's men have discovered some extinguished fires and some thongs in a point of timber where we are having posts cut for the palisades of the new corral. They think that all these recent signs may be an indication of hostile raiders and promise that if the hostile band appears, they will fight them with us. However it may be, recommendations have been made to the teamsters and their escort to redouble their vigilance and to hold themselves always on the alert.

To express to me the need of himself and his people for provisions, Howkah silently uncovered his breast, showing me that he was scarcely more than skin and bones. This silent commentary to his request was not without eloquence. A cannibal could scarcely have found anything to gnaw on his ribs.

Wednesday, April 8: Yesterday in the afternoon died two of our men, one of heart trouble complicated by scurvy, the other of scurvy alone. This disease has noticeably weakened our little garrison during the winter and reached its maximum during the last month. At this time we have in the hospital thirty-two sick of scurvy, and thirteen more are exempted from service with their companies, having only light attacks or being convalescent and on a diet. To this number must be added six employees of the quartermaster who are being treated at the hospital, which makes a total of fifty-one cases of scurvy, equal to a fourth of the garrison.

This regrettable condition is the result of the long deprivation of fresh vegetables and the infrequency of the rations of fresh meat which are distributed but twice a week. The principal food of the men consists of salt pork and salt fish; hence the sickness. . . . Happily the trials are approaching a conclusion, thanks to the impending arrival of the steamboats and the fresh provisions which they carry.

* * *

Saturday, April 11: The news brought from Berthold is no longer as peaceful as it has been. It would appear that the band of hostile Uncpapas have persuaded two other bands (the Blackfoot Sioux and a part of the Minneconjous) to change their good resolutions and join with them in a common plan for war during the coming summer. Some Minneconjous have offered thirty horses to the Three Tribes if they would leave their village and wander on the Plains, renouncing their treaty of friendship with the whites, which they have refused to do. Then some families of Minneconjous, refusing to run the risks attached to a state of war, left their tribe to go and live at Berthold with the Arikaras. I attach little importance to this news. Supposing it true, all that the three bands would be able to undertake would be the stealing of a few mules and the killing of a few teamsters by surprise; but we are taking measures against such a chance, the surprised ones would be these red pillagers on account of the reception which they would receive.

This band of incorrigible Uncpapas is led by four or five chiefs, such as Black Moon, Red Horn, Four Horns, and Sitting Bull. The latter was, several years ago, pierced with bayonet thrusts in a fight. Bloody Knife, who was fighting on the side of the soldiers, seeing that the wounded man still breathed, jumped from his horse and prepared to cut his throat and take his scalp, when the officer in command of the detachment had the ill-timed though philanthropic inspiration of preventing the finishing of the seemingly dying Sitting Bull.[30] The result

[30] The story told here about Sitting Bull and Bloody Knife is recounted in detail by Joseph Henry Taylor in his *Kaleidoscopic Lives*, but the principal characters,

was that the lusty fellow escaped, cured his wounds, and since then, pursuing an insatiable vengeance, has never ceased from working every evil in his power nor of being the soul or rather the arm to strike all the blows attempted or accomplished against us. It is he above all who animates with his own hatred all the others and keeps on the warpath this band of unsurrendered Uncpapas, with whom are always joined some aspiring young men of the other bands in quest of adventure, scalps, and renown.

These young braves make up the turbulent portions of all the tribes, and often the chiefs have a great deal of difficulty in maintaining their authority over them. This is the reason; young men arrived at an age to be classed as warriors can not acquire that position of influence and consideration among their people except through prowess in war. If they are content with being intrepid hunt-

according to his version, were Bloody Knife and Gall, instead of Sitting Bull. The details are the same and there can be no doubt that it is the same story. Which version is correct must remain uncertain. There can, however, be no doubt that the reference to Sitting Bull as leader of the most bitter hostiles is correct. Gall was at first only a warrior, usually a member of Sitting Bull's band, and a follower of that chief until the final retreat to Canada, although he had in the meantime become a chief in his own right. G. F. W.

ers, becoming rich, that is having many
wives depending on them, a dozen horses,
plumes, necklaces and a good supply of
dried meat, they will not be admitted to the
council fire and will not take rank among
the chiefs. For whatever they may have of
ambition they must, then, take to the warpath, and this is what they do on their own
account if their tribe is at peace with the
whites and with their neighbors. Some night
or other they will decamp, perhaps alone,
perhaps in little groups animated with the
same spirit, and will begin to wander over
the Plains. As I have explained before,
bravery for them does not consist in expos-
ing themselves to danger for a difficult or
uncertain result; their exploits are, on the
contrary, counted the more brilliant if they
have gathered many scalps or stolen many
mules or horses with the least possible risk.
So they proceed by ambush and abstain
from attacking openly. Thus has it been
possible for our little two-company post,
exposed on all sides, without defenses of
any sort, separated by six days' march from
Totten, and by four days from Rice, to be
built with impunity and to be maintained
in the heart of the Sioux nation whose
united tribes count some thirty thousand
souls.

But let the solitary man, white or red, beware, should he meet on the Plains one of these bands in search of scalps. Even if his tribe should be at peace with the tribe to which the ruffians belonged, they would have no scruple in murdering him, in stealing his horse and his arms, and in taking away his scalp as a trophy. If the hunt for man should be unsuccessful because their band was not numerous enough, they will find and join some other band and the two will travel over the Plains together or frequent the neighborhood of the military posts to pick off some teamster going for wood or some solitary soldier wandering among the thickets.

When any one of the band has made a fortunate coup, and has brought back a certain number of scalps and some spoils, when the tribe, on his return from his expedition, has danced the scalp dance several times in his honor, celebrated his exploits and honored the memory of them by giving him a name, the aspirant to the title of chief removes all his garments one by one, distributes according to chance all of his horses, his provisions, his ornaments, even his wife, then in the midst of the dance with cries of joy, with improvised songs and beating of the drum, he is proclaimed chief. This does not mean that he will command the tribe or dispossess the second chief or the chief of the warriors. He simply acquires the rank and title of chief; he has entry to the councils; his influence is recognized. He is promoted by brevet as we say in the army, with this difference, that he must do something to obtain the aforesaid brevet, while among us that is the least necessary condition. If, to hunt buffalo, to winter, or for any other reason, the tribe divides into several bands, some families will probably choose his leadership and then he will have the command of a few lodges. His campaigns will be ended for the present, and it may at least be wagered that on a few occasions full of temptation he will keep tranquil.

If, however, his ambition is of a higher order, and if younger rivals come in their turn to acquire by their prowess and renown an influence which threatens to relegate him to the second grade, to maintain his position in the tribe he will undertake another campaign, this time at the head of a few warriors, and will force himself to make some coup sufficient to restore his prestige. He will remain thus on the warpath as long as his ambition is not satisfied, after which, if he attains his goal and is reclothed with a commanding position of sufficient importance, he will rest on his laurels and preach peace to the young men in concert with the elders of the tribe and the retired chiefs. (That is, if in hunting scalps he has not lost his own.)

Warlike exploits are so dominant a consideration in the choice of a tribal chief that nothing else can stand in the way. Thus the old chief of the Gros Ventres, Four Bears, had not in his veins a single drop of blood of the tribe which he ruled. He was an Assiniboine by birth. Made prisoner while still a child and raised among the Gros Ventres or Hidatsa, he grew up among them and so distinguished himself in the combats against the Sioux, to which race he belonged by blood, that he reached the highest rank in the tribe of his adoption and acquired a renown that has long survived him.[31]

[31] The Hidatsa chief, Four Bears, is still remembered and venerated by his people. Only recently his name was prominently mentioned in the course of deciding on a name for the highway bridge lately built across the Missouri at Elbowoods on the Fort Berthold Reservation. An earlier and still more famous Four Bears was the great Mandan chief to whom Catlin devotes so much space, and who died of smallpox at the Fort Clark village in 1837. The fact that the Hidatsa Four Bears was an Assiniboine is not unique. Many adopted members of other tribes achieved distinction and often became chiefs in the tribes into which they were adopted. G. F. W.

It is not even always necessary that there be an election or a proclamation to institute the authority of a chief. Some have imposed themselves on the tribe by their reputation and the vigor of their arms. Some years ago a chief of the Mississippi Sioux (I have forgotten his name) was in this position, and like all usurpers he ruled his band with a rod of iron, using his knife or his warclub at the least sign of insubordination. The final exploit which raised him to the command is sufficiently characteristic.

A numerous band of Arikaras had surprised three Sioux on the prairie and the poor devils had taken refuge in the brush, where none of their assailants, though outnumbering them twenty to one, dared pursue them. The assailants made a great uproar, howling and galloping around; they shot arrows or bullets into the brush, but without venturing in. Two Sioux came upon the scene and informed themselves of the cause of all the noise. Having found out, they dismounted, armed themselves with their knives and tomahawks, and resolutely

The final speech of Four Bears, who died July 30, 1837, has been printed by the present Editor in *Miss. Valley Hist. Rev.*, XVII, 299. It deserves a place in any collection of examples of notable American oratory. M. M. Q.

entered the brush. They killed the three
fugitives, although they were of their own
nation (but not of their tribe); one of the
two died there. The other brought back the
three scalps, and from this deed was considered so heroically brave that on returning
to his tribe he took command without opposition.

Among the hostile Uncpapas nearly all
the chiefs are in the position of being forced
into war, under pain of losing their positions
to the profit of some other more audacious
and more obstinate warrior. Two among
them (Red Horn and Four Horns) were at
one time friendly to the whites and at that
time contributed greatly toward saving the
life of Mr. Gerard, one of the traders at
Berthold.

That was some years ago. At that time
the military posts extended no farther than
Minnesota. Gerard, with some horses and
a wagon loaded with trade merchandise, had
fallen into the hands of the Uncpapas. He
was on their hunting grounds, and his merchandise was unanimously confiscated. Upon
the question of the theft there was no opposition. It was not quite the same on the
question of killing the men. When the pro-
posal was made to put to death the unfortunate whites (there were two of them), some

voices were raised in their favor; but evidently those in favor of death were in the majority, and they were preparing for the execution when Running Antelope came to the rescue.

Running Antelope, it is well to mention, had been in his youth mixed up in an attack on a stage, the seizing of the mail and a large sum in gold, and murder of the guard, the driver, and, I believe, also of several travellers. Pursued and made prisoner by the troops, he was tried and condemned to death. He owed his life only to presidential clemency, by which he was pardoned and permitted to return to his people. He, at least, has shown himself grateful and since then has remained constantly the friend of the whites. "Which does not mean," Mr. Gerard still says, "that I would trust my skin to him any more than to any other Indian in a circumstance where it might be to his interest or advantage to detach my scalp."

However that may be, on this particular occasion Running Antelope leaped upon the captured wagon and harangued the warriors, declaring that Gerard was his friend and he would not permit him to be put to death. At the same time his women and those of his relatives began a certain war song, the object of which was to urge their husbands and

brothers to the fight and to arouse their
ardor under difficult circumstances. At this
appeal the relatives and friends of Running
Antelope ran to their lodges and came forth
armed to range themselves about him. The
opposition party did the same and battle
was immediately joined between the two
factions. Gerard and his companion profited
by getting away with all the speed of their
horses. They lost their goods but escaped with
their lives. There were three or four Uncpapas killed and a good number wounded in the
mixup. After which, the objects of the fight
having escaped, each returned to his tent.

Thus, as this example shows, the Indians
seem to be as ready to fight among themselves as against the whites. From tribe to
tribe wars, or rather hostilities, perpetuate
themselves indefinitely. Twenty times they
will make peace, twenty times they will
smoke together the calumet and bury the
hatchet. These are but momentary truces,
and on the first occasion they will kill each
other, steal from each other with all their
might, provided that one party be much
stronger than the other, and above all, that
on one side or the other they may surprise
a few isolated hunters and raise their scalps
without serious risk.

* * *

Monday, April 13: The band of Medicine Bear, which for some ten days has camped on the banks of Douglas Creek, has taken the trail this morning to go hunting buffalo, their horses being in better condition after this period of rest. Their departure was signalized by one of those acts which demonstrates what I have written above of the lack of discipline of a certain number of the young men in every tribe. Some of these, knowing that camp would be broken early this morning, stole during the night two oxen hitched to Gerard's wagon, near the house which he is building for his goods, at a hundred meters from our quarters. At daylight, when the theft was noticed, the trader and his employees mounted their horses and scoured the prairie.

They found the trail and two of them were following it rapidly when the guilty ones, knowing that they were without doubt pursued, fired the prairie to efface the trail. The pursuers came back to give an account of their efforts and Gerard himself started out with one of his men. Lieutenant Walborn accompanied him with four men mounted. It should not be thought that Medicine Bear himself was an accomplice in the theft, but Gerard thought best to promise him the gift of a horse if the two oxen should be returned to him. Would the chief have enough authority to bring about the restitution or would they get in touch with the thieves before they have killed the oxen to make a great feast? That is the question. Take note that this act of neighborliness is the deed of a friendly band, which has no idea of hostility toward the whites.

P.S. Medicine Bear kept his word. This evening he came back with ten of his warriors, leading one of the oxen and what he had been able to save of the meat of the other. The deed had been done by an Uncpapa and his son who were with the Yanktonais band of Medicine Bear. The latter followed them and caught up in time to save one ox, but too late to get the other. The guilty ones hid in the brush, or so said Medicine Bear, to explain why he had not brought them back. That may be true but I doubt it. At any rate the little band got from Gerard some coffee, sugar, pork, and crackers, and they left very well satisfied with the recompense accorded to them for their virtue.

Tuesday, April 14: . . . We know now that the stealing of the oxen from Gerard was, on the part of the Indians, a punishment inflicted on the trader for having set fire to the prairie several days ago, and thus driving away the game which is their principal source of food.

* * *

Wednesday, April 22: Great agitation at the fort. At nine in the morning the white smoke of a steamboat was observed above the trees, at the point where the river disappears for us behind the hills. At once everyone was outside, all the field glasses were put to use, and in a few moments the movement of the smoke could no longer leave any doubt. Hurrah for the first boat of the season!

* * *

Friday, May 1: . . . Ten Arikara Indians have been enrolled as scouts for six months and will thus serve for the fort or for the escorts which we may have to send out.[32] They

[32] We have here the account of the first enrollment of scouts among the Arikara. From this period until after the battle of the Little Big Horn there were Arikara, Mandans, and Hidatsa enrolled as scouts in the United States service. They acquitted themselves well for the most part and performed dangerous and difficult service with bravery and faithfulness. Volume VI of the North Dakota Historical Society *Collections* gives a full and complete story of the service of the Arikara scouts with Custer. Most of those who served as scouts with the United States Army are now dead, although several of them lived until about 1935. It is a sad commentary on the lack of gratitude of the Government that not a single one of these men was ever able to get the smallest pension. G. F. W.

receive the rations and pay of a soldier and a uniform consisting of a hat with a black plume, upon which they insist, a jacket, overcoat, trousers, and flannel shirt. (All keep their moccasins by habit.) And last, 40 cents per day for the horse which each one furnishes. At the same time Patinaud has been engaged as interpreter. He is a valuable man who has passed thirty years on the Plains and speaks with remarkable facility Canadian French, English, Sioux, Ree, Gros Ventre, Mandan, and Crow. He came into the country at the age of fifteen as an employee of the Choteau Fur Company of St. Louis. At that epoch only a few white men had thus far appeared in Dakota, and all of them for the purpose of trading with the Indians, who invariably received them well. Although the tribes did not cease fighting among themselves, which is an immemorial habit among the redskins, the whites were never included in their quarrels. They might wander over the deserts in safety, without arms, and they were never maltreated. When they met the savages all sat down together around the fire, smoked the calumet of peace, traded a few things, exchanged the news of the day, and separated again as though it had been a meeting of friends. At that period, to the whites nothing could have been more inoffensive than the tribes of the Plains. Among them they received nothing but hospitality; a word given was always religiously kept; and as good faith ruled in their transactions, just so did good feeling rule between individuals. If theft, deceit, murder, and war have succeeded to that state of affairs, the fault is absolutely and solely that of the whites. The trading posts, encouraged by the savages, increased rapidly in numbers, as did the secondary points of rendezvous which were established along the courses of the small streams to meet there the distant tribes who could not without inconvenience bring their furs as far as the banks of the Missouri.

The great profits of the trade engendered rivalries among the traders; these rivalries were translated into all sorts of tricks and schemes by means of which each one sought to attract the Indians to himself and to turn them away from his competitors. It was thus that the whites commenced to stir up the Indians and to urge them to steal in order to get rid of each other. The redskins learned from them bad faith, then theft, then the murder of traders or their employees. Whisky was introduced among them to inflame them to evil doing and so that they might the more easily be despoiled. Pandora's box was thus opened on the Plains and vices, injustice, and bad treatment sown in the Plains by the whites have produced this bloody harvest which for ten years has cost so much in blood and silver. The discovery of the Montana gold mines aggravated all these things by leading into the Plains a crowd of gold-seekers, unbridled bandits, wrapped up in themselves, far from the empire of laws and the domains of civilization. The Minnesota Massacre in 1862 brought on the expulsion of the Santees from their hunting grounds and crowded all the Sioux on the west bank of the Missouri, and their assemblage there under conditions of war with the whites has produced these hostilities which have continued during these last years with so much more activity, since the treaties concluded with the tribes of the Platte have not been observed by the Government. Nevertheless, tired of war, miserable, hungry, harassed, most of the tribes have made their submission, as I have previously related, and the rest, save perhaps a band of Uncpapas, will do the same when the commissioners of the Government are present to conclude a lasting peace on the Upper Missouri.

Here are the names and strength of the Indian tribes of Dakota from the report of the Indian Bureau to Congress in 1866. Without being absolutely exact, the number approaches as near to the truth as it is possible to get among wandering tribes, strangers to all statistics:

		LODGES	PEOPLE
Minneconjou....	Sioux	370	2220
Brulé..........	Sioux	200	1200
Two Kettle.....	Sioux	200	1200
Black Feet......	Sioux	220	1320
Upper Yanktonais...	Sioux	400	2400
Lower Yanktonais...	Sioux	350	2100
Uncpapa........	Sioux	300	1800
Sans Arcs.......	Sioux	280	1680
Oglalla.........	Sioux	350	2100
Mountain Crows.		400	2400
Assiniboines.....		440	2640
Prairie Crows...		250	1500
Gros Ventres of the Plains.....		250	1500
Gros Ventres of the Missouri...	} a common village		400
Arikaras at Berthold......			1500
Mandans at Berthold......			400
		4,060	26,360

This number, to which must be added the tribes of the Mississippi Sioux or what is left of them, Santees, Sissetons, Cutheads, etc., now crowded into Dakota, brings one to a total of some 30,000 Indians (women and children included) in round numbers.

The Gros Ventres or Hidatsa and the Crows are tribes belonging to the same stock, separated by circumstances, but speaking the same language with a little variation. The Mandans come from the same source as the Winnebagos of the Great Lakes region. The Arikaras and the Pawnees of Nebraska have the same origin and belong to the same nation. One of their bands has remained for thirty years in the southern regions, and has preserved there its own language and organization distinct from its neighbors. Another band has no more been heard from. The Arikaras have different names; Arikari in Mandan; Arikarhos in Gros Ventre; Pananris in Sioux; and Rees by abbreviation in American. I have explained before through what catastrophes the Three Tribes at Berthold, formerly powerful and warlike, have been reduced to their present condition.[33]

[33] The list of tribes in Dakota, with their numbers, is interesting and if the figures were correct, nearly all of

Sunday, May 10: Medicine Bear came to the fort to bring a government horse found

the tribes have decreased considerably since then, according to the last official census.

Dr. Roland B. Dixon of Harvard University had charge of the Indian census of 1910 and performed a complete and unusually accurate piece of work. Since 1910 there has been a small gradual increase in most tribes.

The comparable 1910 figures show for the Teton Sioux a total of 10,598 souls. The tribes in De Trobriand's list belonging to this division are Minneconjou, Brulé, Two Kettle, Blackfeet, Uncpapas, Sans Arcs and Oglalla, totalling 11,520 souls. These are now scattered in several states, but it must be remembered that De Trobriand's Dakota included North and South Dakota, much of Montana, and part of Wyoming. Where De Trobriand gives 400 Mandans, the 1910 census shows only 165; the Arikara have shrunk from 1500 to 372; the Hidatsa, however, with 400 in De Trobriand's list, had 418 souls in 1910. The Crows have decreased from 3900 to 1242, the Assiniboines from 2640 to 793, the Atsina or Gros Ventres of the Plains (related to the Blackfoot Tribe), from 1500 to 390. The Yanktonais, with 4500 in the Journal, in 1910 show only 1144. On the other hand, the Oglalla, with 2100 in De Trobriand's list, have, according to the 1910 census, 4168. Some of these decreases and additions may be due to the placing of certain bands under different divisions in the two enumerations.

De Trobriand's account of tribal relationships is entirely correct, although he fails to realize that the Mandan, Hidatsa, Winnebago, Crow, and Dakota are all of the great Siouan stock, to which belong also the Omaha, Oto, Iowa, Kansas, Quapaw, Missouri, Osage, and others in the south and east. G. F. W.

by his people on the prairie. It is an act of honesty and friendship which deserves recompense. I have had given to him a good supply of salt pork, crackers, coffee, and sugar, for himself and the five warriors who came with him. The horse was abandoned some time ago near Dog Den by a detachment of an escort which it could no longer keep up with. It seemed well recovered and is no longer lame.

* * *

Saturday, May 16: . . . The Indians are assembling in great numbers at Fort Rice to meet there the Commission sent by the President to conclude peace with the hostile tribes and renew the treaties with the others, particularly among the Sioux. The Commission, which consists of Generals Sherman, Sheridan, Terry, and Harney, will probably not arrive before June 1. The Indians will pleasantly pass the time of waiting in quarreling, stealing, and fighting among themselves. A few days ago a Mandan was found dead on the prairie, his body gashed with knife wounds and his scalp taken. The poor devil was hunting antelope. It is not yet known who struck the blow, although they suspect the hostile band of Uncpapas which refuses to go to Fort Rice. Always it is the same handful of incorrigible ruffians.

Sunday, May 17: The hostile Uncpapas made today their first appearance before Fort Stevenson. A dozen of them slipping along the coulees stole two or three of the Ree horses which were turned loose to feed on the other side of Douglas Creek. They were hoping, also, to lay heavy hands on Gerard's horses and oxen, but these animals were under the guard of two armed Indians, who received the marauders with gunshots while rounding up the stock. A few soldiers hunting in the vicinity showing themselves just then, the Sioux retired to the hills. The skirmish had attracted our attention. I at once sent twenty-five men led by Lieutenant Ward to reconnoiter the enemy. Our soldiers deployed as skirmishers and mounted to the top of the highest hill without seeing anything. The Uncpapas, seeing them coming, had retreated precipitately toward the east. There they met our Arikara scouts, who were making a reconnaissance in that direction. A few shots were exchanged. Our men, although fewer in number, attacked at once when one of them, Bull Head, was violently thrown by his horse, which was shot under him, on the stony ground. The others could not disengage him and he lay unconscious in the power of the enemy. When word of this was brought to the fort I immediately sent Lieutenant Hooton with his company to rescue the wounded man if he was still alive, or his body if the Sioux had finished him. But soon we perceived our man returning himself in the company of some of his people and ahead of our soldiers. The Sioux were content, during his unconsciousness, with despoiling him of all his clothes and his arms, leaving nothing but his breechclout, which our savages keep, it seems, even under their trousers. By an inexplicable circumstance the Sioux had not scalped him, so that he came out of the affair with only a big bump on his head and another on his thigh. The hostile Sioux had already disappeared.

* * *

Friday, May 22: . . . The mail from Fort Totten is missing. It should have been here Wednesday afternoon but we have no news of it. The convoy under escort of Lieutenant Smith left Tuesday morning to return to Fort Totten, and so followed the mail at an interval of forty-eight hours. The presence of hostile Indians in our neighborhood does nothing to allay some inquietude on our part; but we prefer to suppose that, Colonel Whistler having gone on leave, and the command of Totten having passed to Captain Hill, as a result of some oversight or some error the couriers failed to meet at the halfway station and ours will have been forced to push on to Devils Lake, in which case they could not get back before Sunday evening. These delays in the arrival of the mail are always very vexing for us who invariably await the couriers with great impatience.

* * *

Tuesday, May 26: It was not without reason that we were worried over the failure to return of McDonald and Joe Hamlin, who had left with the mail eight days ago Sunday. Both of them are dead, killed by the Uncpapa Indians who had made their appearance about the post on the afternoon of the same day that the mail left. This is how we learned the sad news:

Day before yesterday two of our couriers left with the weekly mail to meet those from Fort Totten halfway of the trail. They were Brown, an Irishman recently engaged for the government service, and Martin, a half-breed employed since last year, both being perfectly acquainted with the country and speaking Sioux fluently. Toward the evening of the first day they got close to Clear Lake and saw in the distance what appeared to them to be buffalo. They were in reality Indians, who, in order not to arouse

287

suspicion, lay flat on the necks of their horses,
which gave them a resemblance to the animal for which they wished to be taken.
Meanwhile, our men continued on their way,
while the Uncpapas prepared an ambush
for them.

Arrived at a narrow ravine through which
they had to pass, the two couriers suddenly
found themselves enveloped by Sioux pour-
ing in on them from all sides and crying;
"Do not shoot! We some of the people of
Medicine Bear (a friendly chief), We friends,"
and the nearest ones shook hands with Joe
Martin, who was the nearest to them.
Brown's horse, frightened, ran away and
some young men went in pursuit. The mule
which carried the mail sack and the provisions ran away in another direction, with
speed accelerated by fear. When Martin was
so closely surrounded that he could make no
move in his own defense an Indian clapped
his hand on his horse's neck, giving voice
to an exclamation of triumph which the
prisoner could not mistake, and he thought
himself lost. In an instant he was despoiled
of everything, arms, equipment, clothes.
His horse was taken away from him at the
start. Brown, brought back almost at once,
met the same fortune. He had been promptly
overtaken by an enemy riding Charles

McDonald's well known horse, which gave him something to think about. When everything had been taken but their shoes and their drawers the chief gave Martin, to cover himself (for it had poured rain all day and was still raining) an old coat, which he promptly recognized as having belonged to Joe Hamlin. The coat was pierced with two bullet holes in the breast and two tears at the back. The chief asked the prisoners who they were and what they were doing on the prairie. They answered that they were Red River half-breeds hunting on their way back to St. Joseph.[34] The chief then told them that his people had killed two men and a soldier a few days before; our couriers and a man of Lieutenant Smith's convoy. "I would not have had the two Red River men die," said the chief, "but the young men killed them before it was known who they were."

"It was I who killed one of them," said one of the savages, advancing with the 16-shot-rifle (Henry) of Charles McDonald. "I shot an arrow through his body; he fell from his horse and I finished him on the ground with shots from a revolver." The

---

[34] St. Joseph in the Pembina hills, now Walhalla, N. Dak., was an early settlement of the Red River half-breeds and the seat of a trading post in the forties.

prisoners noticed then that the chief wore McDonald's watch chain and recognized several articles of his and Joe Hamlin's clothing on the backs of some of the Indians. "Let us kill them, too," several of them said, "Why waste time in talking? Let us do to them as we did to the others." Then the chief took the two prisoners aside, "The young men are talking badly and are ready to do a bad deed. Profit from the approaching night and save yourselves quickly before it is too late." Our men did not need to be told twice, and, half naked, they scurried away. In place of following the direction they had taken at the start they hurried to hide in some marshy brush, making, in doing so, a circuit calculated to throw off pursuit.

It was well that they took this precaution. The chief had given them their life only on account of the ignorance in which he still was of the fact that they were couriers. The mule that carried the dispatches had run away, as I said above. It had taken some time to get hold of him and the ones that captured him had first feasted on the provisions they found in the saddle bags. When they returned, leading the animal and with the packet of despatches, our men had already left. An immediate search for their tracks was made with the aim, doubtless, of putting them to death; but the night had come, or at least the twilight was already nearly dark, and the tracks could not be found.

They walked part of the night, went astray, and at dawn found that they were still within sight of the enemy. By threading the ravines, hiding themselves as best they could, they hastened along in the direction of Fort Stevenson where, completely tired out, not having eaten a mouthful since the morning of the previous day, they arrived today at sunset without any further misfortune.

McDonald leaves a wife and three young children. He was an excellent man, still young, active, and brave. He had been engaged as chief guide of the couriers with an appointment of $100 per month. His wife's parents live in Minnesota, where they are fairly well-to-do, to the extent, at least, that he does not leave his family in complete destitution. Joe Hamlin was a bachelor and leaves no family behind him. The band which committed the triple murder and rifled and plundered our two last couriers is that of the unsubmitted Uncpapas, who ceaselessly wander through the prairies, pillaging, stealing, and killing the whites, especially all soldiers and government em-

ployees, every chance they get. The principal chief is Sitting Bull, one of the most
dangerous and most ill-disposed Indians in
Dakota. A price has been successively put
upon his head by the authorities of Minnesota and of Montana. Now Dakota has
become the theater for his depredations and
assassinations. It is a fine play, the government leaving us in our posts without cavalry,
without horses, and absolutely in no state to
pursue and chastise him. He can thus wander freely and in all security over the prairies
which he besmears with blood wherever it
seems good to him.

He is a man of forty years, of medium
height, and slightly inclined to obesity, a
rare thing among the Indians. He is sturdy
and wears his hair cut off at the base of his
neck, that is to say short for a Sioux. His
ferocity is hidden under an appearance of
good humor and a conversation flowering
with pleasantry. One would think him the
most inoffensive of Indians, judging from
appearances. In reality he is a fierce beast,
which seems to laugh when it shows its
teeth. When he passed near Fort Berthold
he told some Rees that he was going to stay
for some time along the trail between Stevenson and Totten because there were people
passing that way, whites and soldiers, and

that he would stay so long as he should find an opportunity for some evil doing. It seems that he is keeping his word. He seems to love to talk—for during the little time that our two couriers passed among his people, he entertained them with his exploits and his plans. He is little concerned over the commissioners sent by the government to treat for peace. His business, he said, is to kill the whites, and he intends to kill all of them that he and his band possibly can. He boasts that war is very much more profitable to him than peace; that it brings him arms, ammunition, clothing, and, above all, horses and mules in abundance, while the submitted tribes die in misery of hunger where the whites have placed them. With him is also found Gall, another ferocious bandit. There were in all 32 men and they had with them 54 animals, which included the 4 horses and 2 mules taken from our couriers.

So there are our communications cut off for some time by the way of Totten. That leaves us Rice and the steamboats descending the river.

The Rees and Mandans, that is to say the chiefs accompanied by a few warriors and women, came to ask for some provisions, which I have had distributed to them. To-

morrow it will be the turn of the Gros
Ventres. These poor devils are dying of
hunger because of the disappearance of the
buffalo in this vicinity, and of the severity
and length of the winter, which exhausted
their provisions of corn and left them almost
without resources by spring, when they have
to plant their corn. That business is nearly
finished and now they are going to take up
the hunt, dispersing to pursue whatever they
can find in the way of game.

They will return when the crop is ripe.
It is with savages as with the civilized; "When
the feed rack is empty the horses fight."
Between the Gros Ventres and the Mandans
on one side and the Rees on the other there
seem to be some grievances which embitter
them against each other and which could
degenerate into a bloody quarrel. The former reproach the latter with having profited
by their absence during the winter to tear
down their lodges and use the wood to burn
—which is true—and to steal the reserves of
seed corn, at least in part,—which is probable. We pretend to lead the Indians to live
in peace and friendship with us, even though
those Indians that do live together can not
get along for any length of time with each
other. I do not speak of personal quarrels,
which are always in existence, although

sometimes even they extend to families and give the chiefs much trouble to settle. An individual murder is the most frequent consequence and from it comes a new point of departure for more bloodshed if no recompense is made for it. One of the commonest causes of these quarrels is the boasting with which the warriors are accustomed to speak of their coups or warlike deeds. If one believes himself to have accomplished more honorable acts than another who may not be of the same opinion, to decide which is the better man each enumerates before witnesses what he has done, the number of horses he has stolen, the number of enemies he has killed, of scalps which he has lifted. The one whose superiority is thus established confirms it by picking up a handful of dirt or mud which he throws in the face of his humiliated rival. The latter submits without violence, but not without resentment to this lesson which, however, is not considered as an insult such as must be washed away by blood. But this is not always so; moved by hatred or urged by anger the loser in the tourney hits his adversary or cuts off the locks of hair on the forehead, which habitually descend to the eyebrows. Such an outrage calls for vengeance—unless some fine present accompanied by excuses is offered as recompense—in which case, at the price of a fine horse, for example, the matter is allowed to rest.

Pierre Gareau, the half-breed interpreter at Berthold, had a brother who perished, a victim of personal vengeance. Having quarreled with an Arikara over the relative value of their exploits, and having been declared the better man, he seized a burning stick from the fire and began beating his competitor unmercifully on the back, shoulders, etc.

The latter never moved, spoke not a word, and when the other ceased striking him, he wrapped himself in his buffalo robe and retired to his lodge, without betraying any emotion. From that day forward no one ever saw him among the other members of his tribe; but nearly every day he was seen at a distance, on the summit of some hill dominating the village, alone, crying, imploring the Great Spirit to give him vengeance, and trying to make Him propitious by fasting, vigils, and mutilations. In this way, in the ardor of his supplications, he cut off, successively, the little finger of each hand. He did not re-enter his lodge where his mother lived alone with him except in the darkness of night; then a light meal, the only one in twenty-four hours, and in the morning, before sunrise, he left, again to pursue his sacrifices on the neighboring heights. What he wanted to obtain from the Great Spirit was an opportunity to meet his enemy all alone, in such a way that he might surprise and kill him. He would not have attacked him among his relatives or accompanied by his friends, because they would have executed summary justice upon the murderer, and in that case vengeance would not be satisfied.

Thus months passed. Gareau had gone on a hunt with some Gros Ventres. They returned with a good supply of robes and meat and had camped for the night near the Bad Lands, some seven or eight miles from Fort Berthold. Gareau, more eager to get back to his people than the others, continued on the way alone in spite of the night. As he approached the village he saw a man on foot in the trail ahead of him and without knowing who it was, "Comrade," he said, "step to one side to let pass my horse, which travels faster than your legs can carry you." The Indian spoken to stepped aside without answering and as Gareau was passing him, without thinking that it might be his enemy, the latter, who had at once recognized him, pierced him with an arrow through the body, finished him with his knife, and hacking the body to bits scattered it over the prairie, taking back with him only the liver and heart for his evening meal.

On returning to his lodge he told his mother that the Great Spirit had finally been favorable, that he had killed his enemy, and he advised her to leave the village as soon as possible. For himself, he cooked the cannibal feast the same evening, and ate it with an appetite sharpened by his exultation over a vengeance long and ardently sought and finally accomplished. Before daylight he had left the village, never to return. He went out and joined a Sioux band with which he has ever since lived.

Wednesday, May 27: Yesterday evening two Rees arrived at Berthold from the other side of the river. They were bearers of a letter from Lt. Col. Otis, commander at Fort Rice, which warned me that a strong war party composed of Sioux warriors from the band of Two Kettles and of the lower Yanktonais had just left the vicinity of Fort Sully and Fort Thompson to make an attack on the Gros Ventres, Rees, and Mandans at Berthold. Warned also by a letter from Mr. Galpin, trader at Fort Rice, to Mr. Marsh, trader at Fort Berthold, our Indians have at once called in all their young men to prepare for the battle. Those who came here yesterday to get some provisions departed in haste this morning. The Gros Ventres, who should have come here today, will probably remain at the village, for their enemies must be near. This morning early many Indians were seen crossing over the heights. They are probably scouts for the hostile band. It is a matter between the Indians, for the two opposing parties are equally at peace with and friendly to the whites so that we can only let the affair go on without mixing in it.

* * *

Monday, June 1: In the middle of the night a great disturbance noisily manifested itself among the Ree women and children, who live around the fort on the scraps from the soldiers' table, which they retrieve from waste thrown out from the kitchens. They sleep in the willows at the foot of the bench where the buildings have been constructed. They also engage in fishing, either to eat themselves or to sell. So, after midnight, when all of them are ordinarily asleep, songs and weird cries rose from the willows. There were repeated goings and comings and the screeching of the women mingled with the discord of the men and the barking of the dogs. A messenger had just arrived

from Berthold announcing the victory of
the Three Tribes and the retreat of the
Sioux.

This morning at daybreak I received
more detailed news. The Sioux to the number of 50 or 60 appeared at a gallop on the
prairie and at first succeeded in cutting off
about a score of horses feeding there. The
Gros Ventres, Rees, and Mandans rushed
out after them and there followed one of
those typical Indian combats in which the
warriors on either side scatter in all directions, without any cohesion, and each according to his own inspiration. It resulted
in separate chases of two, three, or four
men, in which the riders played a game,
sometimes pursuing, sometimes pursued,
with exchanges of shots and arrows. The
Indians from Berthold retook part of their
horses, killed five or six of those of the
enemy and, the great triumph of the day,
killed one Sioux. It was a young Mandan,
mounted on an American horse, who made
the coup. Of course he scalped his adversary,
whose body his fellows were unable to carry
away in their flight. Rees, Mandans, and
Gros Ventres at once rushed to the spot and
chopped up the body—what the Canadians
call "retailing." Each one took away a piece
of it and this human debris has figured

prominently in the scalp dance and other ceremonies of the same style by which the victory has been celebrated.[35]

Here, too, we have had the proper celebration. Our scouts, on horseback and in full regalia, presented themselves in front of the post before seven in the morning and gave themselves over to songs and enthusiastic howling. In the afternoon the whole band from the willows presented themselves successively before the quarters of the officers and before the establishments of each of the traders, faces striped black and red, carrying an imitation scalp on the end of a long stick, and presenting ferocious pantomimes with dances and assorted songs, the women taking the chief roles in front of the men, who contented themselves with acting as a chorus. Since it rained heavily the performances were abridged. But what a celebration over a single scalp! Now that they have been attacked at home our Indians are going to launch a campaign to take from the Sioux more horses than they have lost and

[35] The scalp dance, though varied in form, was danced by all the Plains tribes. After the return of the Indian soldiers from the World War it was danced both at Fort Berthold and among the Sioux on the Standing Rock Reservation, presumably over German scalps brought back by some of the young men. G. F. W.

to bring back more scalps. Hence during the summer it is probable that hostilities between the redskins will be actively pursued.

One sees that nothing could be less peaceful than the state of the country at the moment when the government commissioners are about to arrive at Fort Rice to bring a reign of peace to these lands! It is hardly believable that they should succeed. The hostile Sioux will not come at their call and the others, having already submitted, will go to the rendezvous only to voice complaints and ask for favors. What is done for these will be without influence upon those whom they seek to pacify. Father De Smet, who has a great influence on all the Indians of Dakota, came in advance of the Commission. He stopped at Fort Rice to hold a conference with the chiefs located there. Then he buried himself in the Plains with a few interpreters to join, if he can, Sitting Bull and the other hostile Indians who roam the country. He has great courage and great devotion.

The mail by way of Rice left this morning escorted by ten soldiers under a sergeant, in a wagon with six mules. The way is being scouted by two scouts which, with the two couriers and the teamster, makes a force of sixteen armed men. Under such conditions the mail may brave the Sioux; there is no fear of them touching it.

Tuesday, June 2: The *Only Chance* passed here this afternoon, the second boat on its return from Benton. It advised us that the hostile Indians are moving toward Montana. It seems that in that direction some animals have been stolen and some men killed at Fort Shaw. At Fort Union, near Fort Buford, two men, of whom one was a negro, who were going without escort after a cart-load of hay, were surprised and killed by the savages. But whatever may be their hostility toward the whites, they do not practice against them the ferocious butchery which characterizes the fights between themselves. One of the employees of the Northwest Fur Company at Berthold went out the other day with the Gros Ventres to get a shot at the Sioux when they made their attack. They chased them about five or six miles, and it was there that a young Mandan, leaping from his horse, killed with one shot one of the enemy who was rushing upon him. It was a revenge for the death of several men killed last year. The victor had scarcely time to lift the scalp of the vanquished when all the other Gros Ventres, Rees, and

Mandans rushed up and, although the victim still breathed, set to work to cut him up. He literally expired under the knives with which they cut off his hands and feet, opened his belly and chest to draw out the entrails, the heart, the liver, etc., while others disarticulated his limbs. These human fragments were, as I have said, taken in triumph to the village and dragged about through the mud with cords to which the women and children hitched themselves with enthusiasm. One sees that in spite of being our friends and being loyal, the Berthold Indians have lost none of their natural ferocity and savor no less their revenge than if they had never heard the civilized whites spoken of.

* * *

Sunday, June 7: Yesterday evening some suspicious Indians made their appearance on the bluffs and in the night descended along the draws which run close to the corral. A little earlier some Rees came to the post to report that a band of Sioux, apparently of considerable size, was approaching along the higher ground. Our scouts were posted before the corral flat on their bellies in the grass, their eyes and ears alert. The employees who lodge near the corral held themselves ready, and I have given orders to have twenty men besides the guard go to bed fully dressed, their arms ready, so as to be able to get started at a moment's notice. Nevertheless, these precautions were useless. The Indians, who were heard during the night exchanging cries of encouragement, have disappeared and at daybreak there was no sign of them.

An hour later the mail for Totten was on the march. The party is composed of nine soldiers, a sergeant, a corporal, two couriers and an Indian scout. They have a wagon with six mules. With the teamster the total strength is fifteen armed men. They are in sufficient strength to inspire respect in the hostile Indians and they will not permit their passage to be barred.

They were not on the way more than three or four hours when a courier arrived from Fort Totten, the thing that we had least expected. This courier, a white man, young and alert, named Frank Palmer, had consented to risk the journey alone, and had not met a single Indian on the way. He brought me a letter from Captain Hill, who commands the post during the temporary absence of Colonel Whistler. By this means and from the information obtained directly from the courier I have learned the following facts:

On May 17 the two couriers from Totten left as usual and met McDonald and Hamlin half way. They exchanged mail and returned, without having learned anything since of the fate of the two latter.

The convoy commanded by Lieutenant Smith reached Fort Totten after them without having seen anything of their remains. The convoy had been followed by the Uncpapas, who had not dared to attack them. But at Strawberry Lake, where a teamster of the Northwest Fur Company, who had joined the convoy, had stopped behind to water his mules, the Indians, who were on the watch, descended upon the outfit, wounded the man, and got away with the two mules. All this in plain sight of the convoy. Why Lieutenant Smith suffered this insult without chastising the aggressors, without even permitting his men to fire, is something that I can not explain. The official report will perhaps furnish the key to this enigma.

On Sunday, the twenty-fourth, the two couriers sent out without escort saw some Indians, from whom they took flight and returned to Totten without daring to push on. On the same date, from our side, Brown and Martin were captured by Sitting Bull's band, as I have recounted above. Captain

306

Hill then decided to send out the mail again in a wagon under an escort of ten men. They passed the station and got as far as Dog Den. There five Indians came to meet them, exchanged hand-shakes, and told them to go no farther because their band of 17 lodges was a little farther along and would prevent them from passing. Upon this simple warning the sergeant who was in command, and who is, it seems, a great coward, consulted with the couriers and without any further attempt, retraced his steps.

Palmer was one of the couriers. Piqued at the lively chaffing of which he was the object on his return, for having given such advice and failed to attempt to force a passage, he wanted to prove that he had no fear of the Indians, and through pride offered to go out alone and carry a dispatch to Fort Stevenson without escort. This offer was accepted; he left Totten at once and got here today toward noon and had met on the way only our men and their wagon.

* * *

Monday, June 15: I am just back from an impromptu voyage to Fort Berthold. Friday evening the steamboat *War Eagle*, Captain Joseph La Barge, stopped at Fort Stevenson on its way to Fort Berthold where it was taking the annuities for the Three Tribes at that post.[36] Since it was going no farther and must return empty, there was an excellent opportunity to bring here all the grain left in the warehouses of the Northwest Company since last year. Having received instructions on this subject from General Terry, I embarked on the *War Eagle*, taking with me Lieutenant Colonel Norvell, my servant, and Marco, my dog. At the same time I sent by land three wagons and ten men to move the grain from the fort to the landing. The party was accompanied by Patinaud, the interpreter, and five Indian scouts to scout along the way. They arrived before us. Leaving about ten o'clock, we moored the boat at Berthold at three in the afternoon and my men were already at their work, as the pile of sacks of oats rising on the river bank bore witness.

[36] Captain Joseph La Barge and his brother, Captain John B. La Barge, were two of the best known pilots on the Missouri and spent almost their entire lives in its navigation. H. M. Chittenden's book, *History of Early Steamboat Navigation on the Missouri River* (New York, 1903) is practically a biography of Captain Joseph La Barge. The two brothers began their life on the river in the 1830's. Captain Joseph La Barge lived to see the end of steamboating on the river and to tell his story to Chittenden. Captain John La Barge, here mentioned, dropped dead at the wheel of his steamboat just under the Northern Pacific railroad bridge at Bismarck in 1885. G. F. W.

The chiefs, who had already received word of my coming and of the cargo which the boat was bringing for them, came at once to meet me in full dress, some of their warriors painted black as a sign of war, from the occasion of their recent victory over the Sioux. While they were discharging the cargo, which consisted of flour, crackers, pork, plows, wagons, a forge, iron, farm tools and utensils, I went to the fort to estimate approximately the quantity of oats to be loaded, and I decided very quickly that with my ten men and three six-mule wagons, it would require several days. To shorten the time as much as possible I asked for sixty women, twenty from each tribe, and I got immediately more than eighty to load and unload the wagons. Soon, noting that the work still went forward too slowly, I engaged for the next day a trader's cart. The interpreter has done more than I would have asked. He had even the sacks of oats carried by the stronger squaws. Now the weight of each sack varies from 130 to 160 pounds, and the distance from the fort to the boat was not less then 500 or 600 meters. These Indian women are so habituated to hard labor, and particularly to carrying burdens, that the task, although fatiguing, especially under a burning sun, was not apparently considered

by them as especially heavy. They walked
in single file down the hill on which the fort
is situated, following a rather steep path,
bent under the weight which was supported
by a double strap of buffalo hide, crossing
at the same time their forehead and their
shoulders. For this hard labor I had only to
furnish food for them for the duration of the
work. It lasted two full days (Saturday and
Sunday), three hours Friday afternoon, and
two hours this morning, altogether 2½
days, during which 4,039 sacks of oats were
taken out of the warehouse, loaded on the
wagons, and transported to the landing; the
donkey engine had the duty of loading them.
I distributed among the squaws three barrels of crackers and three sides of bacon
weighing 44 pounds each. Then, the work
finished, I had distributed among them 30
sacks of damaged oats, the sacks being
rotten and the grain damp. But what is no
longer fit for our horses and mules is still
good for the Indians, who cook it into oaten
cakes which they regard as a fine windfall,
so commonly does want habitually reign
among them.

* * *

Monday, July 6: The steamboat *Argonaut*
arrived this afternoon...The Captain reports
that there are at this moment from 7,000 to

8,000 Indians camped about the fort. The bluffs along the river are, he says, literally covered with lodges. What has been the result of this great assemblage and of the accompanying conferences? We do not yet know, but we soon shall.

* * *

Thursday July 16: ... The order came to me by the last mail to proceed to Fort Totten to preside at a court martial. Lt. Col. Bowman makes up a part of the court as well as Dr. Gray. The Lt. Col. will probably be here by the first boat. We shall all three leave together about the 25th or 26th, the court opening its sittings on August 3d. I shall take along besides Lt. Marshall, my adjutant, and I shall take the regimental band as escort. This will be, all things considered, a pleasant summer excursion across the plains. The people of the convoy promise us plenty of waterfowl and fish on the way. We shall see.

* * *

Saturday, July 18: ... Three Sioux of Medicine Bear's band came from Fort Rice and announced the conclusion of a general peace. They pretend that Sitting Bull came to the meeting. Red Horn, Four Horns, Gall, and Black Moon did not dare to trust themselves there in person, but had sent their people,

assuring Father De Smet, who had gone out
to find them, that they would accept the
peace as if they themselves were present,
under the conditions agreed on by the other
chiefs. As a guarantee they returned to him
horses, mules, and harness captured from
our murdered men, and in this way we have
come into possession of part of the papers
seized by Sitting Bull from the mail taken
from Brown and Martin. What the Indians
say can not always be accepted without
reserve. We shall wait to learn whether
things really are so satisfactory. The commissioners left Fort Rice eight or ten days
ago, and the crowd of Indians assembled
there has dispersed in all directions, taking
the presents, ammunition, provisions, etc.,
gifts of the Great Father at Washington.
The question now is whether the treaty of
peace will be observed by all the parties
represented, and for how long a time.

Monday, July 20: It does not appear that
the great treaty of peace with the Indians
has produced any immediate effects. Yesterday or day before two whites who were cutting wood for the steamboats were attacked;
their mules were stolen, and a Gros Ventre
who happened to be with them was wounded
by a ball in the foot. The affair occurred

opposite Fort Berthold. The aggressors are unknown but they were necessarily from among the Sioux whom the Government has just fed for more than a month at Rice, to whom it has given presents, ammunition, etc., in exchange for words of peace whose value one can appreciate by this act.

Have I mentioned already that fifteen or twenty days ago seven whites, camped to cut wood above Buford, were massacred by the savages? A steamboat which saw the scalped and mutilated bodies gave them burial.

* * *

Other news: the Indian agent at Berthold, Mr. Wilkinson, informs me that the license of Mr. F. Gerard having expired and not being renewed, he has given orders to his representative to leave with all his goods the Indian territory under his jurisdiction. This representative is Beauchamp, who finds himself much perplexed, and does not know what to do in the absence of his employer. The means are lacking for him to transport the goods here. I have advised him to prepare an inventory and to turn the keys over to Wilkinson, who can scarcely refuse to take charge of them. The other employees of Gerard will easily find employment with Mr. Anderson, who has need of additional men to hasten the delivery of the wood and hay. The cause of this severity is a report which Gerard sent at the beginning of last winter to Washington, setting forth the claims of the Rees who complained of having been robbed by Agent Wilkinson in the distribution of their annuities. The political influence of Wilkinson's friends has secured for him the renewal of his commission as Indian agent without the charges against him having been given any consideration, and now he uses his power for personal revenge against Fred Gerard by refusing to sign his new license, and ordering him, at the expiration of the old, to evacuate Berthold with all his goods. The buildings constructed by Gerard as residence and warehouses would be without doubt very convenient for him to use for his personnel and part of the materials of his agency. The expulsion from Berthold extends to all the white employees and residents except those who are in the pay of the Agency or of the Fur Company of Durfee and Peck. It is a monopoly of two which, by removing all surveillance, delivers the Indians and their interests, without possible recourse, to the good pleasure of Mr. Wilkinson and Mr. Marsh, the trader. I believe that it is not very difficult to foresee the conclusion, or

314

rather what the immediate consequences
will be. What may be divined of the result-
ing consequences among the Indians is a
serious enough matter. And it is thus that
all the efforts and expenditures of the Government and its commissioners are continually compromised by political meddling
and particularly speculation in the Indian
Bureau. The power given to the agents to
keep or expel whosoever seems good to them
is too great and must give rise to the most
serious abuses, when its exercise is not surrounded by guarantees of justice.

It is the day for happenings; the stock
had scarcely arrived with its escort of a
mounted company, under the command of
Captain Stanley (a brave officer who lost
his left arm at Cold Harbor) when 300
lodges of Indians from Rice appeared on the
horizon. These 300 lodges comprise 1200
or 1500 persons, being parts of seven bands
whose chiefs are Medicine Bear, Black Eyes,
My Red Horse, Ouanata (meaning unknown), All Black, Carrying Buffalo, and
Crying Buffalo. With them is the son of
Black Catfish who died last winter. His
name is Bear's Nose. All these people come
from Rice and are going after buffalo which,
it is reported, are coming down from the
Yellowstone.

Camp pitched, the chiefs, followed by 200 or 300 of their people, came to see me—needless to say for what purpose. Among the Indians it is always a matter of getting some provisions. But it is impossible to get them to ask for something to eat except in the form of a peroration to a discourse running always in the same pattern, and of which I would not know how to present here a new specimen without repetition. I was obliged therefore to receive the seven chiefs and to endure their eloquence. Four among them had not yet made my acquaintance, a particular reason for employing their oratorical talents. There was nothing lacking in the presentation. The only relief I have found in the affair has been the examination of the original of a treaty of peace concluded with the Indians in 1820 on the Three Rivers at the Sioux Crossing, which was then in the open desert and which is today so far back in the States that even the interpreters knew nothing about its location. This treaty, signed by a score of officers and twenty-seven chiefs or important Indians, contains nothing which has been carried out on either one side or the other; but those who signed it have long been dead and will not return to make complaint. This document was given me to read by Crying

Buffalo, whose grandfather was one of the principal signers.[37]

In conclusion I had distributed twenty-two boxes of crackers, three for each band and one to divide among the seven chiefs who besides received each a pound of coffee, two pounds of sugar and a piece of salt pork.

* * *

Sunday, July 26: . . . Lieutenant Colonel Bowman has not yet appeared; he should be here today. I shall wait for him no longer before going to Fort Totten, where I must preside over a court martial of which Dr. Gray is also a member.

JOURNEY TO FORT TOTTEN
(DEVILS LAKE)

Tuesday, July 28: Lieutenant Colonel Bowman has arrived from Fort Buford in a small boat which the first steamboat going up-river will return there with the men who made up the crew. This was yesterday; and having no one else to wait for, we set out

[37]Apparently this was the treaty negotiated by General Henry Atkinson and Indian Agent Benjamin O'Fallon, June 22, 1825, and printed in *U. S. Stats. at Large*, VII, 250–52. Its principal purpose was to take the several Sioux bands who signed it under the protection of the United States, and to provide for the conduct of future relations with them. Fort Lookout was a post of the

today in the afternoon to avoid the heat of the middle of the day. The little expedition consists of four officers: myself, Lieutenant Colonel Bowman, the Surgeon Major, Dr. Gray, and Lieutenant J. Marshall. The latter is not a member of the court martial, but I am taking him in the capacity of Acting Assistant Adjutant General of the District, of which the Headquarters is moved with me to Fort Totten during the time I shall stay here. The chief clerk of the office accompanies us for the same reason. Three servants and a cook complete the personnel except for five teamsters and the regimental band (19 men) which form the escort and are on duty en route. In all, 33 persons, in an ambulance, a wagonette, and three wagons. In such numbers, and armed as we are, the hostile Indians, if they meet us, will respectfully let us pass.

Columbia Fur Company, built in 1822. It stood on the west bank of the Missouri near the junction of the southern boundary of the Lower Brulé reservation with the river. The three Rivers of the Sioux Pass enter the Missouri from the east in Buffalo County, South Dakota; their present-day names are Wall, Campbell, and Soldier creeks. Fort Lookout was a few miles up-river from present-day Chamberlain. A new Fort Lookout was erected by General Nathaniel Lyon in 1856, but soon gave place to Fort Randall. See Doane Robinson, *Encyclopaedia of South Dakota*. M. M. Q.

I have no intention of hurrying. Water-fowl are very abundant along the way at this season of the year; the court does not open its sittings until Monday, August 3d, and we have therefore time enough to make this journey a pleasure excursion.

* * *

Saturday, August 1: ... Toward noon we reached the end of Devils Lake, whose blue waters had already been in sight for some time. From this point it extends to the north as far as the eye can see, bordered along its edges by prairie. Trees cover a few islands and peninsulas along the side which the trail follows. There, too, the banks are shaded by oaks. Soon we left the edge of the lake to make a short cut in the direction of Fort Totten, where we arrived about one o'clock, happy to be at last at our destination and to have finished with that long drive through the monotonous uniformity of the vast prairies.

Fort Totten does not present exactly an enchanting aspect despite the fact that the lake serves it as a setting. It is a long parallelogram formed by a palisade; at one end are the guard house, the prison, the saddlery, and the lodgings of the mule drivers; along the sides are the stables, the company barracks, the hospital, the warehouses and the offices, and opposite the entrance at the back of the parallelogram the officers' quarters. These last are arranged very much the same as at Stevenson; two lodgings to a house, separated by a common corridor. At Stevenson each lodging has its own corridor and is entirely separated from the other by a thick partition. The corral for the cattle is on the side opposite that by which one enters, at the foot of the elevated plateau where the fort is situated and at the edge of the water. All the buildings are uniformly log houses, that is to say built of tree trunks and mud, which is not a particularly pleasing sight. Altogether, seen at a distance, Fort Totten resembles a set of vast stables. When one arrives there the impression changes because of the lake and its borders shaded by trees which dominate the view. Again, to see the lake and trees well it is necessary to get outside the palisade which surrounds you on all sides. This precaution of the palisade, which we have always disdained at Fort Stevenson, does not seem to me necessary. It gives to the post the disagreeable air of a prison. Living on the open prairie without barriers of any kind, I felt as if I were constricted and breathe less easily though the fort is twice the size of Stevenson.

Tuesday, August 4: The Court Martial opened its session today.

* * *

Sunday, August 9: A courier from Stevenson informs me that the hostile Indians attacked my cattle the day after my departure, but they were repulsed and quickly chased away without driving off a single animal. The Rees conducted themselves well. Lieutenant Cusick, who came with fifty men to get the 210 head intended for Buford, also had a skirmish with the Indians, a skirmish without any other results. The treaty of peace with the redskins has apparently produced no great effect.

* * *

Thursday, August 13: The provision train has come back from Fort Stevenson. The first division arrived yesterday, the second today. Lieutenant Leonard also arrived this afternoon, coming from Fort Stevenson. He is called as a witness. Last Sunday as the steamboat *Lina Leotti*, on which Lieutenant Leonard was a passenger, stopped at Fort Berthold, forty Sioux appeared suddenly on the opposite bank and fired several volleys at the boat. No one was hit except a Mandan who was on the bank. The passengers, who were armed with rifles, replied in lively fashion. The Indians of Berthold did the same and the assailants retired precipitately into the draws where they disappeared. No doubt that the firearms employed by the Sioux are a part of those which the Peace Commission so benevolently distributed among them. The effects of the absurd policies of the government develop more and more. Hostilities have been revived among the Sioux, who are supposed to have been disarmed by a generosity which they very naturally take for fear. They have accepted everything that one wished to give them, and they make use of the gifts in making war with greater confidence and energy. The only way to bring the thing to an end is, before all else, to chastise them thoroughly. From the moment when they become convinced that we are the stronger, they will keep quiet. Until then, no.

Monday, August 24: The mail which left for Stevenson today was attacked by Indians about noon at the Grand Coulee. The men had unharnessed the mules from the wagon and with that blind imprudence which characterizes the soldier when left to himself, when the danger is not most apparent, they had left their arms in the vehicle. The sergeant had placed no sentry, thus disobeying orders received. This disobedience cost him his life as well as the lives of two of his men. Six Indians, ambushed near there, seeing the negligence of our men in guarding themselves, waited till they were all seated on the ground eating their dinner, to approach, crouching, up to the back of a rock situated at only a score of paces. From there they fired all together at the group, and, as I have just said, they killed three men, the sergeant among them.

The three others ran for their arms, but it was too late. They could only shoot at their assailants from a distance, the latter having fled, profiting by the irregularities in the terrain, with the mules which had been stampeded. Palmer, one of the couriers, arrived last night bringing the fateful news. Immediately Colonel Whistler sent Captain Hill with thirty men in three wagons to bring back the wagon with the mail if it had not been destroyed, as well as the soldiers who escaped the attack. But the latter arrived in their turn in the evening. They had left intact on the spot the wagon, the mail, and the bodies of their three comrades, whose arms they hid so as not to fall into the hands of the Indians if they should return, which is probable.

Tuesday, August 25: Captain Hill returned this morning, bringing the three bodies which had not been mutilated by the savages. The latter were content to appropriate whatever they found in the wagon that suited their taste. They left there the letters, official correspondence, and papers which were all brought back today and with which we shall charge ourselves on returning to Fort Stevenson. A part of our detachment has gone on ahead with the mail for Stevenson which they are taking along. Taught by what has occurred, our men will be on the alert and will so guard themselves as to leave the Indians no chance to repeat.

The session of the general court martial, of which I was the president, has closed. So without losing any time I have decided to leave tomorrow for my general quarters.

* * *

Wednesday, August 26: . . . And here am I on the way back to Fort Stevenson. I feel the pleasure of the traveller who is going back home. The sojourn at Fort Totten, in spite of the hunting, the fishing, the lake, and the woods, has not inspired in me any regret that Headquarters for the district are not transferred there. Taking everything into consideration I prefer Stevenson. The passage of the steamboats, the new figures which one sees on them from time to time, the reports which they make to us from Montana or from the States, produce there a spirit which does not exist at Fort Totten. One feels attached to civilized life through those who go and come. It is like a thread which for six months ties us to Sioux City, Omaha, St. Louis and through them to the rest of the world.

On Saturday (August 29) we arrived. Having left July 28, we have therefore been gone a month. Nothing extraordinary has distinguished our return trip except that, at a short distance from Fort Totten, we met the mail from Stevenson for which Captain Hill had sent a dozen men and a wagon.

The sack was opened to extract the dispatches which might be found there addressed to me. The most important had been placed in the care of the sergeant who carried it upon his person and presented himself to give it to me, saying that it had been brought from Buford by two Indian messengers with instructions to get it to me without delay. It was marked "Important" and the contents justified this inscription. It was a summary report of an attack by hostile Indians and the carrying away of nearly all of the herd of cattle sent for the purpose of providing fresh meat to the garrison during the coming winter and spring, and at the same time a requisition for another herd of 200 steers to be sent in haste before

325

the cold weather. I at once signed and approved the requisition and returned it to the sergeant to be expedited the next morning to the quartermaster of the department.

Now here are the facts in substance, as contained in a second and detailed report which arrived here by steamboat.

On August 20 about three in the afternoon two or three hundred Indians, divided into two bands, burst suddenly from the ravines in the neighborhood of Buford, in the bad lands, near which the herd was that day feeding. The guards on horseback hurried at the first sign of attack to push the animals toward the fort; but they were soon compelled to turn and face the band of redskins who had come up with them. There were only twenty men against 100 or 150; still they would have been able to hold out against their assailants long enough to save the cattle, if the second band which they had not yet perceived had not made its eruption between the cattle and the fort. These last comers uttering furious whoops, shaking their buffalo robes, shooting in front of their noses, threw the cattle into disorder and panic and they returned pell mell upon the drivers through whom they tore, crazy with terror, pursued by the redskins. The

326

two bands then united to envelop the twenty guards, while others urged the steers along into the defiles of the Bad Lands. Our men fought bravely and at close quarters for several were hit by skull crackers, among them Lieutenant Cusick, officer of the day, who had rushed out at the first alarm. But all they could do was to fall back, fighting a passage through the Indians, upon the infantry who had turned out to the rescue.

At Fort Buford as at Fort Stevenson they are in the midst of building. All the men were at work. They ran at once to arms and rushed toward the assailants, but the latter were all mounted and they could not overtake them. They had, therefore, to confine themselves to recovering all they could of the steers who had separated from the herd. Part of the cattle were more or less seriously wounded, others had been killed by the Indians, who shot the stragglers with arrows.

Major Dickey, commanding the post in the absence of Lieutenant Colonel Bowman, immediately mounted all the men he could on the horses which he had collected and the pursuit continued for a matter of several miles, skirmishing on the way. It was all useless. They were able to save only some 40 beasts out of 240 or 250 which the herd totalled.

The next day Brevet Major Little was
sent with two companies to try and gather
up such remnants as might remain along
the route. He found only a number of car-
casses. The herd had been taken in the evening of the previous day or early in the
morning to the other side of the Missouri.
Besides the loss of 200 steers this affair has
cost three men killed and three grievously
wounded. Lieutenant Cusick came out of
it very fortunately.

It is told that he owes his life to one of
his men who ran to help him as he was engaged at close quarters with the redskins
and who was killed as a result of this act of
devotion.

Although the first dispatch received en
route did not contain all these details, the
known result was not of a nature to cheer
our return. It was a day of evil omen. Toward noon (August 26) or one o'clock we
arrived at the Grand Coulee where the three
men from Totten had been killed three days
before. My first care was to alight and examine the terrain. The place of the murder
was clearly indicated by three spots of blood
where the victims had been struck and
whence the bodies had been retrieved by
Captain Hill. It was on a little jutting plateau surrounded on nearly all sides by a

ravine. The six Indians had slipped up the slope and had crawled up to a large rock whence they had fired at 20 paces upon the group of soldiers nonchalantly eating their dinner, seated on the ground near the un-hitched wagon. Not one of them had his gun. The arms were left in the wagon. One of the couriers who was going to water his horse at a nearby spring, taking his gun with him, had been, in fact, made an object of joking by the soldiers. Was he then afraid that Indians might come and attack him? He was a very cautious man, etc. And five minutes had barely passed when three of the jokers were struck by shots from Indian guns. They perished victims of their own complete negligence in guarding themselves and of their disobedience to the orders re-ceived. If the sergeant had only placed a single sentinel at the edge of the plateau not a single Indian could have approached with-out being seen, for the ravine is as bare as the hand, without a bush or a rabbit hole even. But the Indians, posted somewhere in the vicinity, promptly recognizing that our men were without their arms and had no idea of watching around them, conceived the idea of surprising them, and that in full day, on the open plain, and though only six of them against eight. It is probable they had planned that if they were discovered they would advance as friends, exchange handshakes, and beg some bribes of provisions. But everything succeeded as they wished, they made their coup, and fled driving the mules, frightened at the discharge of the guns.

* * *

Friday, September 4: ... This morning seven Sioux, believing themselves sufficiently protected by the river, came to the bank opposite Berthold, more through bravado than anything else, and fired some shots at those of our Indians who were on the bank on this side. Immediately the warriors of the Gros Ventres, Rees, and Mandans ran for their horses and crossing in bullboats over the Missouri, gave chase to the imprudent seven. They caught up with one of them across from the Bad Lands and according to their custom killed, scalped, and mutilated him. The steamboat *North Alabama* passed Berthold at the moment when they were returning in triumph, bearing the scalp and the hands of the victim. It is in that way that we had the first details of the affair. There will be dances and rejoicing at Berthold for a week. An odd fact is that the one who killed the Sioux is the same young Mandan who killed the other one at the beginning of the summer. There is a young fellow who will become a chief if his career is not arrested.

Tuesday, September 8: The steamboat *Andrew Ackley* brings us news that the Indians have attacked five men established below Buford to cut wood for the steamboats. The captain having stopped near there to make some repairs, heard the fusillade and sent his yawl with a dozen armed men to the aid of the wood choppers. Two of the latter were already seriously wounded, no longer with arrows, but with balls and buckshot. The steamboat took them all to Buford where the two wounded are in the hands of the surgeon. I have prepared a long report to General Terry and to Lieutenant General Sherman on the hostilities of which my district is the theater and in which I do not mince the verities as to the evil effects of the policy adopted by the Government and the deplorable consequences of the distribution of arms and ammunition among the Indians, especially after the weakness which has been shown in abandoning, in the face of their threats of open hostilities the three posts built at great expense in the valley of Powder River. Will this report have any effect? I do not know. In any case I shall have done my duty in pointing out the evil, even if the high authorities supply no remedy.

Thursday, September 10: A band of Indians, evidently friendly, since they had with them their lodges and families, appeared this morning on the hills some distance from the fort. Soon a number approached on foot with the apparent intention of coming to the post. They were promptly met by Lieutenant Leonard, officer of the day, who, accompanied by the interpreter, went out to find out who they were. A few soldiers without arms, a part of the provision train, the first section of which arrived yesterday, went with them and so found themselves among the Indians, who were not expecting this visit. There the men from Totten were quick to recognize several redskins who were in the band which, at the beginning of the summer, tried by a sudden attack to run off the mules at Devils Lake. One especially, White Faced Bear, was positively recognized by one of the soldiers. More, they had with them three beeves which must necessarily have come from the herd stolen at Fort Buford, whence the band had come, and two mules branded U. S., property of the United States Government. The officer of the day took from one Indian a Sharp's rifle which he pre-

tended to have bought from Galpin, the
trader at Fort Rice. But when he wanted to
take the mules he met lively opposition, and
the friendly Indians began to load their
guns; since the officer of the day was alone
with three or four unarmed men and since
the Indians promised, as soon as their camp
was pitched, themselves to bring the animals and explain to me how they came into
possession of them, he left them and came
back to make his report. Hardly was his
back turned when the Indians, instead of
making camp as they had announced, left
in all haste and disappeared with their booty.
And now would you like to know what band
it is in which are found men who took part
in hostilities against our posts, and stole our
horses and cattle? It is the band of Black
Eyes, those friendly Yanktonais who dwell
at Rice where the Government feeds them,
clothes them, and arms them. Black Eyes
himself was with them, Black Eyes, that
inveterate beggar among beggars, an Indian
who goes from post to post with his hand
out, and protests his devotion to the whites
to obtain provisions. It was his fourth visit
to Fort Stevenson; but this one was of short
duration and brought him little, as has been
seen. If he comes again I shall make him
disgusted for good with these visits of self

interest. While waiting, I am going to denounce him in a new report to the district headquarters. We shall see what comes of it, and whether Lieutenant General Sherman, now named Superintendent of Indian Affairs, will authorize me to chastise these impudent vagabonds who come and parade around our post the animals stolen at other posts under my command.

P. S. The Sharp's rifle seized in the hands of a Yanktonais Indian and deposited with me has been recognized as the same one that Sitting Bull's band had taken from Joe Martin, one of our couriers, when with Brown he was captured near Dog Den at the end of last May. Joe Martin recognized it at first glance and showed me a double letter scratched with a knife on the butt, a mark which makes any error impossible. Another proof of the connivance which exists between most of the friendly Indians and the Indians who are declared enemies. Supposing, on the other hand, that the man might have told the truth (which is hardly probable) and that he had bought this arm of Galpin, it would be interesting to make an inquiry into what sort of commerce it is through which, at Fort Rice, a government arm stolen by hostile Indians, was sold to a friendly Indian, by a trader employed by the Government.

Monday, September 28: . . . By the *Bertha* I have just had a report from Major Dickey who informs me that on the 18th four soldiers, who were hunting near the fort at about a kilometer from what is left of the herd of cattle, were attacked in a surprise by a dozen Indians. One of them was mortally wounded and the others would probably likewise have lost their lives if the guards with the steers, who were mounted, had not rushed to their aid. The Indians were pursued, but uselessly. They crossed the river in haste and left nothing but one of their bullboats in the hands of their pursuers.

* * *

Monday, October 5: Today I took possession of my new house. At last! I am sleeping there for the first time tonight. It is a great change, leaving that dark cave where I have spent more than nine months between walls made of logs and mud, under a low roof, squat, of sods of earth where the mice have set up their domicile, where they have multiplied rapidly, and where they dance their witches' dance each night, running over the old pieces of canvas which take the place of a ceiling.[38] From that

[38] The play of the field mice is not at all exaggerated. It is unlikely that the common mouse was at the post so soon after its inception. The field mice will play by

dreary and sordid lodging, behold I am moved to one at least comfortable and presentable. My house is composed of five rooms. It is divided into two parts by a hall; on the right the parlor, the dining room, and the kitchen; at the left two bed rooms. Upstairs the rooms of the servants and the loft serving for a store room. The walls are painted with oil paint as is the woodwork, but with different colors of course; the woodwork is white, like the ceilings; the walls in the parlor are chestnut brown, in the bedroom lilac gray; in the dining room reddish grey. My furniture is quite sufficient. In brief, here I am conveniently and agreeably installed for the winter; it is a grand thing.

* * *

Saturday, October 31: The second half of the month has slipped by without incident. The hostile Uncpapas came, as they had announced, to trade with our Indians at Berthold. They brought their women and their lodges, which guaranteed pacific intentions on their part, made their camp on the other side of the Missouri, and for several days the going and coming from one

the hour on the roof of a tent, climbing up and sliding down the sloping roof time after time. They will also deposit in shoes pebbles, prune stones, and various treasures which they may gather in the night. G. F. W.

bank of the river to the other in bullboats has been very active. The Three Tribes have acquired fifty horses in exchange for corn, after which they separated and the Uncpapas took their way toward the Little Missouri.

I have explained before that these truces are customary between the savages when it is to the interest of both parties to trade peacefully at a given rendezvous. They smoke the pipe of peace; they exchange handclasps and benevolent speeches. Then, as soon as they have separated, they kill and scalp when they meet as if nothing to the contrary had ever happened.

It would have been a fine occasion to strike a heavy blow and to chastise in exemplary fashion the Uncpapas for their misdeeds; so much the more since the famous Sitting Bull, the Man Who Jumps into the Fight, Red Horn, and several other chiefs were of the party. But for that there must have been at our disposal 150 or 200 men. We might have crossed the river at Stevenson, marched at night, and at daybreak surrounded the Indian camp and then swept the tables. Unfortunately the whole first company was on the way to Buford, 45 men from Co. F had been discharged from service, and nearly all the rest were actively engaged at the work which must positively be completed before winter, which gives us no time to lose. Besides, in the absence of exact orders, it is without doubt better at this time not to put our hands into the business further than the Government is prepared to back us up. The war which is actively pursued against the Indians in Kansas and Arkansas, the Cheyennes, Arapahoes, Kiowas, Comanches, etc.; the expedition directed against them by Sheridan, and the mobile columns sent to protect the sutlers, all this absorbs the military forces which might have been at the disposition of the Missouri division, and there remains nothing but our feeble garrisons in Dakota in case of a mass rising of the Sioux. Let us then have patience; everything in its own time. Encouraged by the security which they have enjoyed this time, the hostile Indians will come again next year, in circumstances from which we shall be able to profit. For further information, the peaceful visit of the Uncpapas to Berthold has not been without some results. It enabled us to learn that the three soldiers killed at Grand Coulee on August 24 were assassinated by six so-called friendly Indians from Fort Rice, three Black Feet Sioux, and three Yanktonais, and that the attack and theft of the cattle at Fort

Buford was the work of the Tetons and different wandering bands united for that purpose.

* * *

Tuesday, November 3: Colonel Wright, the paymaster, has lost no time. Although the season is still fine and we have been greatly enjoying for about three weeks St. Martin's summer, he fears a change in the weather and an early opening of winter. With this fear at his heels, a fear not without justice, he has paid everyone during the day and is already on his way back to Rice and thence to Sully, Randall, Dakota, Sioux City, and Omaha, paying the troops at each of these posts on his way. His departure was signalized by an occurrence of which I do not yet know what the consequences may be, and of which, therefore, I shall put over the recital until tomorrow.

The event to which I alluded yesterday was an immense fire in the prairies, which the wind drove toward us and which we watched with disquietude as it approached. It was first heralded in the afternoon by a mass of smoke which, floating in the air, formed an enormous yellow-colored cloud which the wind pushed from the northwest. The wind increased from moment to moment and it was very difficult to determine just how far away the fire was. One thing, nevertheless, was very evident; whatever the distance might be that separated us, the extent of the conflagration was very great. Indeed, on the horizon, beyond the bluffs, whenever a gust of wind raised or tore the vast curtain of smoke which commenced to obscure the sun, one saw distinctly twisting columns rise, white, red, brown, in a long line, under the feet of the wind. Thus the matter stood at sunset when the paymaster and his escort, commanded by Brevet Major Nelson of the Twenty-Second Infantry, started out. He was returning to Fort Rice, which is to say in a direction opposite to that whence the fire was coming, and he counted on a start of two or three hours to get to the other side of Snake Creek and there make camp in such a way as to be entirely protected by the course of the creek. But he was scarcely gone when the first tongues of flame appeared along the summit of the bluffs. Almost immediately, with a rapidity of which no one could have any idea without having seen fire driven across the prairies by a high wind, the flames ran over the crest of the ridge and all the line of the hills was crowned with a splendid illumination, so much more splendid since night had already fallen. The flaming line

reached Snake Creek much more rapidly
than any harnessed horse could reach there,
so that we began to feel serious disquietude
for the paymaster and his escort, which we
expected to see return at full speed every
minute. When the flames had descended
the hills, and, crossing the prairie, gained
the bank of the Missouri east of Fort Stevenson without the detachment having appeared, the impossibility of retracing their
steps was far from reassuring to us, and we
understood that their only chance was in
gaining with all speed the mouth of the little
creek, there, if they have time enough, casting themselves on the sands which in that
direction border in places the edges of the
Missouri River. Our own preoccupations,
however, quickly changed their direction,
for we soon had enough to think about on our
own account.

The first flames which appeared on the
bluffs were seen directly to the north at
about a mile from the fort. Since the wind
blew toward the east-southeast they did not
come down into our pasture lands, and while
their advance guard devoured everything
in the direction of Snake Creek the rear
guard was extinguished for want of material
upon which to feed, and the center descended
the hills on a slant in the direction of the

wind about two miles away. The fort then was safe, but what inspired in us even greater disquietude, the four enormous stacks of hay containing 300 tons, the corral and the stables, and the sawmill for fire wood, all of this was nearer to the fire (by 200 to 300 meters) than our buildings.

And then just at the hour when we thought ourselves to be done with the fire after a not very dangerous alarm, a new conflagration appeared with the wind with a great red glow whose flame and heat grew and intensified more and more from minute to minute. Everyone had their eyes fixed on this new enemy, which advanced no less rapidly than the first. But the general opinion was that this second fire, or rather this second column of fire, would stop of itself at the edge of the terrain already burnt over, and where there remained not a spear of grass to burn. This calculation appeared doubtful to me, for the fire this time was travelling straight toward us; it could come to the crest of the hills on this side of the burned area, descend onto the flat and then—. At any rate I gave the necessary orders so that everyone would be prepared to rush out at the first notice. All the men were held in their quarters, although it was not yet the hour for tattoo, and all the officers held themselves ready. It was well that I was moved to take these precautions.

A quarter of an hour had scarcely passed before the fire was running down the hills like a torrent of lava from a row of craters. It engulfed the pasturage and on one side rushed crackling toward the traders' buildings, on the other toward our hay stacks.

My servant was the first to warn me. I ran out at once and a glance sufficed to show me clearly the extent of the danger. I rushed onto the parade ground and in my loudest voice called, "Outside everyone!" The officer of the day, who came out of the guard house, ran immediately to his company quarters. I ran to the other barracks, and roughly opening the door, repeated my command to the men, who, grouped, talking, about the stoves, had not at first heard. All of the officers came from their quarters at this moment; the sergeants formed the men into squads. They ran first to a pile of dogwood which I had had cut below the fort by the prisoners, at the first appearance of the fire, and which they had piled up near the guard house. Each man took an armful with which to beat the fire. Those who did not have them, armed themselves with whatever they could find, old sacks, old brooms, switches, etc., and upon my order they ran toward the fire to fight it as far away as possible. Naturally, the men divided into two groups to meet the enemy at the two points of advance. I led one band myself to the point where the fire was most threatening to the stacks. The other band, with the greater part of the officers, ran in the direction where the danger was greatest to the traders' buildings, their wood, and forage. You may believe that the 60 or 80 men who worked under my eyes and personal direction did not spare themselves in their efforts; but it is a difficult task to extinguish dry grass on fire when a strong wind is blowing. Each one whipped the flames, tramped on the burning cinders, scratched at the burning grass, using the long dogwood sticks like brooms, or attacked it with empty sacks, but in vain. The fire, beaten out at one point, burst out at once in another place. When the wind dropped for a moment or veered a little in a way to throw the flames back among the cinders, the whole line went out at the same time; the plague was for a moment mastered. But then came a fresh gust which rolled the flames toward us, and blinded, suffocated, burned, we were put to rout, to return to the charge as soon as we had inhaled a few lungsful of air, especially when the fire got to the places where

344

the grass was the thinnest from having been tramped over or eaten off by the cattle. In spite of all our efforts the fire gained on us more and more and forced us back. We had retreated for a hundred meters or more. Wishing to give an example to the men, I had breathed the fiery and suffocating smoke till for a moment I nearly fainted, to the point of seeing everything as red and even of not seeing at all. What could we accomplish in this kind of a struggle? We came to a trail made by the wagons hauling stones from the hills for the masonry of the fort. I saw that it was our best chance and, calling to me all the men who were fighting the fire on that side, I placed them along the line of the trail to which the advance of the flames came diagonally. This first line fought the fire so that it stopped at the edge of the trail and a second line stationed behind put out all the little embers and sparks which, whipped by the wind, would have unfailingly relighted the fire on the other side in the dry grass. Once the head was beaten we advanced again and, the terrain there being in a more favorable condition, we finally stopped and put out all the fire on this side.

What we did on this side the other detachment did on the traders' side, but since the grass was more beaten down and scattered on their side, their task was less arduous. In spite of everything, they were only able to stop the fire at the cemetery, at 200 meters from the first building, and farther on the fire, crossing two beaten trails, did not stop except at the edge of the slope below which are the dogwood thickets. There it went out, and what had been our danger became our protection. In fact the fort henceforth was completely surrounded on three sides by a wide zone of ashes and burnt-over ground. The fourth side being formed by the Missouri and its sand banks, the fire might for the future go wherever it would in the prairie. From whatever direction the wind might blow it could not approach us any longer and must perforce die at the edge of this black sea of charred earth, in the midst of which Fort Stevenson and the land surrounding it for a radius of several hundred meters rises like an island. Our isolation becomes henceforth our security. I stayed till the last with a few men to extinguish the little fires which still smoldered for an hour or two under the ashes, in the roots or tufts of grass, or in the dried manure. At the hour of tattoo (8 o'clock) everything had returned to its usual calm. Everyone could go to bed without worry in full security.

The paymaster and his escort were also safe on the other side of the mouth of Snake Creek, on the sands of the river. Two Indians sent out in search of them reported to us this satisfactory news.

* * *

Wednesday, November 11: The cold continues. Very soon the soldiers will cease escorting the mail wagon which our couriers will transport with teams of dogs on the small sledges for that purpose. So I have sent today a detachment of four wagons and a dozen men to build three cabins for stations, the first at Sulphur Spring Lake, the second at Strawberry Lake, and the third at Stony Creek. At the same time I am sending orders to Colonel Whistler to send from his direction another detachment to build a cabin at the halfway station and at other intermediate points between there and Totten. The men are hauling all the necessary materials; the cabins are to be built of slabs under the direction of Brown. The river is running full of ice. It will not be long in freezing if the cold continues.

* * *

Monday, November 16: The cold took hold again yesterday more than ever; the river, almost free of ice, begins to cover over again. Brown and his men have returned after having built their three shelters. They saw not a single Indian. The season has come now when we are rid of them till spring.

* * *

Monday, November 23: Lieutenant Walborn died this morning after a sickness of several days. We shall bury him tomorrow with military honors. He leaves here a young widow and two very young boys. At this season of the year the poor woman can not return to her family. She will have to remain here all winter near the temporary grave of her husband whose body, I believe, she intends to take with her when the first boat returning from Fort Benton shall offer her a means of transport. In any case that can not be before the month of June.

A report from Berthold announces that three Gros Ventres have been killed by the Sioux on the other side of the river. The Sioux in small numbers have appeared on the bluffs opposite the fort, disguised as buffalo, that is to say lying flat on the necks of their horses wrapped in buffalo robes, which at a distance presents and can be mistaken for a silhouette of that animal. Our three Gros Ventres fell into the trap and, going out to hunt the pretended animals, did not return. Nevertheless, since their bodies have not been found the tale demands confirmation and their death is not yet proven.

Wednesday, November 25: White Shield, the Arikara chief, having come to Berthold from his winter quarters to get a supply of corn, pushed on here to make me a call of condolence on account of the death of Lieutenant Walborn, whom we buried yesterday. He made a brief discourse on this subject which was not lacking in character, recalling that Lieutenant Walborn had been the chief of the Indian scouts, and that the chief's Ree children had been commanded by him.

The chief called at my house, into which he had not entered before since it was finished. In spite of the habitual Indian reserve he was not able to conceal his astonishment or his admiration for what the whites were able to do in this direction. He advised me that the three Gros Ventres represented as dead are instead in very good health. Not finding any game they continued their excursion farther than they had intended, and in consequence were a longer time absent; but in fact they had not met any enemy. The only verified fact is that twelve horses were stolen from the Rees during the night. This theft could only have been committed by a party of Sioux; hence the prompt supposition that the three Gros Ventres were dead. White Shield went off with a little present of sugar and coffee, as usual. This prospect was perhaps at least as much in the idea of his visit as the death of Lieutenant Walborn. Savage and civilized resemble each other on more than one point.

* * *

JOURNAL FOR 1869

Sunday, February 7: The special courier who brought the last dispatches from Fort Buford is called Kelly. He is a very young man, a tall, vigorous, fine lad, with a very intelligent and intrepid air. There is in his life a mysterious story the details of which are unknown but of which something has been noised over the plains. What is known is that Kelly, Irish and Catholic, was intended for the priesthood. On completing school he entered a seminary with that end in view; there he either wholly or in part completed the course. It is a fact that his education, which includes Latin, is indeed high in contrast with what the pioneers of civilization on the Upper Missouri possess in that line. They claim, I do not know on what grounds, that he at that time fell headlong in love with a young girl who, because of her own position or through reverence for or antipathy toward the robe of the seminarian, did not accept his love. The story always is that Kelly threw aside the frock and, like many another wounded and despairing heart, shook the dust of civilization from his shoes and plunged into the deserts of the West in search of adventure and danger. He found both. He has already been famous for some time for the careless intrepidity with which, alone and without bravado, he travels over the plains with his rifle and revolver without a thought for hostile Indians, appearing one day at Fort Berthold, another at Fort Buford, and again at Fort Benton, stopping here and there according to his fancy, and leaving without warning, as he has arrived, when he considers that he has rested long enough. Surely it would have been a pity had all this adventurous energy been lost under the priest's frock.[39]

[39] The "very young man"—he was nineteen at this time—was Luther S. Kelly, better known as Yellowstone Kelly. While still under sixteen he had left the Academy at Lima, N. Y., to enlist in the regular army, and at the close of the Civil War was sent to the Upper Missouri, where his term of enlistment expired in 1868. He became one of the most successful men of his type in the history of the American Border, in 1876, when still in his twenties, becoming General Miles' chief of scouts. In comparison with his career the much-vaunted

Army Life in Dakota

Having brought the dispatches from Buford and having rested several days here, where I kept him to await the arrival of the mail from the east, he left Wednesday afternoon, his horse and arms in good condition.

Yesterday morning an Indian from Fort Berthold brought the news here that Kelly had killed two Sioux near the Grand Detour (a point on the Missouri), that some Mandans who happened to be in the vicinity had taken the scalps and cut up the bodies, and that they were going to have a grand scalp dance in the village. The reports of the Indians are to be taken with much caution so I preserved sufficiently strong doubts as to the correctness of this tale when this afternoon the return of Kelly served to confirm it and complete the details. Here is what happened to him; I give his own words:

"Near the Grand Detour about forty miles on the other side of Berthold the trail follows a sort of narrow passage between the foot of the bluff on one side and on the other

exploits of such a character as Billy the Kid pale to insignificance. Kelly's own personal narrative, edited by the present writer, was published by the Yale University Press in 1926. Of his interview with Colonel De Trobriand he merely records that he was "a portly man with a pleasant face." The story of Kelly's supposed study for the priesthood and his blighted romance finds no support in his own narrative. M. M. Q.

the strip of willow thicket on the edge of the
river. I had reached there when in turning
an elbow in the trail I found myself unex-
pectedly face to face with two Indians coming toward me and from whom I was
scarcely distant more than forty yards. On
seeing me they reined in their horses sharply
and leaped to the ground. I also stopped
but remained in the saddle, merely drawing
my rifle from its sheath. Seeing this the two
Indians threw themselves into the brush.
One was armed with a good double-barreled
gun, the other had only a bow and arrows.
Their actions seemed to me suspicious and I
called to them in Sioux, asking who they
were and what they wanted. They called
back not to shoot, that they were friends,
Mandans, and that they belonged to a party
from Fort Berthold that was cutting wood a
few miles from there. I saw at once that
they were lying; because of their speech and
of their general appearance I recognized
them for Sioux. Almost at the same time a
shot came from behind a tree and my horse
began to turn and jump. I saw at once that
the shot had struck him and that it would be
impossible to hold him quiet so I quickly
jumped to the ground. In jumping I fell at
full length and while I was trying to get
upon my feet one of the Sioux ran up to

within six feet, took a sight at me, and fired. I would have been dead had the charge exploded but the cap did not fire and I lost no time in replying and my adversary fell dead with a ball through his head. Then it was like a duel with the other one, who kept himself covered behind a tree trunk whence he shot down at me with arrows as you see (showing me a double hole in the folds of his coat). I was entirely in the open so, keeping my gun always ready, I hunted and found a rise in the ground behind which I was better posted. From there, having still fifteen shots to fire without reloading (Kelly was armed with a Henry rifle), I began in turn to touch up my man with care. The tree behind which he stood was not big enough to cover him all at once. On one side or the other there showed at intervals an arm, a shoulder, or a thigh so that after having barked the tree without knowing what other effect my shots had had, I ended by breaking his arm below the shoulder. Soon he dropped to the ground, and approaching I saw that besides the broken arm he had several other balls in his body. He admitted to me then that he and his comrade were Sioux belonging to a band of 15 or 20 lodges of Uncpapas who were in the vicinity and for whom they were serving as scouts when I met them. My

354

horse was dying; theirs had run into the brush so, without wasting time in running after them, I went on foot to the point where I knew the Mandans were. I was some five or six miles away.

"When I told them what had happened to me, the better mounted leaped on their horses and rushed to the place of the fight. They found there the dead man and the wounded one, lifted their scalps and dismembered the two bodies, after which we made a good meal on the flesh of my horse and returned altogether to Fort Berthold. There I met two couriers from Fort Buford with whom I have come here to make my report."

Monday, February 8: There is a great celebration at Berthold where they are dancing the scalp dance with enthusiasm around the chopped-up pieces of the two Sioux. Kelly will return Thursday to Buford along with the two couriers who arrived yesterday. The mail which they brought is without important news.

* * *

Sunday, February 28: Upon receiving news that an epidemic is declared to exist among my Berthold Indians, especially the Rees, I have sent Dr. Goddard to make sure of the

355

fact and to identify the disease. He has returned this morning announcing that it was
a matter of the scurvy which has made serious ravages during the past two weeks.
Twenty or twenty-five of the Indians, mostly
old people, have died of it and thirty-two
are still sick with it. I immediately requi-
sitioned a wagon from the agency and I have
sent to Berthold ten kegs of sauer kraut,
gherkins, and anti-scorbutic pickles to be
distributed from day to day among the Indians. These poor devils do not cease to
surprise me with their honesty and good intentions, a very great contrast with the character of the Sioux. The scurvy among them
is a result of their privation and sufferings;
they have suffered especially from cold and
hunger, having nothing but a very little
corn to sustain life, and withal the beef herd
of the agency is not shut up but wanders
among the willows and the tall grass of the
river banks. They are unguarded, within
reach of all, especially at night. And these
poor Indians die of hunger near these cattle
rather than touch them, when the flesh of a
single beast would make a royal meal for a
very large number of them. I certainly
would not trust to the honesty of whites
under such conditions. And these are the
Indians who are pillaged, plundered, and op-

pressed without mercy by the government agents. Let us hope that all this rubbish in the Indian Bureau will soon be swept out to be replaced by military authority.

* * *

Tuesday, March 9: It seems that the Indians at Berthold have succumbed at last to the unfair temptation that the subagent has placed before them since the beginning of winter. At the end of patience and endurance, half-dead with hunger and misery, one of them has killed a young calf that had been allowed to roam with the rest of the herd on the bank of the river. Whereupon Mr. Marsh, who replaces Mr. Wilkinson, wrote me *ab irato* to demand that I arrest the culprit and keep him in my guard house for thirty days. I refused. The post is not a penitentiary to be used for delinquent redskins. Especially as I consider that in this case the agent is more at fault than the poor devil who killed the calf. If the greater part of the supplies that were sent to our Indians by the Government had not been stolen by the agent with the connivance of the traders, they would not have been reduced to this horrible misery and would not have killed the calf for food.

The scurvy is checked by the vinegary supplies that I sent. Since then no more

have died and the sick are getting better.
I am about to send another cart load of
sauer kraut and pickled cucumbers.

* * *

Monday, March 22: A day marked with a
white cross! The mail that arrived today
brings us the official information of the
changes of garrison ordered by the General
Headquarters. As concerns my regiment,
we shall be relieved by the seventh which
will come up the river as soon as navigation
is opened. On its arrival, I am ordered to
transfer to its contingent those of the soldiers who still remain in my companies, and
to report with my officers, non-commissioned officers and corporals, and my military band, at Newport Barracks opposite
Cincinnati on the Ohio. There I shall receive fresh orders for an ultimate destination when the ranks of the regiment shall
have been refilled. Thus we leave the desert
plains of Dakota, and the Indian tribes, to
re-enter the States. May Heaven be praised!

* * *

The general jubilation has been shadowed
somewhat by another piece of news brought
by the same courier. The party composed of
Richter, Vogel, Bittner, and Shank, under
the leadership of Brown, the guide, is lost
in the snow near Big Coulee. Only two of

them have been found by the mail couriers,
Richter and Brown, half-dead of cold and
hunger, their limbs frozen, etc., near their
dog sled, burned to make a little fire. As
for the three others, being anxious to force
their way on, they disappeared, and no one
knows, or rather one knows only too well,
what has happened to them, for they left
their buffalo robes and their blankets behind
them in the sled, and had nothing with which
to build a fire. Except by a miracle they are
dead.

* * *

Sunday, April 4: "Ma foi! A great fool is
he who trusts the future!" The mail arrived this afternoon, bringing us all the news
that we were expecting, and more, one piece
that we did not expect; the latter is what
affects us most directly. All is changed as to
the announced movement of the troops. The
order is revoked by reason of an Act of Congress, which, among other provisions, reduces the Infantry of the Army from 45 to
25 regiments. A new general order of the
Commander-in-Chief (now W. T. Sherman
in place of U. S. Grant) prescribes the con-
solidation of the regiments among themselves, and designates the officers continued
on the active list. I am among the 25 colonels chosen and am transferred to the com-

mand of the Thirteenth Regiment of Infantry, the Thirty-First being consolidated with the Twenty-Second, which is our neighbor in Dakota.

My new regiment, stationed in Montana, does not change garrison. So, instead of returning to the States, I plunge more deeply into the Territories; instead of getting any nearer to my family, I am going farther away by some thousand miles. My headquarters are at Fort Shaw, sixty miles beyond Fort Benton which is the highest navigable point on the Missouri.

Nevertheless distance is not everything; means of communication are many, and in this regard I gain by the change. At Fort Shaw there is a regular daily mail service. Letters and newspapers come by the Pacific Railroad and the stage line from Salt Lake, the city of the Mormons. They take less time to come than to Stevenson. Fort Shaw is also half-way between Fort Benton and Helena, keeps its communications open all the year round, and the climate is much milder than in these regions.

* * *

My stay in this new post should complete my studies of life in the Far West in all its phases. I have already lived for two years among the redskins, whom I shall know henceforward thoroughly. It remains for me now to make acquaintance with the miners and gold-seekers who people Montana. Come on! Perhaps it is all for the best in the end. Let us obey Destiny without a murmur.

The mail from Totten brings also a detailed report on the deplorable fate that overtook Vogel and his companions. On receipt of the first news of what had happened, Colonel Whistler immediately sent out scouts to hunt for the missing travellers. Two of them were found dead in the snow; one only three miles away from Fort Totten, the other at eight miles. These were Shank and Bittner. At the time of writing Vogel has not yet been found.

* * *

Thursday, April 15: Twelve or thirteen days ago a party of seventeen Arikaras coming from Fort Berthold passed in front of the fort going down the river in bullboats. They were painted and armed for war, and in fact they reached the neighborhood of Fort Rice with the intention of surprising the Sioux there, and striking a good blow. Today they returned. Towards the middle of the day, columns of smoke rose on the horizon on the bank of the river (for a moment they were taken for the smoke of a steamboat) announcing their return. They come back triumphant, and this evening there is great rejoicing in the quarters of the scouts, where the victors are singing their chants and dancing the scalp dance. They bring back two scalps and a horse. They killed one warrior from whom they took his scalp and his weapons, and (which is not the prettiest side of the affair) one squaw. But such are the redskins. In war, neither age nor sex rejoices in any immunity, and they kill children, old people, or women as they would the warriors. The victory of the Rees in this instance was won at a high price. They have brought back two of their number seriously wounded, one in the thigh and the other in the rump; both still have the bullet imbedded in the wound. They are in the hospital where the doctor will operate to extract the bullets. A third is also slightly wounded, having a finger of the left hand skinned on the knuckle by a bullet. All the Rees were on foot; the Sioux whom they fought were mounted. (They were Yankton-ais from the band of Two Bears). To have brought off their wounded, and to have despoiled the enemy, the Rees must have fought bravely and skillfully.

* * *

Sunday, April 25: The orders that we have waited for during three weeks have at last arrived from the Headquarters of the Department. The principal dispositions that affect me are that I am relieved from the command of the Middle District and appointed to the command of the District of Montana, where I am ordered to proceed without unnecessary delay. The Thirty-First is consolidated into five companies with the Twenty-Second, to form the new Twenty-Second Regiment. Fort Buford is transferred to the district of Montana and will be held by three companies of the Thirteenth, who go from Benton by the first boat to relieve the present garrison. All the new posts of the new Middle District will have two companies each.

Accordingly, I am proceeding with my preparations for departure: the transfer of the government property, packing, etc., after which, en route by the first boat that can give me proper passage. My former adjutant, Mr. Marshall, will await orders from General Stanley to bring to Fort Sully the non-commissioned staff and the band, and to transport there the files of official papers, etc., of the former district.

So for a time I close my diary.

Appendix to Dakota Notes

By George F. Will

THOSE who have read the preceding
pages of General de Trobriand's diary
can not avoid being impressed by the
humiliating and exasperating position in
which he found himself, from his utter in-
ability to punish the marauding bands of
hostile Indians with the infantry forces at
his command. To a man who had commanded a division in a great war, to be held
practically in a state of siege by a few hand-
fuls of savages; his communications interrupted, often entirely cut off from the
outer world; his men murdered from ambush; and even the government cattle run
off within sight of his army posts, was not
only a constant irritation, but a source of
deep humiliation. Over and over again in
his notes he refers to the hopelessness of
pursuing and capturing these mounted bands
of marauders in the open prairie by men on
foot, and even by regular cavalry mounted
on grain-fed horses, burdened with the arms
and accoutrements of civilized warfare. He

constantly refers to what might be done to punish the bandits, and to protect the country against their depredations had the means and opportunity been granted him.

On his transfer to the command of the District of Montana, he found much the same condition prevailing there. The young Bloods, under the lead of several outlaw chiefs, refused to obey the orders of the older heads of the tribes, and roved the country at will, murdering, stealing, and raiding until life and property were in constant peril from their activities.

But General De Trobriand's experience had not only given him the knowledge of how to cope with the situation, but had taught him that there were good Indians as well as bad ones, and his chief anxiety was to take no action that would harm the law-abiding members of the tribes, while dealing a decisive and crushing blow to the outlaws. Therefore it was necessary for him to wait until the bands had gone into their winter quarters, and the identity of the various bands and the exact location of their camps had been verified. Although the entire white community was crying out against his apparent inactivity, he refused to make any statement as to his intentions or proposed plan of campaign.

Appendix

When the time came for action, he had exact information as to the location of every camp of the Indians, friendly as well as hostile, and his orders included not only the plan of attack to destroy the outlaws, but to protect the law-abiding bands from any possible damage through error of the punitive forces. When he struck, he struck so wisely and forcibly that although every band of outlaws was destroyed, not one friendly Indian was injured. Though the bandits were killed or driven out of the territory, no feeling of resentment was engendered among the friendly chiefs; on the contrary they were rather pleased that those who had defied their authority in the tribes had been punished, and their own prestige restored.

The result was that a lasting peace was restored to the Territory; life and property was once more safe, and in the words of the General's report: " . . . The peace and security of the Territory may therefore be considered as restored, at least for a pretty long time, and may be forever, if judicious measures are taken to prevent occasions of new troubles as well from lawless *white men* as from wild Indians." (The italics are the editor's, to emphasize the thought which was always in the General's mind that, often, the white man was quite as blameworthy as the red.)

Appendix

The official reports of the expedition against the hostile Piegans are set forth in full in *Life and Memoirs of Comte Régis de Trobriand*, and will not be repeated here. But the following article in a Montana paper so briefly and succinctly describes the expedition that I feel that it should be added to the Diary.

(Article from a Montana paper, dated January 30, 1870.)

THE INDIAN EXPEDITION—COMPLETE AND SUCCESSFUL RESULTS

And now from a number of private letters, some of them from official sources, placed in our hands by different friends, we are able to announce that the expedition against the Indians was a complete success; that the camps struck were the hostile camps, and that the Indians have been taught the sharpest and most bitter lesson ever received by them in this northern country.

The expedition, as we understand it, surprised Bear Chief's camp and cleaned that out; then went for Mountain Chief's camp and captured that, killing a number of the members while others barely escaped with their lives; then went to the "Blood" camp, where no fighting was done, as the Bloods peaceably delivered up all the stock in their

368

possession. A letter from high authority,
dated Fort Shaw, Jan. 28th, gives the result
as follows:

"One hundred and seventy-five Indians
(Piegans) killed—left upon the field—and
over three hundred horses captured. All the
horses taken from the white people, and in
the hands of the Bloods, were delivered over
by them to Colonel Baker."

Besides this, the utter destruction of their
villages, their winter stores, their furs, and
everything that goes to constitute an Indian's property, all going to make it a
terrible and fatal blow at the impudent and
bloody marauders that have during the past
summer ravaged our northern frontier.

Col. Baker was in immediate command
of the expedition, which was organized by
Gen. de Trobriand, commander of this
Military District. He has been its head and
projector, as Baker has been its right arm.
To them hundreds of men, women and
children in Montana, who can now go to
sleep with a greater feeling of security than
ever before, can render their thanks; and to
the gallant officers and men of the command
that faced the open prairie in the midst of
winter to hunt these savages in their lair.

In our issue of December 27th we stated
that Gen. de Trobriand, having chafed all

summer against his forced inactivity for
want of troops, an inactivity for which he
was by some unjustly censured had been
aching ever since the means had been put at
his command to get at these red marauders.
At that time he was preparing and planning
and endeavoring to get permission to organ-
ize this expedition, and show the people that
it was no lack of zeal and energy that kept
him inactive. As infantry came in he moved
the cavalry from Ellis, and Benton gulch,
organized the expedition at Fort Shaw. He
did all this as secretly as possible, having
requested the silence of the press, while, as
we then said, he was engaged in a movement
that would convince the people that he was
the right man in the right place. Everything
was finally ripe for a movement; the Indians
had all the time for repentance that the
Indian Department could ask. Gen. Hardie
came up to satisfy himself of the situation,
and Gen. de Trobriand was all ready for action. Then came the late snow storm and
the bitter cold weather. Pretty rough time
for camping let alone marching over the
bleak, timberless and wind-swept prairie.
Gen. de Trobriand could have had good excuse for abandoning the expedition under
the fear of another such storm overtaking the
troops on the prairie; but as soon as the

weather moderated he took the responsi-
bility and started them out. Fortunately,
they were favored with good weather, and
being active, vigilant and quick of movement, well supplied with scouts, guides, and
information, they surprised the Indians and
achieved a complete victory.

The thanks of the people of Montana are
due to Gen. de Trobriand, to Col. Baker and
the officers and men of the expedition. We
could not wish for better officers nor braver
soldiers to defend our settlements and protect our frontiers.

Immediately after the Piegan expedition,
the remnants of the tribe sued for peace
which was granted on condition that they
deliver up the two murderers still at large,
Mountain Chief and Pete. The former had,
however, escaped over the border into the
British possessions. The second, Pete, was
found by his people dying of smallpox in a
far off retreat. To bring him alive was
troublesome, and finding his death too lin-
gering, they hastened the end by cutting off
his head which was brought in a bag to
prove the sincerity of their desire for peace.

Index

Index

Index

Index

377

Index

Index

Index

Gros Ventre (Hidatsa) Indians, characterized, xxx–
xxxii, 39–40; warfare with Sioux, 44, 303–304,
348–49; attend council, 72–86, 239–49; rescue mail-
carrier, 231–33; relation to Crows, 282. See also
Three Tribes, Mandans, Arikara, and Indians.

HALF-breeds, families reared, xxvi, 35, 65–67; employed, 36; trading activities, 93; sell liquor to Indians, 116, 129; carry mail, 157, 186–89, 195–98, 213–
15, 217–22; Indians kill, 289. See also Red River.

Hamlin, Joe, slain, 287–91; carries mail, 306.

Hampson, Major Jesse A., commands Fort Wadsworth,
94.

Harney, Gen. Wm. S., establishes Fort Randall, 16; influence with Bear's Ribs, 118, 123–24; member of
Peace Commission, 284.

Heat. See Weather.

He Who Wears Beautiful Things, visits Fort Stevenson, 166.

Hidatsa Indians. See Gros Ventre Indians.

Hill, Capt. ——, commands Fort Totten, 286, 305;
leads detachment, 323; sends escort, 325.

Hooton, Lieut. Mott, fights Sioux, 286.

Horses, stolen, 121–23, 133–34, 285, 349; traded, 337.

Howkah, visits Fort Stevenson, 145–54, 166–69, 262.

Howell, ——, in Indian attack, 110.

ILLINOIS, prairies described, 7–8.

Indians, of North Dakota area, xx–xxi, xxiv, xxvi,
xxix–xxxv, 281–83; Minnesota massacres, xx, xxvi,
90–92, 151, 231, 280; marry whites, xxvi, 65–67;
methods of warfare, xxxiii–xxxiv, 46–54, 266–64;
attack river boats, 25, 27; burial methods, 27; as
army scouts, 43–44, 57–58, 94, 159–60, 277–78,
285–86, 304; migrations, 92–94, 114, 124, 131, 141,
162, 170, 177, 182, 239, 255, 257–59, 262, 275, 303,
315, 336–37; councils with, 73–86, 94–97, 123–28,
145–54, 170–74, 177–79, 240–49; self-torture, 62–64;

Index

Index

Index

Index

Index

Index

Index